Schelling's Naturalism

New Perspectives in Ontology
Series Editors: Peter Gratton and Sean J. McGrath, Memorial
University of Newfoundland, Canada

Publishes the best new work on the nature of being

After the fundamental modesty of much post-Heideggerian Continental philosophy, the time is now for a renaissance in ontology after the rise of the new realisms and new materialisms. This new series aims to be an interdisciplinary forum for this work, challenging old divisions while borrowing from the ontological frameworks of post-humanism, ecological studies, critical animal studies, and other post-constructivist areas of endeavour. While often working within the Continental tradition, the books in this series will move beyond the stale hermeneutics and phenomenologies of the past, with authors boldly reopening the oldest questions of existence through a contemporary lens.

Editorial Advisory Board

Thomas J.J. Altizer, Maurizio Farraris, Paul Franks, Iain Hamilton Grant, Garth Green, Adrian Johnston, Catherine Malabou, Jeff Malpas, Marie-Eve Morin, Jeffrey Reid, Susan Ruddick, Michael Schulz, Hasana Sharp, Alison Stone, Peter Trawny, Uwe Voigt, Jason Wirth, Günter Zöller

Books available

The Political Theology of Schelling, Saitya Brata Das
Continental Realism and Its Discontents, edited by Marie-Eve Morin
The Contingency of Necessity: Reason and God as Matters of Fact, Tyler Tritten
The Problem of Nature in Hegel's Final System, Wes Furlotte
Schelling's Naturalism: Motion, Space and the Volition of Thought, Ben Woodard
Thinking Nature: An Essay in Negative Ecology, Sean J. McGrath

Books forthcoming

The Late Schelling and the End of Christianity, Sean J. McGrath
The 1801 Schelling–Eschenmayer Controversy: Nature and Identity, Benjamin Berger and Daniel Whistler
Schelling's Ontology of Powers, Charlotte Alderwick
Heidegger and the Groundwork of Evental Ontology, James Bahoh
Hölderlin's Philosophy of Nature, edited by Rochelle Tobias

www.edinburghuniversitypress.com/series/epnpio

Schelling's Naturalism

Motion, Space and the Volition of Thought

BEN WOODARD

EDINBURGH
University Press

Edinburgh University Press is one of the leading university presses in the UK. We publish academic books and journals in our selected subject areas across the humanities and social sciences, combining cutting-edge scholarship with high editorial and production values to produce academic works of lasting importance. For more information visit our website: edinburghuniversitypress.com

© Ben Woodard, 2019, 2020

Edinburgh University Press Ltd
The Tun – Holyrood Road
12(2f) Jackson's Entry
Edinburgh EH8 8PJ

First published in hardback by Edinburgh University Press 2019

Typeset in 11/13 Adobe Garamond Pro by
IDSUK (DataConnection) Ltd, and
printed and bound by CPI Group (UK) Ltd,
Croydon, CR0 4YY

A CIP record for this book is available from the British Library

ISBN 978 1 4744 3817 9 (hardback)
ISBN 978 1 4744 3818 6 (paperback)
ISBN 978 1 4744 3819 3 (webready PDF)
ISBN 978 1 4744 3820 9 (epub)

The right of Ben Woodard to be identified as the author of this work has been asserted in accordance with the Copyright, Designs and Patents Act 1988, and the Copyright and Related Rights Regulations 2003 (SI No. 2498).

Contents

Acknowledgements

During the two years in which I wrote this book, I lived in over twenty cities across ten countries. Given that its theme is space and motion, that now seems like a perfectly appropriate, if exhausting, choice. It also means that these acknowledgements are longer than is generally acceptable.

First, deepest thanks to Tilottama Rajan and Joan Steigerwald for their extraordinary patience and rigour in bringing this book's first dissertation form into being. The finer pages no doubt reflect their cautious and clear remarks while, as far as the rougher patches are concerned, I have only myself to blame. Much gratitude to fellow students who challenged and encouraged me in equal measure: Svitlana Mativyenko, and especially Karen Dewart McEwen. Thanks to Nandita Biswas-Mellamphy and Dan Mellamphy for luring me to Western in the first place. Thanks are also due to Alisha Vasquez for always listening, and to Jillian Traskos for going with me anywhere and everywhere.

I also owe special thanks to Diana Khamis who edited the entire manuscript with a keen Schellingian eye and proved invaluable in bringing the second draft into good shape.

I owe many and scattered thanks for the indefinable assistance of a ragtag and international community of brilliant minds who taught me much while tolerating my rants about Schelling, and who, in many cases, fed, transported and hosted me globally: Lendl Barcelos, Ray Brassier, Katrina Burch, Edia Connole, Florin Flueras, Irina Gheorghe, Teresa Gillespie, Matt Hare, Amy Ireland, Heather and Nicola Masciandaro, Anna Mikkola, Silvia Mollicchi, Reza Negarestani, Alina Popa, Patricia Reed and Pete Wolfendale. Thanks also are due to my fellow Schellingians: G. Anthony Bruno, Marcela Garcia, Tyler Tritten, Daniel Whistler and, most of all, to Iain Hamilton Grant and Diana Khamis. You are a university unto yourselves.

I am very grateful to everyone at the Performing Arts Forum who made my long stay in Saint Erme equally welcoming, rewarding and interesting: Perrine Ballieux, Stéphanie Barbier, Daniela Berhsan, Ed Clive, Marcus Doverud, Fiona James, Dan Lucas, Jean Félix Marecaux, Alex Napier, Jan Ritsema, Mike Schmid and Christian Töpfner. I owe too much to the oracular wisdom and kindness of Valentina Desideri. *Ciao Bella.* Also thanks to Ada for letting me read Plato to you, if only to put you to sleep.

I would be beyond remiss, and against nature, to not thank Melanie Caldwell Clark without whom the Theory Centre, where much of this work was done, would cease to function and, perhaps, disappear altogether. Thank you for answering three or four questions when I thought there were only two or none at all.

To my family Cathy Schanerberger, Andrew Woodard and Gary Woodard, thank you for a lifetime of filling my head with ideas about chemistry, technology and physics.

Lastly, I want to dedicate this text to Vanessa Ohlraun for keeping me both grounded and ungrounded at the right times.

Change is the diet on which all subsist
Created changeable, and change at last
Destroys them. Skies uncertain, now the heat
Transmitting cloudless, and the solar beam
Now quenching in a boundless sea of clouds,
Calm and alternate storm, moisture and drought,
Invigorate by turns the springs of life
In all that live, plant, animal, and man,
And in conclusion mar them. Nature's threads,
Fine, passing thought, even in her coarsest works,
Delight in agitation, yet sustain
The force that agitates not unimpaired,
But worn by frequent impulse, to the cause
Of their best tone their dissolution owe.

William Cowper, 'Yardly Oak'

Nature, who has played so many queer tricks upon us, making us so unequally of clay and diamonds, of rainbow and granite, and stuffed them into a case, often of the most incongruous, for the poet has a butcher's face and the butcher a poet's; nature, who delights in muddle and mystery, so that even now (the first of November, 1927) we know not why we go upstairs, or why we come down again, our most daily movements are like the passage of a ship on an unknown sea, and the sailors at the mast-head ask, pointing their glasses to the horizon: Is there land or is there none? to which, if we are prophets, we make answer 'Yes'; if we are truthful we say 'No'; nature, who has so much to answer for besides the perhaps unwieldy length of this sentence, has further complicated her task and added to our confusion by providing not only a perfect ragbag of odds and ends within us – a piece of a policeman's trousers lying cheek by jowl with Queen Alexandra's wedding veil – but has contrived that the whole assortment shall be lightly stitched together by a single thread. Memory is the seamstress, and a capricious one at that. Memory runs her needle in and out, up and down, hither and thither. We know not what comes next, or what follows after. Thus, the most ordinary movement in the world, such as sitting down at a table and pulling the inkstand towards one, may agitate a thousand odd, disconnected fragments, now bright, now dim, hanging and bobbing and dipping and flaunting, like the underlinen of a family of fourteen on a line in a gale of wind. Instead of being a single, downright, bluff piece of work of which no man need feel ashamed, our commonest deeds are set about with a fluttering and flickering of wings, a rising and falling of lights.

Virginia Woolf, *Orlando*

Introduction

This book is centrally concerned with the concept of nature and the ways nature is considered within modern and contemporary philosophy and science. Secondarily, it investigates how the work of F. W. J. von Schelling is pivotal in understanding this concept. The concept of nature I take from Schelling is not the one that immediately springs to mind for many: by 'nature', I do not mean great expanses of water, patches of forest, the creatures that reside in the desert, or even the more general concept of ecosystem. In this book, 'nature' will instead be used to signify the open series of nested physical systems that comprise the cosmos. Nature is thus not some local part of the universe, wild and untouched, but the processes that constitute the productive, stabilising and diversifying attributes of existence. The interactions and processes that allow you to perceive a bird on a branch are as natural as the bird and the branch and the brain in your head perceiving them.

Beginning here has several consequences, two of which are the collapse of the natural–unnatural distinction and the naturalisation of cognition along with other human-centric capacities. The result of the former is that one must articulate and advocate the coherency of local domains of inquiry in place of such a split: the biological, the physical and the chemical are far more instructive divisions and do not carry the normative threat of easily dividing the natural and the unnatural. The result of the latter, which is a general de- or anti-anthropocentric move, is one I accept but with an extensive caveat. Many non-anthropocentric trends in contemporary philosophy (which will be addressed below) often, albeit not always, carry an ecological edge, endorsing an ethical, political and/or ontological flattening of the human and the non-human: everything exists equally, or becomes equally important, or equally capable. However, I think that such flattening is ill-informed and ecologically dangerous. In this book I am not overtly interested in the ethical and political claims of ecology but in the concept of nature that makes such claims possible. As a result, I do not see how jettisoning the concerns of epistemology, of how and why humans know and think differently from other creatures, leads anyone on a path away from ecological disaster (to say nothing of other political disasters).

Humans have a capacity that does not seem as extensively present in any other known species – that for thinking and technologically embodying thought. I do not say this to endorse any human supremacy, but to acknowledge that our cognitive capacities carry extra responsibility in the ecological and political domain. I do not see how ontological flattening benefits ecological thinking, I do not see how ignoring or outright rejecting the authority of the sciences is a viable option in a world in which we are dependent upon the nature that we think and that thinks through us.

Furthermore, I do not wish merely to defend nature as an object of inquiry that is only for philosophy (as a mere concept), but, following Schelling, I hope to demonstrate that philosophy (or any form of thought) is not possible without nature, a nature that necessarily grounds yet exceeds philosophical (and for that matter scientific) conceptualisation. This is not to endorse the all too easy move of writing off the physical sciences as foolishly reductive, but to show that philosophy is challenged and invigorated by developments in the physical sciences, especially those that explore the generative capacities of the various physical systems we have discovered.

Lastly and very importantly, the above discussion does not mean that philosophy, or human thought more generally, should be *a priori* limited by nature, but rather that thought is part of nature's spatially and temporally expanding continuum. This too is a kind of limitation, but to grasp such a limitation fully would be to know in advance what nature is when, in fact, attempting to know what nature is expands the distant boundary of what we thought it was.

In order to address this rather abstract starting ground, I focus on the sub-themes of motion and space. Before approaching these particular topics, I will sketch an outline of the contemporary state of philosophy (focused on realisms and materialisms since my emphasis is nature) and give some reasons as to why I believe the work of F. W. J. von Schelling has a useful role to play in contemporary philosophy thus understood.

Schelling and contemporary philosophy

> The entire new European philosophy since its beginning (with Descartes) has the common defect that nature is not available for it and that it lacks a living ground. Spinoza's realism is thereby as abstract as the idealism of Leibniz. Idealism is the soul of philosophy; realism is the body; only both together can constitute a living whole.[1]

In the following I outline my general approach to F. W. J. von Schelling as a philosopher concerned with the problem of nature, as well as the way in which modern philosophy has, historically, ignored this problem. While any sketch of contemporary philosophy I could provide would be provisional and biased, since it would be informed by my own viewpoint, I am specifically interested in how contemporary philosophy, both analytic and continental, has returned to questions of materialism and realism while somehow largely avoiding nature as a topic or problem *for philosophy*. This is not to say they have avoided ecological concerns, but that ecology has also, somewhat impossibly, forgotten nature in a realist sense. Even more specifically, I wish to diagnose this avoidance of nature in contemporary philosophy within the ranks of current thinkers who specifically address German Idealism and Schelling, both positively and negatively. I then examine recent Schelling scholarship and my project's relation to it, before going into Schelling's general approach to philosophy as a system, as well as into his methodology. Lastly, I provide a chapter by chapter outline of the book.

The above epigraph, which features on the back cover of Iain Hamilton Grant's *Philosophies of Nature after Schelling*, marks one of the central concerns of this book as well. Unsurprisingly, this flags this study's fidelity to Grant's interpretation while, simultaneously, generating the necessity of differentiating this book from his. Or, in a proper Schellingian fashion, identity between two objects does not mean equivalence but indicates an asymmetrical relation of dependence and independence. In other words, for a difference to be true to its origin, it must stretch its consequences to test the ground's, or origin's, elastic essence. Explicitly put: I share the concern that nature is indeed left out of much modern and contemporary philosophy, and take this lack of engagement with nature as an impetus to investigation. However, while Grant's task is often a historical one, since Schelling's project requires rescuing from obscurity, fragmentation and misinterpretation, my project here is more to bring Schelling, and the Schelling resurrected by Grant as well as by Daniel Whistler, Bruce Matthews, Jason Wirth and others, into contact with specific strands of contemporary continental and analytic philosophy. This requires some brief qualifications.

By contemporary philosophy I mean philosophy from the last decade, and not, as is too often the case, simply post-Heideggerian philosophy, although these recent strains have roots reaching further back. In this regard, I define contemporary continental philosophy as following the rise of Alain Badiou and Slavoj Žižek (at least in the English-speaking world), the emergence of Speculative Realism, and the various 'turns' to materialism, metaphysics, affect and ontology. A parallel, though differently motivated, move can be observed in the halls of analytic philosophy whereby the increasing complexity and conceptual ramifications of the physical sciences have prompted more adventurous forays into dispositions

(Stephen Mumford, Stephen Molnar, David Ellis), modality and possible worlds (David Lewis), process metaphysics (Johanna Seibt) and research on grounding (Kit Fine, Fabrice Correira). While one could easily state that analytic philosophy has ignored nature as potentially exceeding its concept as noted above, particularly in the philosophy of science or in science and technology studies, I believe that there has been a general trend to limit nature's influence in analytic strands of thought which have taken up German Idealism without reference to Schelling.

While the weight of their particular disciplinary histories no doubt plays different guiding roles, a turn towards the outside, in grander and more speculative philosophical gestures, can be readily observed in both continental and analytic philosophy. This move, however, is couched in quite different, often opposed, methods or ethics. Many figures of New Materialism for instance (Jane Bennett, William Connolly and Karen Barad in her related agential realism) take Derrida and Deleuze as inspirations or, at least, as figures whose general critiques cannot be bypassed. The newness of the New Materialists, then, comes from the fact that they are attempting to do materialism while accepting the critiques of Derrida, and the notion of materialism following Deleuze (that matter is material 'stuff' and is inseparable from things *that matter* such as politics, ethics, etc.). Thus, for them, as well as for other ontological liberalists (such as Bruno Latour, Graham Harman, Maurizio Ferraris and Markus Gabriel), the argument, broadly put, is that everything has being and, simultaneously, worth, equally. Liberal ontology situates philosophy as far-reaching but, while adopting a veneer of modesty, it pursues an ontology or metaphysics out of political, aesthetic or logical *fairness*, that is, based on non-philosophical demands. My question here is: how can all of these approaches eschew any serious discussion of nature as defined above?[2]

Alain Badiou, in tandem with the ever-increasingly popular Slavoj Žižek, on the other hand, both triumphantly embrace the traditional bravado of classical philosophy's speculative reach, albeit supplanting it with finer, non-philosophical tools; mathematics (in the form of Cantorian set theory) for Badiou, and Lacanian psychoanalysis for Žižek. However, while Badiou and Žižek propose and work out massive systems of philosophical inquiry, unsurprisingly with and against Hegel and his French reception, they nevertheless remain focused upon the problematic of the subject, whether political or otherwise, whereas the aforementioned New Materialists generally see the post-Kantian or psychoanalytic fixation on the subject as a residue of anthropocentricism.

It is from this tumultuous cauldron of Deleuze versus Badiou, or Derrida versus Žižek, that Speculative Realism emerged in the mid-2000s. Following Quentin Meillassoux's *After Finitude*, Ray Brassier, who translated the text, came into contact with Graham Harman's Object-Oriented Ontology and was already aware of Iain Hamilton Grant's nascent Schellingian naturalism. While never self-identifying as a coherent movement, these thinkers shared something of an antipathy to what Meillassoux (interestingly a student of Badiou) had deemed correlationism, namely, that subject and object, following Kant, were always-already caught in a co-determining, and thus inescapable, loop. As Meillassoux defines it: 'Correlationism consists in disqualifying the claim that it is possible to consider the realms of subjectivity and objectivity independently of one another.'[3] In addition to this definition, Meillassoux names two variants of correlationism: weak correlationism and strong correlationism. Weak correlationism, of which Kant is the flag-bearer, asserts the co-determination of subjectivity and objectivity while maintaining the conceivability of the in-itself, whereas strong correlationism dismisses any possibility of thinking the in-itself.[4]

The four figures mentioned, each in their own way, attempted to propose methods of escaping such an epistemic circle. The only other feature they shared, except for Harman, was a general interest in the consequences of the contemporary sciences that led Meillassoux, Grant and Brassier to engage contemporary analytic philosophy as well. The insistence that nature exists prior to human thinking, and that it forms and impinges on human action and thought, goes against decades of hermeneutic, phenomenological and post-modern *doxa* which would otherwise relegate nature to the status of 'just another discourse', grand narrative, master signifier or pre-critical fantasy. While analytic philosophy has been markedly less anti-realist, or at least anti-physicalist, numerous moves in ethics and philosophy of mind have been stalwartly internalist and/or normativist, against the advances of both scientific and philosophical naturalism.[5] Idealism broadly understood, and German Idealism in particular, have been used to staunchly defend a normativist view.

It is here that Schelling's place in contemporary philosophy and his potential importance can begin to be articulated. *Contra* many traditional readings, Iain Hamilton Grant refuses to temporalise the periods of Schelling's thought into two, three or four separate slices, and instead argues that his thinking is, through and through, a philosophy of nature. For one, this immediately retaliates against the consistent dismissal of Schelling by Hegelians, who take the latter at his word regarding the former. While Deleuze showed some sympathy for Schelling, both Badiou and Žižek repeat the gesture of making Schelling a mere historical note, a stepping stone between Fichte and Hegel. I will address this issue in the following chapter. In addition, Grant's claim, which I will refer to as the continuity thesis, runs against much of the scholarship on Schelling, both past and current. More recently, however, Daniel Whistler has taken up the continuity thesis as well, whereas Bruce Matthews, Jason Wirth and Markus Gabriel, while arguing for philosophical continuity across Schelling's texts, do not define this continuity as a strictly *Naturphilosophical* one.

If one accepts the continuity thesis, then a broad comparison of Schelling to Hegel is instructive. Is it simply the case that Schelling's ramshackle method scares would-be Schellingians away and into Hegel's embrace? Or do those who cherry-pick and chop up Schelling's work into periods do it *because* he seems to present an anti-Hegelian style of philosophy, because he is a protean or pre-post-modern thinker? One cannot, in good faith, justify either claim in my view. As to the former, Schelling and Hegel were equally extensive when it came to the topics of their philosophical investigations, but it remains possible that methodological difference is the primary deterrent. Regarding the latter claim, Schelling's approach to philosophy cannot be classified as simply anti-systematic or non-systematic, but, as I will argue below, he adheres to a notion of systematicity that is is ablative. The reason for this is not the same one that generally motivates post-structuralist claims about knowledge, that is, that there is no master discourse, but rather because there is already a system that pre-exists any system of knowledge, that is, the cosmos or nature. It is this assertion regarding the primacy of nature over thinking that makes Schelling, following Grant's reading, into a non-correlationist: he claims that nature *is* whether or not we humans exist to think it. I discuss what exactly ablative systematicity means for Schelling below.

But since we do exist, how are we to think this nature which pre-dates us? It is here that Schelling appears both modest and grand in his general philosophical approach. While he believes that the physical sciences provide invaluable knowledge regarding nature, he also believes that philosophy is in a position to identify conceptual biases, as well as local practical limitations, in any given investigation. Hence philosophy is broad and grand, yet its tests, like the hypotheses and experiments of any scientific endeavour, require the locality of an action or deed. Philosophy, for Schelling, consists in testing and mapping the consequences of any given act, whether practical or noetic, philosophical or scientific. This model of thought is apparent in Schelling's hyper-constructive method, which I briefly examine below.

The argument that Schelling's philosophy is continuously a philosophy of nature has consequences for the practice of philosophy itself. Namely, for Schelling, taking nature as an open set of nested processes (of which thought is one) means that philosophy studies forces or powers, and treats things or objects as secondary. This move empowers and localises the resources of idealism, simultaneously problematising the resources of realism generally and, for our purposes here, naturalism in particular. If everything is ideal and a part of a nature that has no outer boundary, then our responsibility for our actions is deepened. Ignoring the productive ground of nature arises not in the form of an ethical imperative, but as an ontologically, and formally, pre-existing ground. Furthermore, this installs a minimal difference between 'philosophy of nature' and *Naturphilosophie*. While both disciplines philosophise about nature, the latter also attempts to explore how nature philosophises, and how thinking nature is impossible without a concept of nature as thinking through us. Given this schema, following from the generally continuous and/or *Naturphilosophical* readings of Schelling, it is worth providing a brief survey of other past and current literature on Schelling.

The first wave of secondary literature (in English, German and French) is perhaps better known through its reputation than by its actual content. It has become a standard trope of anglophone Schelling scholarship in the last few decades, as already indicated, to begin by lamenting the fragmentary treatment of Schelling in the initial wave of secondary literature.[6] This strategy is often justified, by both its proponents and its detractors, as necessary given Schelling's 'wild and protean nature'. That is, since Schelling's own work was seen as rife with inconsistency and changing form, one was given *carte blanche* to pick and choose from his various texts and phases. *The Essay on Human Freedom* is a privileged choice, due to the attention it has been given by Heidegger, Nancy, Derrida and others. Alan White's book *Schelling: An Introduction to the System of Freedom* (1983) was one of the first well-known secondary English texts to follow this mode. Bruce Matthews suggests that, apart from White's *Schelling*, only three other of these works deserve mention: Andrew Bowie's *Schelling and Modern European Philosophy* (1993), Edward Beach's *The Potencies of the God(s): Schelling's Philosophy of Mythology* (1994) and Dale Snow's *Schelling and the End of Idealism* (1996).[7]

While I agree with Matthews's assessment that all these authors are guilty of 'cherry-picking', this does not detract from many of the broader claims they make with regard to Schelling's wider thought, although these are made from the perspective of a particular form of Schelling's thinking. Given the focus of Matthews's own project (being organicism) however, the accusation of cherry-picking raises the question of whether any account of Schelling's thought can be totalising. Following the abductive logic of C. S. Peirce, with whom we will engage below, it seems that the best means of addressing Schelling's work is to begin from a particular field and, following Grant's discussion of extensity in *Philosophies of Nature after Schelling*, push the field to its limit in order to grasp a snapshot, however imperfect, of the absolute (or what I will argue should be discussed simply as nature). Similarly, while I am largely convinced by the general outline of the German Idealist project put forth by Paul Franks's *All or Nothing*, his assertion that Schelling was in pursuit of one complete system seems questionable to me.[8]

Matthews does not, however, mention the tendency, beginning most notably with Slavoj Žižek in *The Indivisible Remainder* (2007), of placing Schelling in a psychoanalytic context. This has been followed by treatments of Schelling in this vein by Adrian Johnston, Sean McGrath and, to a lesser extent, Markus Gabriel. While this trend has shed light on, and expanded knowledge of, Schelling, I would argue that it often, though not always, has the tendency of placing Schelling closer to both Hegel and Kant by moulding his *Naturphilosophical* speculations into theories of subjectivity without adequate justification. These texts which, again following Žižek, are largely supplemented by Lacan and Hegel, tend to focus on the *Ages of the World* and *The Essay on Human Freedom*, at the expense of all others.

There is also, however, a variant of this tradition which is less critical of Schelling and, on the other hand, focuses more on the Freudian aspects of his thought than the Lacanian ones. Here one can mention Sean McGrath's *The Dark Ground of Spirit: Schelling and the Unconscious* (2011) as well as Matt ffytche's *The Foundation of the Unconscious: Schelling, Freud, and the Birth of the Modern Psyche* (2011). While these psychoanalytic approaches can serve to deepen our understanding of Schelling, they risk placing him too firmly in the context of psychoanalysis.

The third wave of Schelling scholarship, in which we are now engaged (and in which I would place this book), rejects the fragmentary view of Schelling and argues that the breadth of his work is unified by a singular principle. These works are characterised then, not surprisingly, by the central theme they choose. I would argue that this begins with Jason Wirth's *The Conspiracy of Life* (2003) which, while in many ways mirroring the pre-post-modern reading of Schelling found in Bowie, attempts to concentrate around the theme of life. Wirth's concept of life is heavily theological and reads life not in its organic form but in terms of human or divine existence. Iain Hamilton Grant's *Philosophies of Nature after Schelling* (2006), which takes the form of *Naturphilosophie* itself as the uniting theme in Schelling's work, belongs in this third wave as well. Like Matthews, Grant pays particular attention to Schelling's engagement with Plato and his use of Plato against Kant in order to articulate his one-world physics of both thought and nature.

Most recently, Bruce Matthews's *Schelling's Organic Form of Philosophy* (2011) can be taken as a kind of synthesis between Wirth's and Grant's approaches, as it argues that life, taken in terms of its organic form, is the unifying theme in Schelling's thought. Like Grant, Matthews spends considerable time in tying this organic form of thinking to Schelling's utilisation of Plato's *Timaeus*. Other studies that have attempted to analyse

Schelling's entire body of work via a unifying theme are Bernard Freyd-berg's *Schelling's Dialogical Freedom Essay* (2008) and Devin Zane Shaw's *Freedom and Nature in Schelling's Philosophy of Art* (2011). One can also add Daniel Whistler's *Schelling's Theory of Symbolic Language* (2013) as well as Tyler Tritten's *Beyond Presence* (2012) to this list.

While this covers the majority of book-length studies of Schelling's work, there have been other texts and essays that have dealt extensively with his corpus, though not always directly. Numerous essays by Arran Garre place Schelling's work in the context of Whitehead's process philosophy. Robert Richards, Timothy Lenoir, David Farrel Krell, Christopher Lauer, Tilottama Rajan and, more recently, Dalia Nassar have produced excellent works placing Schelling in the broader context of German Idealism and Romantic thought.

Outside the strictures of Continental Philosophy proper, numerous works on the history of science and technology have provided interesting treatments of Schelling. Gilles Châtelet's *Figuring Space* (1999) devotes a third of its pages to discussing the relation of Schelling's work to modern mathematics and physics. L. Pearce Williams argues that Schelling's role cannot be excised from any coherent attempt at developing the history of modern physics in his *The Origins of Field Theory* (1966). Furthermore, Joan Steigerwald's and Marie-Luise Heuser-Kessler's numerous essays are invaluable sources for placing Schelling in the context of romantic science.

In analytic philosophy, Schelling's day has not, and may never, come. While in the last few years, interest in Schelling's once-friend and eventual nemesis Hegel has been piqued (most notably in the work of the so-called left Sellarsians Robert Brandom and Robert Pippin), Schelling, as Andrew Bowie has most openly lamented, is left out of the picture. This is not too surprising given that the form of Hegel adopted by the thinkers mentioned tends to draw overwhelmingly on his logic.

However, an avenue for probing and cultivating the possible analytic roots entangled with Schelling's thought can be found in Peirce's abductive logic and his praise of Schelling's *Naturphilosophie*, as well as the way Schelling, via Peirce, feeds into contemporary uses of asymptotic thinking in philosophies of science. To put it provisionally, Peirce emphasises the centrality of thought as inherently experimental and hypothetical such that one's interaction with the object of inquiry can always be tightened or sharpened as one attempts more and more investigative surveys. This slightly more analytic interpretation of Schelling is supported by the connections that can be drawn from his use of identity in relation to theories of the continuum and to theories in the natural sciences, which, relying on Peirce, investigate the importance of the systematically continuous over that of the analytically discrete.

Schelling's ablative systematicity

> Nothing upsets the philosophical mind more than when he hears that from now on all philosophy is supposed to lie caught in the shackles of one system. Never has he felt greater than when he sees before him the infinitude of knowledge. The entire dignity of his science consists in the fact that it will never be completed. In that moment in which he would believe to have completed his system, he would become unbearable to himself. He would, in that moment, cease to be a *creator*, and would instead descend to being an instrument of his creation.[9]

> To what extent is a system ever possible? I would answer that long before man decided to create a system, there already existed one, that of the cosmos. Hence our proper task consists in discovering that system. The true system can never be *created* but only uncovered as one that is already *inherent* in itself.[10]

> The idea or the endeavour of finding a system of human knowledge, or, put differently and more appropriately, of contemplating human knowledge within a system, with a form of coexistence, presupposes, of course, that originally and of itself it does not exist in a system, hence that is an [*asystaton*] – something whose elements do not coexist, but rather something that is in inner conflict.[11]

Given the above sketch of the contemporary philosophical climate, as well as the current forms of secondary literature on Schelling, I believe that the way Schelling's thought regarding systematicity functions is even more relevant now than it was in his time. As Paul Franks illustrates in his impressive book *All or Nothing*, systematicity, the demand that philosophy function as an organised whole, was central to Fichte's, Schelling's and Hegel's projects following Kant. Franks argues that this requirement for *a* system often alienates analytic philosophers, and, I would add, most contemporary continental ones, from addressing any of the German Idealists other than as idealists or defenders of the normative order.[12] It is prevalent in post-Heideggerian thought (to take one example) to characterise Hegel in particular as the arch-enemy of free thought, as the demon who wished to totalise the world. Franks complicates this caricature by articulating what exactly the German Idealists saw as systems and by pointing out why they sought systematicity in the first place. First, Franks claims that in attempting to provide the premises for Kant's critical conclusions, the German Idealists qualified any notion of system with two demands: namely, that any system must be both holistic (and thus heterogeneous) and monistic (and thus unified). Franks defines them thus: '*the holistic condition* [is] that every particular (object, fact, or judgment) be determined through its role within the whole and not through any intrinsic properties; and the *monistic condition* that the whole be grounded in an absolute principle that is immanent and not transcendent'.[13]

Quite simply, the positive aspect of German Idealist systematicity lay in its aspirations to construct a system that would be as solid and far-reaching as Spinoza's infamous equation of Nature and God (that, at least, is how the German Idealists understood Spinoza via the pantheism controversy discussed below), and yet would still adhere to Kantian strictures for knowing. The negative aspect, as a result of the pantheism controversy, was a deepening of philosophical scepticism following both the revival of Spinoza's immanence and Kant's championing of reason. Put simply, the German Idealists wanted there to be a unified world, but one unified in a way that neither undermined nor justified reason alone.

While I will address the pantheism controversy in the following chapter, its main thrust was simply that both rationalism and transcendentalism forced one to decide the limits of the power of reason *vis-à-vis* faith since without such a delimiting decision, one would either forgo the cognitive fortunes gained from the Enlightenment, or, on the other side, fall into a Godless nihilism. Franks then steps back from the historical details and formulates the problem of systematicity and reason's potentiality in terms of the Agrippean or Munchausen trilemma. The trilemma, which has to do with ultimately justifying knowledge in general, claims that there are only three kinds of possible justification, none unproblematic. It goes like this:[14]

1. *Argument by circularity*: Thought makes a justification that simply relies on its own logic (this we can see as part of the fundamental logic of correlationism mentioned above, which is reduced to its purest form via facticity in Meillassoux) as in: a fact is a fact because it is a fact.
2. *Regressive argument*: Every statement of thought requires a further proof which in turn requires further proof *ad infinitum* (this is accepted by the ontological liberalists mentioned above, accepting, to various admitted degrees, infinite regress supported by philosophy as description).
3. *Axiomatic argument*: One grounds thought in an axiom which is supported by 'accepted' percepts in that it borrows from another authority such as mathematics or psychoanalysis (both Badiou and Žižek are central thinkers in this regard).

Here are the possible critical responses to advocating these forms. Quoting extensively from Franks:

> 1 You have failed to answer the question until you manage to answer the why-question in a way that falls into none of the three options. Unless that happens, there is no reason to assume that you have given any justification whatsoever, and indeed there is no reason to assume that any justification whatsoever is available.

2 In at least some cases, there must be an answer to the question that falls into none of the three options, even if you have not yet succeeded in giving it. For if there is no reason to assume that justifications are sometimes available, then there is no reason for anything.

3 Even if you answer the question in a way that falls into one of the three options, your answer may still be satisfying. The two previous responses assume that no adequate justification can be, without further reason, infinitely regressive or circular. But this assumption is mistaken. The fact that some line of response to a why-question is vulnerable to the [Munchausen] trilemma does not mean that it is an inadequate line of response, and it provides no ground for skepticism.[15]

While, as Franks argues, this ancient trilemma resurfaced and was the negative condition for the emergence of German Idealism, we can say that contemporary continental and analytic reactions to German Idealism indicate that such scepticism has deepened, but also transformed. Regardless of whether one agrees with the solutions that, say, Meillassoux proposes, it is hard to deny that he highlighted a particular bias widespread in contemporary philosophy, one that is very much centred on anti-systematicity. Correlationism, one could argue, is the application of this methodological scepticism brought into the very structure of thought itself. That is, correlationism is a scepticism that is not sceptical about itself, because any statement stands as long as it fits within the circle of subject and object. This means that much contemporary philosophy struggles to axiomatise or otherwise justify philosophy's broad reach without as much as *appearing* totalising, à la a naïve view of German Idealism. Badiou's return to Truth and Platonism is only possible through a mathematics of *incompleteness* while, similarly, Žižek can be Hegelian only by attaching idealism to Lacanian psychoanalysis, emphasising the latter's discussions of the subject as rupture, break, symptom, thereby leaving the ontological order incomplete.

The three epigraphs from Schelling above indicate how his view of systematicity not only anticipates scepticism applied to the all (as both Fichte and Hegel did), but stipulates that it should be applied also to philosophical authority itself. Schelling is not merely against systems, since he asserts that they exist. The problem is, of course, that there are many systems in conflict with one another. A system must then be universal in such a way that its principles are applicable outside of its particular domain (whether it be nature, art, science, mythology, etc.) and, at the same time, are necessarily able to identify particular shifts and differences within their domain to do justice to them. Or, put simply, a system must be open to its materials and to the possibility of being ruined or reimagined by them, yet must hold its form sufficiently to be compared with, and attached to, other systems.

It is in this sense that I must disagree with Franks's articulation of the heterogeneous and monistic demands as applying straightforwardly to Schelling. While Schelling admits that all determinations, all *things*, determine each other, he does not view this as a closed system, that is, he is not a straightforward holist.[16] This non-holism follows from his rearticulation of the transcendental against the limitations of Spinozist immanence in that the transcendental is the *a priori* as a generative motion unconstrained by sheerly human conception. Put succinctly in Schelling's own terms: 'It is not because there is thinking there is being but because there is being there is thinking.'[17] Furthermore, Franks sees Schelling's abandonment of universal validity, that is, his rejection of the claim that there must be *one system* that universally applies, as irrational or elitist.[18] Yet the uncertainty of the practice of philosophy is difficult because of its obscurity, and Schelling offers no prerequisite for the successful pursuit of philosophy other than a stoic-like abandonment of all one's earthly comforts. Thus, and once again to turn to the epigraphs above, Schelling's assertion that we must collect systems that are always in disarray in order to even attempt to discover the traces of the cosmos as a pre-exisiting system demonstrates, if anything, a humility, but one that does not hide behind the claim to humility as a philosophical justification in and of itself.

In the wake of a return to 'grand' philosophy (Badiou, Žižek) followed by an explosion of ontological and metaphysical speculation, Schelling's ablative notion of systematicity as that which degrades itself to protect what lies beneath (philosophy as such, nature as such) seems to be an important model. The tension in the above epigraphs is that between creation and discovery, between acting in a way that augments knowledge, and discovering that knowledge which already exists *in order to augment it*. It is here that I now turn to Schelling's method of construction.

Schelling's constructive method

The poet Heinrich Heine once compared Schelling and his followers to whirling dervishes who 'continue spinning round in a circle until objective and subjective worlds become lost to them'.[19] Heine's comment no doubt stems from Schelling's attempts to complicate, through his concept of identity already mentioned, the relation of subject and object, to deprive them of their thing-hood and, instead, to extrapolate their synthetic and positional nature. This spinning, which ends in absolute confusion, has haunted Schelling, marking him as a thinker of (apparent) motionless identity, an advocate of absolutising a black night devoid of all difference, or worse. Yet Schelling's notion of identity is not one that nullifies difference, but one in which difference follows from a primordial continuity, a meontological (force-based) continuity that makes possible a unitary approach to his thought. While meon means non-being, Schelling interprets this as meaning that becoming precedes being, yet becoming also acts, as a force, by producing beings. In this sense meon should not be interpreted merely as being against being, but as advocating a philosophy where non-being is the interplay of being and becoming.

To say that everything is composed of forces is not to reduce everything to the same thing or matter or to the same force. Philosophy necessarily isolates and divides this synthetic field in order to think it, yet this does not explain how nature as force-composed arises in us, that is, both how nature creates thoughts in us and how we then come to have abstract concepts about nature, which can be locally applied to manipulate natural phenomena. Or, to refer to points made above, philosophy can only discover by constructing and testing these constructions against other systems and against the world as it appears. This disarray of systems, of thoughts, is part of the world, but, to complicate things further, this world is not one of closed immanence (Spinoza) or only of physical objects (crude naturalism), but one always augmented and populated by *Potenzen* (or powers). A direct way of seeing how these problems lead to Schelling's constructive method is to focus, as I said at the outset, on space and motion.

In terms of motion, in a lecture given in Erlangen entitled 'The Nature of Philosophy as a Science' (1821), Schelling begins by discussing how the first cause of nature (insofar as that can be speculated) is an infinite motion, if it is to be claimed that the world begins in disarray, but can be later thought and systematised. Following this, Schelling points out that the assumption of an absolute movement is always a consequent absolute since everything is activity, having a past and unknown trajectory. Furthermore, the synthetic distinctions we make are relative to a relatively fixed frame and to ourselves. It is a mark of intellectual laziness on behalf of his critics, Schelling argues, that they jump to claiming this to be naïve idealism when, in fact, it speaks to being caught in the momentum of the world and in nature, which necessitates the reality of the ideal. As Daniel Whistler has noted, Schelling's brief text 'On the True Concept of the Philosophy of Nature and the Correct Way of Solving its Problems' (1802) not only clearly states the importance of nature in Schelling's thought but also serves as a response to Heine and the double relativity above:

> Without doubt, there is a reason for the *fact* that I separate philosophy of nature and transcendental philosophy from one another and have tried to generate the latter in a quite different direction than the former. If the reason for this fact has not been extensively dealt with in this journal before now, then

this is merely because for the time being the journal is devoted more to the internal culture of this science than to investigating and proving its possibility (of which I am personally certain), and also because this proof can be achieved successfully only in a general presentation of philosophy. [. . .] If there is to be an idealistic type of explanation (or rather construction), then this is not to be found in the philosophy of nature as I have established it. – But then was it just a matter of that? – I have expressly proposed the opposite. If therefore the idealistic construction of nature as I establish it is to be judged then it must be judged according to my *System of Transcendental Idealism*, but not my *Outline of Philosophy of Nature.* But why then is this not idealist? And is there even (and the author agrees with this) any type of philosophising other than the idealist? Above all, I hope that this expression is to be further determined [in what follows] that it has been up until now. There is an idealism of nature and an idealism of the I. For me, the former is original the latter is derived.[20]

The aforementioned dizziness of Heine is remedied by understanding that while the momentum of nature is original, we, as beings capable of philosophy, experience the momentum of ideality *first*. But, against Franks and other critics, Schelling argues that one breaks out of the 'magic circle of consciousness' by turning it against itself; the rotations of the mind are capable of depotentiating objects, of thinking of their essence as if thought did not exist. In essence, the highest form of abstraction is what gets us closest to a sense of the objective (or the physical) in a world that is continuously constructed, that is, endlessly produced by the hands of nature. Or, since one is already in the world, one is already being affected by it and, as a consequence, one is already thinking according to it. The only way of thinking the world, while being composed by it, is to acknowledge that pure epistemological escape is impossible and that, instead, one pushes and stresses the material in order to discover what it is 'originally', while acknowledging that this origin and, for that matter, any particular end have already been decided by other powers.

Attempts to read Schelling's method have generally emphasised its intuitive nature (Förster, Franks), its temporal form (Beach, Beiser, Tritten), or its constructive aspect (Matthews, Nassar). Given the discussion of Franks above, I believe that the intuitionist approach – the claim that intuition is Schelling's only method – generally comes from an inability to see any method whatsoever. Heine's critique of Schelling as a dizzy or indiscriminate thinker emerges from a general stereotype of romanticists and, to a lesser extent, German Idealists, in that they believed that thought and the world could simply be merged by wanting it to be so. While I argue that intuition, as one form of thinking, is indispensable for Schelling, it does not describe his entire method. Intuition, for Schelling, is a capacity that helps one pivot between multiple methods distributed between

Naturphilosophie and transcendental philosophy. I discuss Forster's particularly dismissive account of intuition in Chapter 5 below and set the matter aside for the moment. The second and third approaches, while having more promise, ignore the proto-pragmatic and locative aspect of Schelling's thought, that is, its properly *spatial* character. In my reading of intuition below, it functions not as an immediate and direct connection between mind and nature, but as an indirect and vague attempt at thinking the continuity between nature and mind in a very localised and minimal sense.

Edward Beach in his *Potencies of the God(s)* emphasises the temporal character of Schelling's method, coupled with what he sees as a voluntarism, or emphasis on will, via Schelling's concept of the potencies. While I discuss this at length in Chapter 4, for now the important aspect is the fact that Beach sees Schelling as pursuing a method based on all-inclusive succession.[21] While I see merit in Beach's emphasis on temporalisation, I believe that he overemphasises the notion of will or subject, and turns it into a particular human being, while I take Schelling's account of subjectivity and the potencies to be more generic. Frederick Beiser argues that Schelling is heavily indebted to Kant but merely in that he takes Kant's deduction beyond the law, or perhaps, in Schelling's case, under and beyond the stable ground that Kant thought was practical. That is, Beiser seems to suggest that Schelling's method is deduction beyond the particularly straightforward function of the transcendental ideal. Beiser argues that, in this sense, Schelling's method is a hybrid between an *a priori* method, that of simply digging for ever deeper grounds, and one supported through and challenged by empirical findings in the natural sciences.[22]

This methodological split is also stressed by Tyler Tritten in his *Beyond Presence*, although he emphasises the late work as opposed to the earlier texts on which Beiser focuses. Tritten argues that Schelling's method is one that oscillates between the *a priori* and the *a posteriori*. Specifically, Schelling's method can be viewed as broadly intuitive in that it acknowledges the *a priori* as a problem and as a focus for negative philosophy, or a philosophy of pure reason, while also acknowledging that philosophy must attend to the accidental or the contingent category of experience.[23] This oscillation between reason and action, as already suggested above, is what allows thinking agents to test their own grasp of a concept and its expression through, yet beyond, that singular expression of it.

Bruce Matthews focuses on the constructive aspect of Schelling's method, namely, that Schelling's emphasis on freedom necessitates that we construct *with* nature in order to discover its structure. He writes: 'In direct violation of Kant's doctrine of method, Schelling adopts the procedure of construction as the methodology for his philosophy. Only this productive method of construction can supply the possibility of envisioning the dynamic dualisms of our estranged existence.'[24] Matthews goes on to state that Schelling does not violate Kant's prohibition on construction (as belonging only to mathematics) simply to oppose Kant, but because, as Schelling sees it, Kant cannot even construct the schema on which he relies without such an intuitive notion of construction.[25]

In other words, how do we construct construction without construction as non-rational element? Whereas Dalia Nassar argues that Schelling's method is constructive, for her it is constructive in two opposed ways. Nassar takes Schelling's method to be caught between philosophy and mathematics, or between demonstrating logically the succession of states that mirrors nature and consciousness, and the more Spinozistic method of the *Presentations*.[26] Franks also endorses a constructive reading, but one tied to intuition – construction, for him, takes place in solitary intuition as opposed to a more broadly applicable, or more social, Hegelian dialectic.[27] Franks also suggests that Schelling aligns construction with exhibition (*Darstellung*) too quickly, thereby erasing the methodological difficulties, and the role of reason, in the act of construction itself.[28]

Franks's comment reflects a typical, and often Hegelian, gesture with regard to Schelling. The idea that Schelling generated multiple systems because of his own protean (or indecisive) style is a claim that can only be made by overlooking his central concerns, which is to say, reducing him to a moment in the history of philosophy leading up to Hegel. Furthermore, it would be more than tragic if our choice was between having no system, or having noetic totalitarianism.

With specific regard to intuition, many of the above readings, I would argue, would benefit from analysing, and taking seriously, the aforementioned continuity thesis. To elaborate here: by 'continuity thesis' I mean two interrelated claims. First, Schelling's meontology of potencies asserts that there is an underlying, if difficult to access, continuity composing and connecting all things. Things are, at bottom, expressions of this continuity, but they are dynamically free, or individual, in how they express the potencies, or forces, out of which they are built. Secondly, the continuity thesis expresses Schelling's series of philosophical systems as necessarily interconnected and built upon one another. Meontology, at least in Schelling's usage, is a discourse on being that is neither non-being (*Ouk*), nor existence, nor inexistence, nor essence (*Wesen*). My aim is to work out these differences across this entire book, though most intensely in Chapter 4. For now it can be said that Schelling doubles each basic distinction within being in order to paint a complex notion of being, existence and essence. While being can be without existence, as soon as a being is specifiable as a 'that', it has existence. In a similar manner, essences have being but can remain potential, but once they become actual they produce existing things.[29]

These discussions are central to how Schelling understands objects or things that are only thoughts or more than thoughts (more than merely ideal). While ideas do not always have actuality they do once they are put into practice. For this reason, Schelling would think it absurd to deny ideas being, since we can refer to them and since they can direct our actions and the target of our actions. Following these layers of being and existence and variable ontological status, the capacities of the mind become transformed according to their level of access and the level at which they can produce ideas.

In this vein, Schelling's intuition, or productive imagination as Matthews calls it, cannot be viewed as merely an exercise in abstract philosophising, as the armchair philosopher deciding what constitutes the cosmos.[30] The form of isolation that such a notion would require is, for Schelling, impossible. That is, given that we are simultaneously produced by nature and in nature, every act requires its potential consequences to be rigorously traced. Philosophy in general, as Schelling's constructivism via the space of intuition emphasises, is meant to model and simulate these actions before we take them, not to replace or nullify action *tout court*. As I will discuss below, this applies to both productive and intellectual intuition, that is, to the tacit knowledge of a craftsperson constructing in the former case, and to the philosopher tacitly abstracting in the latter case.

More generally, my aim in this book is to demonstrate that nature, as an open set of nested physical systems, is a topic that continental philosophy has largely minimised over the last fifty years. While this is a broad claim, my hope is that by outlining the use of German Idealism in the contemporary moment, I will demonstrate why and how Schelling's thought as a form of naturalism should be taken up alongside Hegel's. What Schelling offers is a complex way of addressing how to adequately grasp what it is we think nature is – not only to do philosophy, but to continue to exist as thinking entities that are composed by, and of, such a nature. Because such a task is colossal, I further restrict myself to the notions of space and motion, especially in their relation to the genesis of thought, as well as to thought's relation to action, across Schelling's work.

Chapter outline

In Chapter 1, I begin by outlining how Schelling conceives of thought as a species of motion – a particular form of motion which we humans have access to. This access, while incomplete, demonstrates that we *participate* in thought but cannot claim to *have* it. I demonstrate how this rather speculative argument leads Schelling in a satisfactorily continuous way away from Kant, Fichte and Spinoza because of their shared insufficiency regarding the combination of nature and freedom or the relation of world and thought. By naturalising thought, that is, by making thought a process, but one that has a pressure or a volition outside of us, Schelling is able to claim that Kant's dismissal of teleology is unwarranted if the teleology in question is merely an objective fact about a nature that has no determinable beginning or end. That is, Schelling naturalises thinking which, in effect, destabilises teleology, since if nature has a goal to its creation, it is only to create endlessly, or so it would appear to our limited mental capacities.

To further articulate this naturalisation, I then turn to J. G. Fichte, Schelling's mentor, who inspires Schelling in creating a more active form of thought than Kant, that is, in arguing that thought must be a capacity with uncertain boundaries. But whereas Fichte saw philosophy as beginning, and ending, with an extreme form of subjectivism, Schelling sees Fichte's treatment of the I or the subject to be erasing nature as external world in order to grant thought maximum freedom. I then examine how Schelling's reaction to the immanent concept of nature in Spinoza exhibits the opposite concern, namely, that Spinoza's mechanistic and deterministic articulation of nature does not allow for an adequate articulation of human freedom. However, rather than merely asserting human freedom over nature as Fichte arguably does, Schelling suggests a maximally expansive form of naturalism that allows for nature to be dynamically constituted by forces, one of which is thought. I close the chapter by examining Schelling's peculiar utilisation of Platonic cosmology and Aristotelian naturalism, in order to further support his argument concerning the motive, or volitional nature, of thought. Specifically, I claim that Schelling utilises Plato and Aristotle to demonstrate how unifying an abstract image of universal motion (from Plato's *Timaeus*) with a naturalistic ethological view of animal movement (taken from Aristotle's *De Anima*) allows one to naturalise abstraction while demonstrating how seemingly abstract ideas, such as dimension, can emerge naturalistically.

In Chapter 2, I continue to investigate the resources that Schelling utilises to construct his dynamic concept of nature *vis-à-vis* the thinking subject. Instead of focusing on the general activity of thought, however, I analyse how the problem of being in a nature that we seem to be able to contain in thought becomes apparent in the relation between sense and construction-in-thought (whether in terms of imagination, intuition, etc.) as well as between those and notions of space. The figures whim I engage here are Kant and the post-Kantian philosopher Salomon Maimon. With regard to Kant, I analyse his remarkable text 'What Does It Mean to Orient Oneself in Thinking?' which defends and describes the function of reason in *navigational* terms. Kant uses the term 'navigation' as shorthand for the synthesis of motion and space between the numerous capacities of inner navigation (experience, intuition, reason, speculation) and those of outer structure (space, horizon, direction, magnitude, etc.). To put it differently: the way in which navigation is described in Kant can be taken as a measure of the tensions between the inner and outer grounding of space and motion, and of how the bridge from inner to outer is constructed and considered either analytic (as self-evidently external) or synthetic (as provisionally internal). In this chapter, I argue that Kant begins to lean upon naturalistic modes of explanation while disavowing them, that is, Kant relies on the reasoner-as-navigator through the physical medium of the body and its resulting feelings.

Following this, I move on to Kant's somewhat controversial *Opus Postumum*. In the *Opus Postumum* Kant expands the navigational model of the orientation essay by returning to the relation between human knowledge and the form of the physical sciences that he had previously explored in *The Metaphysical Foundations of Natural Science*. I examine warring interpretations of Kant's final text in order to lay down the foundation of Schelling's further dynamisation of nature, as well as thinking itself. Following this, I address how Salomon Maimon's critique of Kant's synthetic *a priori*, supported by his discussions of mathematics, suggests that speculation, such as the speculation in which Kant engages in the *Opus*, breaks the critical system, but in a way that allows for a synthesis of the natural and mental in a fashion that inspires Schelling's dynamic treatment of nature. This dynamic treatment centres on the problematic relation of the qualitative to the quantitative, primarily in terms of magnitude. The question here is, namely, that of how is it that the intensive and the extensive can interact, measure and be measured from a purportedly neutral location. Maimon's law of determinability, in what appears to be a proto-Schellingian fashion, attempts to combine a genetic or asymmetrical creation of objectivity on the one hand, with a polarity between intuition and conceptualisation on the other. The notion of the genetic, which accompanies that of determination, is imperative for maintaining difference in any situation where dualisms (mind and nature, inner and outer) are questioned. Maimon's attempt at being speculative, yet empirical, presents a particularly helpful way of leaving the gravity-well of Kant's system, while still recognising the veracity of the transcendental beyond the merely normative. I conclude by arguing that a physicalisation of Kant's perspectival mode, conjoined with Maimon's discussion of magnitudes, creates a historically indirect, but conceptually fertile, ground for Schelling's reconstruction of nature via powers or *Potenzen*.

In Chapter 3, I outline Schelling's concept of mathematics in order to address how intuition, space and continuity function in his thought. I argue that Schelling's engagement with geometry, in conjunction with his utilisation of K. A. Eschenmayer's notion of *Potenz* as algebraic exponential, speaks to an early form of intuitionist mathematics which is important to Schelling's thought in (at least) two areas: first, in discussing the relation of quantity to quality, and, second, in constructing and describing thought as a species of motion. Looking at the geometrical and algebraic themes across Schelling's thought allows one to view his intuitive, yet continuous, concept of space as functioning to map the difference between kinds (via geometry), and a difference in intensities (via algebra), in a nature composed of continuous forces. These pursuits, in different but bound ways, illustrate the complex form by which Schelling integrates human thought into nature through naturalising that which seems most artificial: the synthetic creations of mathematical intuition. To unpack these claims, I contrast and compare Schelling's concept of number as indicator of force, via Maimon, to his fellow *Naturphilosoph* Lorenz Oken, who argued that numbers themselves were endowed with substance. In order to address the geometrical tendencies of graphical demonstration, I examine how Schelling utilises the geometric line to exhibit forces and polarities in nature. Following Gilles Châtelet's reading of Schelling's *Naturphilosophie*, I argue that the geometrical and the diagrammatic dimensions allow Schelling to avoid an over-utilisation of logic, and the normative or scientist separability of the logical domain, and to demonstrate how the tracing of nature, via geometry, adds to nature's very expression. I then return to the question of combining the diagrammatic and the algebraic to discuss the relation of powers, intuition and space.

In Chapter 4, I build on the previous chapters' focus on Schelling's sources and his divergences from those sources in an attempt to address the meontological core of his work overall – namely, his theory of powers (or the *Potenzen*). The systematic need for these powers, which cannot be equated with either modalities or possibilities, follows consequently from Schelling's explorations of dynamics via Kant and Spinoza on the one hand, and from the articulation of thought-as-activity via Fichte on the other. That is, I explore how the *Potenzen* are pivotal to naturalising thought and dynamicising nature in that they keep nature and thought interconnected but not fully co-determining. Schelling's utilisation of the *Potenzen*, I argue, functions to combine the stability of identity as form with the creativity and contingency of freedom-as-dynamics. For Schelling, an unavoidable ramification of this freedom, particularly when glancing over the history of philosophy, is the free construction of philosophical systems.

My more specific goal in producing a historical survey of Schelling's *Potenzen* is to demonstrate how Schelling attempts to construct and maintain a minimal difference between motion and space – or, more generally in the terms of the *Potenzen*, between creation and structure. This key to this difference is determining the status of the *Potenzen* as forming a a domain of *inexistent necessity*. Inexistent necessity, or the contingent necessity of necessity, is the cornerstone Schelling's argument for an original (but *consequently* original) momentum to creation which, because of its inexistence, is necessarily ungraspable (or unprethinkable) *for us*, yet is the condition of all forms of creation, noetic and otherwise. This does not mean that nature as such or the *Potenzen* as such are the unprethinkable (i.e. taking the unprethinkable as an entity) but that 'finding' them in thought, in what seems to be *for us*, potentially has ontological consequences. However, just because we discover the *Potenzen in thought* does not mean that thought exhaustively *contains* nature or the *Potenzen*. It rather means simply that the construction of the *Potenzenlehre* (as always being in thought *qua* constructed) is how we create a provisionally minimalistic meontology. Thus, to say that a *Potenz* or power *is*, only means that there are general classes of can-be-states (or dispositions, or tendencies) that function across numerous dimensions. In approaching Schelling's use of powers or potencies historically I have two subsequent aims. First, I intend to uphold and do justice to the continuity thesis, that is, the idea that Schelling's work is not absolutely fractured into periods, but only as regards its focus. Secondly, by moving historically through Schelling's use of the *Potenzen*, I hope to demonstrate how their lack of domain-specificity (whether in thought, art, material production, natural processes, etc.) exhibits their basic functional use as opposed to them being viewed as metaphysically fundamental or ontologically superfluous.

In Chapter 5, I address the apparently problematic status of epistemology in Schelling's work. Given the (at times) overblown emphasis on Schelling's purported anti-Kantianism, there would seem to be little hope in articulating anything like a theory of knowledge across his *oeuvre*. I emphasise knowledge's spatial and navigational functions in Schelling's texts – in particular, how the navigational locates, and constructively constrains, the capacity of the subject to synthesise. This is accomplished, I will argue, via a spatialised reading of Schelling's concept of intellectual intuition and its relation to construction. Against a generic or naïve reading of intuition, I argue that it is a rudimentary form of non-intentional abstraction, a genesis of temporary and experimental immediate conceptual space. This intuitive spatialisation of epistemology in Schelling can be viewed as the problem of location and synthesis on two axes. The first vertical axis is the purportedly asymmetrically causal or generative axis of nature represented by Schelling as the *Stufenfolge* (or graduated stages of nature). The second axis is the horizontal representation of nature in terms of fields or domains of knowledge. Or, put otherwise, Schelling's epistemology must deal with the vertical axis of the transcendental method which manifests as the *Stufenfolge*, as well as the horizontal axis which manifests itself as fields or the scientific classification of the progression of the potencies (*Potenzen*) via a form of Peircean abduction. One could imagine the transcendental mode as a geology of the world's creation and the horizontal mode as the map of the sciences.

I then examine how the horizontal or field-based view of Schelling's thought can be elaborated with the assistance of Robert Batterman's work on inter-theoretical relations between scientific theories when it comes to emergent phenomena. Batterman demonstrates how even a hardcore realism is left with competing theories which then each require often indirect methods for examining what seems apparently the case according to our senses. I then turn to another vein of interpretation regarding Schelling's theory of knowledge – that of facticity and fact-based ontologies. Against an overly epistemological reading of Schelling, I examine Markus Gabriel's use of Schelling to argue for a fact-based transcendental ontology. Gabriel's view, in my opinion, far too quickly erases the *Naturphilosophical* roots of Schelling's project in order to make him compatible with, but critical of, contemporary analytic philosophy. I engage the work of Gilles Châtelet in order to demonstrate the importance of Schelling's 'indifference points' for examining the relation between intuition and construction, between scientific theories, and between philosophy and science. Schelling's combination of construction-as-dynamics and intuition as recognition of those dynamics is best illustrated by Châtelet's analysis of his influence on field theory and the diagrammatic tools required to capture fields made of forces. Put more generally, Chapter 5 attempts to discern where Schelling's claim to knowledge falls between reliance on spatial intuition, facticity (the status of facts as facts), and the faculties of sense as a physical domain.

In Chapter 6, I demonstrate how Schelling's emphasis on motion and space, coupled with his particular mode of philosophical speculation, leads to a form of proto-pragmatism. I work this pragmatism out via Schelling's turn towards Aristotle in the 1821 *Erlangen* lecture ('On the Nature of Philosophy as a Science') by moving through the connections between the great American pragmatist C. S. Peirce and Schelling. Specifically, I argue that Peirce's fondness for Schelling demonstrates the links between speculation and pragmatism generally, in addition to indicating how Schelling's use of intuition is an early and imperfect version of Peircean abduction.

I then compare Schelling's proto-pragmatism with the analytic thinkers who have taken German Idealism, in conjunction with the pragmatic legacy of Peirce as well as Sellars, to imply a philosophy that emphasises normativity at the cost of nature, namely, McDowell and Brandom (referred to as left Sellarsians or Pittsburgh Hegelians). I close by appealing to the contemporary pragmatist Mark Wilson, who operates between the scientific considerations of Peirce and the communicative and practical pragmatism of the Pittsburgh Hegelians, synthesising the two. Wilson, through a focus on classical concepts in the physical sciences and especially engineering, demonstrates the limitations of a normative approach to human thought. Specifically with regard to the pragmatic use of concepts, Wilson attempts to argue for a navigational approach to cognition that steers clear of both the normativity of the Pittsburgh Hegelians and the more hard-nosed neuroscientific articulations of consciousness in the work of Daniel Dennett and Patricia and Paul Churchland (categorised as right Sellarsians); the former emphasise reason as *sui generis* in the naturalistic context, whereas the latter investigate the impact of the natural sciences arguably at the cost of normativity. Peirce, Sellars and, as I will argue, Schelling attempt, all in their own ways, to construct a philosophy where the division between the capacity to articulate particularly human concerns and the capacity to adequately describe and situate our place in the natural world are not incompatible endeavours.

Notes

1. F. W. J. von Schelling, *Philosophical Investigations into the Essence of Human Freedom*, trans. Jeff Love and Johannes Schmidt (Albany, NY: SUNY Press, 2006), 26.
2. For a general critique of this trend, see Pete Wolfendale, *The Noumena's New Clothes* (Falmouth: Urbanomic, 2014), ch. 3.4.
3. Quentin Meillassoux, *After Finitude: An Essay on the Necessity of Contingency*, trans. Ray Brassier (London: Continuum, 2008), 5.
4. Ibid., 66.
5. Thus I would argue that Schelling fits into an externalist strain of thought, albeit one that is not anti-representationalist – an example of such thought can be found in the work of Fred Dretske.
6. This would seem to exclude early secondary literature written by many English thinkers in the late nineteenth century. Numerous students, in part inspired by Samuel Coleridge, attended Schelling's lectures in the early to mid-nineteenth century and no doubt began a series of critiques and accounts of his work. These accounts, such as Henry Crabb Robinson's and John Watson's account of Schelling's Transcendental Idealism, while scattered, often attempt to grasp the whole of Schelling's system. This is also true in Henrik Steffens's autobiography *The Story of My Career*, trans. William Gage (Boston: Gould and Lincoln, 1863).

7. Bruce Matthews, *Schelling's Organic Form of Philosophy: Life as the Schema of Freedom* (Albany, NY: SUNY Press, 2011), 226–7.
8. Nowhere is this clearer than in Schelling's discussion of philosophy as an *asystaton* in F. W. J. von Schelling, 'On the Nature of Philosophy as a Science', in *German Idealist Philosophy*, ed. Rudiger Bubner (London: Penguin, 1997), 168.
9. Quoted in F. W. J. von Schelling, *The Grounding of Positive Philosophy*, trans. Bruce Matthews (Albany, NY: SUNY Press, 2007), 3.
10. F. W. J. von Schelling, 'Stuttgart Seminars', in *Idealism and the Endgame of Theory*, trans. and ed. Thomas Pfau (Albany, NY: SUNY Press, 1994), 197.
11. Schelling, 'On the Nature of Philosophy as a Science', 168.
12. Paul Franks, *All or Nothing: Systematicity, Transcendental Arguments, and Skepticism in German Idealism* (Cambridge, MA: Harvard University Press, 2005), 1–2.
13. Ibid., 9–10.
14. Ibid., 10–11.
15. Ibid., 18.
16. Franks repeatedly stresses Schelling's Spinozism despite the former's critiques of the latter. Furthermore, Franks argues that Schelling's *Potenzen* are analogous to Spinoza's attributes which, as I attempt to show in Chapter 4, is a critical misreading of Schelling's philosophy. See ibid., 137–8.
17. Schelling quoted in Iain Hamilton Grant, 'Prospects for Post-Copernican Dogmatism: The Antinomies of Transcendental Naturalism', *Collapse: Philosophical Research and Development*, 5 (2009): 415.
18. Franks, *All or Nothing*, 375.
19. Quoted in Jason Wirth, *The Conspiracy of Life: Meditations on Schelling and His Time* (Albany, NY: SUNY Press, 2003), 106.
20. F. W. J. von Schelling, 'On the True Concept of Philosophy of Nature and the Correct Way of Solving its Problems', trans. Judith Kahl and Daniel Whistler, *PLI: The Warwick Journal of Philosophy*, 26 (2014): 11.
21. Edward Allen Beach, *Potencies of the God(s): Schelling's Philosophy of Mythology* (Albany, NY: SUNY Press, 1994), 147–8.
22. Frederick Beiser, *German Idealism: The Struggle Against Subjectivism, 1781–1801* (Cambridge, MA: Harvard University Press, 2008), 526–8.
23. Tyler Tritten, *Beyond Presence: The Late F.W.J. Schelling's Criticism of Metaphysics* (Boston: De Gruyter, 2012), 64–5.
24. Matthews, *Schelling's Organic Form*, 191.
25. Ibid., 193–4.
26. Dalia Nassar, *The Romantic Absolute: Being and Knowing in Early Romantic Philosophy, 1795–1804* (Chicago: University of Chicago Press, 2013), 158–9.
27. Franks, *All or Nothing*, 339.
28. Ibid., 373.
29. For a helpful discussion of Schelling's use of being and non-being, see Manfred Frank, 'Schelling and Sartre on Being and Nothingness', in *The New Schelling*, ed. Judith Norman and Alistair Welchman (London: Continuum, 2004), 151–66.
30. Matthews, *Schelling's Organic Form*, 195–6.

Chapter 1

The Natural Forge of the Transcendental: The Movement of Thought and the Space of Nature

How and why does Schelling conceive of thought as a species of motion? Conceiving thought as motion and subsequently giving it a spatial character is, for him, one means of naturalising thought while still doing justice to its abstract function. Discussing thought as motion is Schelling's way of naturalising thought without calcifying it into a product or substance or dissipating it into a vague process without root.

This approach to thought is not articulated directly by Schelling but, as I will argue, it arises from three engagements and dissatisfactions internal to his intellectual upbringing. These are, first, Schelling's interest in, and critique of, Kant's use of teleology in the *Critique of Judgment*; secondly, his adoption and critique of the activity of the 'I' in Fichte's system; and finally, his critique of the immanent concept of nature found in Spinoza. These concerns can be translated into simple interrelated questions. First, how can Kant argue for a mechanistic world while simultaneously inferring that there are natural purposes (teleologies)? Secondly, why does Fichte's attempt to get away from Kant's conception of a world in itself, radically external to us, necessitate that only the human element become a pure activity? Thirdly, does being completely *within* nature and determined by it require that nature be understood as substantive or immanent only?

The early struggle with these problems led Schelling to construct a form of maximally expansive or transcendental naturalism, in which nature as such is an open system, itself made of self-augmenting open systems. While this model will be fleshed out throughout this entire book, this chapter explores and emphasises how Schelling's uptake of Kant's concerns with inner space via teleology, Fichte's activity *contra* a static concept of the noumenal, and Spinoza's active notion of nature all lead him to fixate on thought as a motion that traverses an open, or unbound, nature. This motion, which cuts across space while synthesising and augmenting what it encounters along the way, can be taken as a naturalised notion of the Kantian transcendental (hence, of understanding nature itself as processes and constraints that are productive of experience).

The final question is: What does Schelling's transcendental (or non-eliminative) naturalism mean for the status of thought and the status of nature when both are described in terms of motion and space?[1] I attempt to answer this question by sketching Schelling's very particular selection of concepts from Plato's cosmology and Aristotle's naturalism in the final section. These ancient ideas on the construction of the cosmos are brought in to cure Schelling's seemingly eclectic sampling of his teachers and contemporaries.

Thought as direction: Schelling via Kant

In his early text 'Of the I as a Principle of Philosophy' (1795) Schelling notes his fascination with a particular passage of Kant's 1790 *Critique of the Power of Judgment*. I quote Schelling at length:

> Since there is no imperative for the absolute I, no practical possibility, then, if the finite could ever fulfill its entire task, the law of freedom (of the imperative) would attain the form of a law of nature (of being). And vice versa, since then the law [241] of the finite's being would have become constitutive only through freedom, and this law itself would inherently be a law of freedom. Therefore, the ultimate to which philosophy leads is not an objective but an immanent principle of preestablished harmony, in which freedom and nature are identical, and this principle is nothing but the absolute I, from which all philosophy has emanated. Just as there are no possibility, no necessity, and no contingency for the nonfinite I, so likewise it does not know of any purposes to be attained (*Zweckverknüpfung*) in the world. If, for the nonfinite I, there were any mechanism or any technique of nature, then, for that I, technique would be mechanism and mechanism would be technique, that is, both would coincide in its absolute being. Accordingly, even the theoretical inquiry must regard the teleological as mechanical, and the mechanical as teleological, and both as comprehended in one principle of unity, although nowhere realizable (as an object). Yet the inquiry must presuppose that unity, in order to comprehend the unity of the two contrasting principles (the mechanical and the teleological) – which is impossible in the objects themselves – in one principle that is sublimely above all objects. Just as practical reason is compelled to unify the contrast between laws of freedom and laws of nature in a higher principle in which freedom itself is nature and nature freedom, so must theoretical [242] reason in its teleological use come upon a higher principle in which finality and mechanism coincide, but

which, on that very account, cannot be determinable as an object at all. What is absolute harmony for the absolute I is for the finite I elicited harmony, and the principle of unity is for the former the constitutive principle of immanent unity but for the latter only a regulative principle of objective unity which ought to become immanent. Therefore the finite I ought to strive to elicit in the world that which is actuality in the nonfinite, and which is man's highest vocation – to turn the unity of aims in the world into mechanism, and to turn mechanism into a unity of aims.[2]

The young Schelling is here beginning to question whether Kant can so strongly infer that the teleological principle of nature is an adequate defence against a dynamic form of nature that, for Kant, too readily threatens the grounds of practical action. Furthermore, Schelling is sceptical as to whether any teleology of this form can be inferred at all. In other words, Schelling is uncertain as to how Kant can claim that the strangeness of biological creatures leads to a regulative concept of natural purposes, and why such purposes, even merely as regulative ideals, apply only to the biological. For Schelling, Kant's selective use of teleology, even as a mere regulative ideal, is question-begging if it serves largely to keep the dynamism of nature at bay, to fit biological creatures in a necessarily mechanistic universe. Furthermore, Schelling suggests that a form of unity between nature and freedom would remove the artificial barriers that Kant had constructed, barriers that had largely failed to dispel the unease he had sought to vanquish.[3] While this could be read as Schelling simply toeing the Fichtean line, that is, that Kant should have merely removed the world in itself and focused on the determining power of the subject, Schelling is rather claiming that nature is more dynamic than either Kant or Fichte could ever allow.

It will be helpful to flesh out the Kantian remark that Schelling is alluding to. Ostensibly this remark seems largely to reaffirm the division between the understanding and judgement using the concept of purposiveness as an example. This remark is an addendum to passage 75 which is entitled 'The Concept of an objective purposiveness of nature is a critical principle of reason for the reflecting power of judgment.' The consequences of Schelling's claim are quite extensive as he, even at this incredibly early stage in his life, is attempting to demolish the ontological (or at least anthropological) certainty of inner space – of a notion of a normative subject distinct from the outside natural world. One possible ground of this certainty is traceable to Kant's thoroughgoing anxiety about the status of the biological *vis-à-vis* the ground of reason. That is, one could argue that Kant has to give life-forms an ontological excessiveness and a purposiveness, in order to subsequently ground the forms of reason that can potentially emerge out of them. The function of biological purposiveness would, for Kant, 'pre-ground' the schematic function of reason in perpetuity. Yet as Schelling goes on to explore in his *First Outline* in particular, he does not find such an internally defined ground for the organism (or for any phenomenal product or *Scheinprodukt*, for that matter) plausible. Organisms, or any form of individuated entities, are merely meta-stable events composed and decomposed by the forces of nature in which they are nested.

However, rather than engaging at length with the differences between Kant and Schelling at the level of the organism, I wish to focus on the interior space that the organism requires for Kant in order not only for purposiveness in nature to hold, but also so that this purposiveness can be cleanly translated into moral imperatives (purposiveness becomes teleology proper). The specific focus here is the construction of an inner space, a kind of spatial orientation inherent to the subject and independent from nature. This inner space is necessary, for Kant, to root teleology, so that nature be properly navigable and human constructs be appropriately compatible with the natural world. This imperative, this goal of making nature navigable, is central to Schelling as well, but he is willing to sacrifice this interior space, or minimal safe distance, which Kant insists upon for the sake of compatibility – Kant's priorities are the reverse. This lack of an inner barrier between nature and the human in Schelling points to the related but, in the end, rather different notions of the transcendental in both him and Kant.

Schelling's worries at this early stage are repeated and transformed many decades later in his letures on modern philosophy. In a footnote in the section on Kant and early modern philosophy Schelling writes:

[Dogmatism] sought to restore the freedom of the philosophising subject against the object and to assert, not by again making the empirical subject into the point of departure, but by presupposing in the understanding certain given, universal, transcendental concepts, via which all being (*Seyn*), thus including the being of the Absolute, would be determined. As these concepts were, on the one hand, concepts of the pure understanding, on the other hand, however, they had objective significance and supposedly the power themselves to determine the Absolute, then it was as if a mediator had been found by this, whereby both the Absolute and the philosophising subject could exist; there was, if this was successful, a free relationship between the philosophising subject and its object. But this hope was destroyed and thwarted by Kant, by his declaring precisely those pure and general concepts to be concepts of a merely subjective understanding, and by his denying every possible transition from them, denying every possible breakthrough into the objective. There was no alternative here, if one did not wish to move once again into the absolute object which destroys everything free in the subject, than to move to the opposite – to the all-destroying subject, which was now no longer the empirical subject of Descartes, but only the absolute subject, the transcendental. Already for Kant, the transcendental unity of apperception, which was nothing other than transcendental egoity (*Ichheit*), was the only last principle or creator of the only knowledge which he admitted as real, knowledge through experience, Fichte raised this I from the partially obscuring surroundings it had in Kant, and put it absolutely as the sole principle at the highest point of philosophy, and thereby became the creator of transcendental idealism. Since this I was not the empirical I, then for Fichte the *I am*, which he made into the highest principle of philosophy, could also not be in an empirical fact – Fichte declared it to be an action (*Thathandlung* [literally 'deed-action']), and showed how the I could in no way exist independently of this action as a dead, immobile thing, but only in this act of self-positing, in which he recognised not just a temporal, and also not just a transitory beginning which had begun the movement at some time, but the beginning which was always equally eternal – thus that, wherever and whenever one wanted to begin, this act of self-positing always had to be the beginning.[4]

In this quote I believe Schelling is largely historicising the concern quoted above from 'Of the I as a Principle of Philosophy' regarding Kant's treatment of freedom in relation to nature. Kant's transcendental philosophy, concerned with fundamentally determining the conditions of the possibility of experience, is often criticised as a self-justifying juridical model. Or, in other words, the criticism is made that Kant wants merely to solidify the power of his own (or ostensibly anyone's) brandishing of the sceptre of reason via subjective judgement. My critique of Kant's concept of the transcendental, particularly as it applies to judgement, does not share these motivations. I believe judgement can be taken up as a form of categorisation at worst, and as a simultaneously exploratory and simplifying machine of reason at best. While I believe that this view potentially sells Kant's notion of judgement short, it is somewhat easy to see the troubling legislative aspect of his transcendental conditions as they apply to nature. In the *Critique of the Power of Judgment*, Kant goes to great lengths to limit the power of nature through the power of reflection. In the section on the dynamic sublime, he quickly squelches any possibility of a dynamic nature by stating that nature has power over us, but never dominion, because our safety in the face of an immense natural occurrence (mountain, tidal wave, volcanic eruption, etc.) simply increases our own vital powers.[5] In other words, the fact that we can rationally think this overwhelming phenomenon reasserts the power of reason over and above nature.

This passage is indicative of the way in which Kant discusses nature as mechanical, purposive and lawful, from the very beginning of the *Critique of Judgment*. Furthermore, Kant immediately divides nature and freedom via a separation of the scientific and the practical.[6] For Kant, nature necessarily conforms to our power of judgement.[7] As Kant writes: 'The special principle of the power of judgment is thus: nature specifies its general laws into empirical ones, in accordance with the form of a logical system, on behalf of the power of judgment.'[8] Thus as Kant's closed interzone of inner space protects the figure of the thinker from the wrath of exterior nature, while simultaneously providing a stable ground from which judgement can sort out experience from the formal *a priori* structures that make experience possible, the notion of interior space has an earlier and more physical grounding, as well as one to which Kant, as I argue in the following chapter, returns in the *Opus Postumum* (1802).

In his early text, 'Concerning the Ultimate Ground of the Differentiation of Directions in Space' (1768), Kant builds the safety zone of inner space in an altogether different manner. As Eckhart Förster points out, this text marks the end of Kant's long-held agreement with Leibniz over the generation of space by way of entities. Whereas Kant had previously held, with Leibniz and against Newton, that absolute space was an implausible notion in that it relied upon an arbitrary decision of the creator as to the location of the universe, in 'Concerning the Ultimate Ground' he criticises Leibniz's relative notion of space as unable to address the problem of direction. Kant writes, referring to Leibniz's mentioned, but never published, *analysis situs*:

> What I am seeking to philosophically determine here is the ultimate ground of the possibility of that which Leibniz was intending to determine the magnitudes mathematically. For the positions of the parts of space in reference to each other presuppose the direction in which they are ordered in such a relation. In the most abstract sense of the term, direction does not consist in the reference of one thing in space to another – that is really the concept of position – but in the relation of the system of these positions to the absolute space of the universe.[9]

Kant goes on to state that he is attempting to determine whether or not the unity of space has an existence outside of the relations between parts. Kant quickly adds a caveat – namely, that the absolute space that he seeks to determine is not one made of matter, or otherwise physical in any strict sense, but that he seeks to construct a form of absolute space not for engineers, but for geometers.[10] Kant begins to construct this notion of direction (focusing on the relation of right to left and left to right) by appealing to spiral patterns in organisms and the weather, as well as the celestial motions. Kant argues that these motions are anchored to our bodies using, for instance, the example of the compass – east and west must be translated into left and right in order for cardinal directions to have any import on our understanding and subsequent actions. Strangely, Kant converts this natural skew of right over left into an argument to the effect that the mechanics of nature provide us with a *feeling* whereby we consequently emphasise the right over the left. Kant then writes: 'What we are trying to demonstrate, then, is the following claim. The ground of the complete determination of a corporeal form does not depend simply on the relation and position of its parts to each other; it also depends on the reference of that physical form to universal absolute space, as it is conceived by the geometers.'[11]

Kant's example, one to which he returns and which will be discussed in the following chapter in relation to magnitudes, is that of chirality, or handedness, or put technically, the non-superimposability of mirror images. Kant argues that some internal ground is necessary in order for the bodily tendency of left and right to make sense and that, furthermore, this inner ground points to a notion of absolute space, or fixed reference, by which right and left make sense. That is, right and left cannot determine themselves only in relation to the other, for this says nothing as to why their orientations are mirrors or, as Kant puts it, incongruent counterparts of one another.

Kant's absolutisation of space, however, did not hold for long. In the *Critique of Pure Reason* (1781) he argues against the reality of space yet maintains the importance of absolute inner space, although this space becomes slowly transcendentalised. As Christian Kerslake skilfully outlines it:

> So why did Kant soon deny the reality of absolute space, and affirm its ideal-ity? In *The Critique of Pure Reason* he gives two arguments against the reality of space. First, the Newtonians create an absurd proliferation of entities when they think of real things coexisting with an 'eternal and infinite self-subsisting nonentity, which exist[s] (yet without there being anything real)' (A39/B56). Second, geometry is threatened by the reality of space, as its *apriority* would no longer be immediately guaranteed. But there is a clue from a late set of lectures on metaphysics that Kant has another anxiety. 'If we consider space as real, we assume Spinoza's system. He believed only in one substance, and all the substances in the world he held for its divinely inhering determinations (he called space the phenomenon of the divine omnipresence)' (LM 368, AK. 28:666).[12]

We can begin to see how teleology is co-determinate with Kant's concept of internal ground. This internal ground is essentially a navigationally necessary microcosm of absolute space, that is, one's sense of direction cannot, for Kant, merely be that of moving within a world, as that movement requires a notion of orientation by which the absolute space of the world is, at least minimally, fixed for the subject. But instead of arguing this fixity through either a mental screening, or a manipulation of feelings and external sensations, or an appeal to the situated and navigational development of the organism as an organism of a particular species, Kant threads inner space and movement into purposiveness and teleology, relying on them to fix the parameters of space. That is, Kant makes *a priori* regulations of what could be described as naturalistic derivations from the position of human reason.

Schelling takes up and modifies both of these claims by addressing teleology in his early work, and the orientation of the organism, first abstractly, as we have seen in the *First Outline* (1799), and then more specifically in his later Aristotelian work – the lectures on *Pure Rational Philosophy* (1847–52).[13] With regard to Kant's strange purposive threading, Schelling writes in the *First Outline*:

> To Philosophize about nature means to heave it out of the dead mechanism to which it seems predisposed, to quicken it with freedom and to set it into its own free development – to philosophize about nature means, in other words, to tear yourself away from the common view which discerns in nature only what 'happens' – and which, at most, views the act as a factum, not the action itself in its acting.[14]

One could compare this sentiment with that of Kant, albeit at a later stage. In the *Opus* he writes:

> it is we who first provide the data out of which cognitions can be woven (into the cognitions possible from them): e.g. attraction, for the sake of determinations and laws of its relation in space and time. *He who would know the world must first manufacture it* – in his own self, indeed.[15]

We see that Schelling emphasises a perspectival view altogether different from Kant's, a view that he will articulate throughout his career. For Schelling, one approaches an embodied perspective not by immediately determining what inner ground is necessary for small determinations, but in arguing that only an overview, or abstracted perspective, built nonetheless from small determinations, is capable of viewing subjectivity as a problem for, and not a solution to, nature's dynamism. These small determinations, or forms of dependence, are exactly those components of nature on which our cognitive architecture rests. This point is clear in Schelling's above-mentioned lectures on *Pure Rational Philosophy* where, in opposition to Kant, he asserts the species-specificity of dimensionality:

> What accords with the progressivity of organic forms stands in direct proportion to the separation and actual differentiation of dimensions. The slightest change in their relations changes the entire type. The same muscles that draw

an animal's head earthward, when reversed, posited as the past as it were, direct the human apex above. Throughout the entire ascending line of the animal kingdom we may note how the heart is increasingly transposed from the right or the middle towards the left. With this guiding thread in hand it becomes easier to demonstrate the progressive transformation of one and the same primal form through the entire series of organic beings.[16]

Thus, while for Kant right and left must index an inner ground that necessarily computes right and left into all visual activities, for Schelling, whether or not certain motions are privileged has to do with the physical constraints the species (or even inorganic entities) engaged in those motions have prior to learning to move according to (or perhaps against) them.

While much more can be said to address how Schelling utilises and augments the Aristotelian-inspired discussion of dimensionality arising from corporeal constraints, I am specifically interested in how the speculation regarding dimensions, rather than leading to worries about finding immediate ground as in the case of Kant's 'Concerning the Ultimate Ground', instead leads Schelling to suspend the immediate or ultimate ground as a subject in the name of further experimentation. The structure of the subject is far less important for Schelling then what the subject, or subjectivity at a location where it manifests as human, can do. The problem Schelling intends to investigate, one that he inherits from Fichte, is the question of how one can best think human thought as an activity when its ultimate ground belongs elsewhere – or perhaps nowhere, so that it has no final ground at all. While Fichte's and Schelling's philosophical trajectories quickly diverge, the pressure of the act is a concept that Schelling adapts wholeheartedly, as will be discussed below.

Thought as activity: Schelling via Fichte

There is a fairly well-known saying about the German Idealists (primarily Fichte, Schelling and Hegel) running through the door that Kant had only wished to peek through. This speaks to, among other things, the cautious uncertainty of Kant's position being 'ruined' by the German Idealists who wanted to explicate 'things-in-themselves' or, in various ways, to get rid of the things-in-themselves altogether and expand the Kantian ground outwards, as a defence against accusations of both dogmatism and scepticism. Whereas Slavoj Žižek has argued that Hegel effectively ontologises that which Kant had recognised without really recognising (namely that the subject comes to be substance through a kind of indirect self-recognition),[17] the contemporary Pittsburgh Hegelians take both Fichte's and Hegel's idealisms to be grounding the stability of the starting subject position as rational agent in the efficacy of the normative, which is *sui generis* and separate from what John McDowell calls, following Wilfrid Sellars, the logical space of nature.[18]

In essence, the problem of how mind and world (or thought and nature) interact in Fichte and Hegel is based upon a self-sustaining space of reasons where, via linguistic structures, habit and rearing, a subject in that space needs to be able to confirm, on its own terms, that the world is 'thus and so' in relation to a community of reasoners being able to agree that the world 'is thus and so'. This capacity cannot, following Brandom and McDowell, be anchored in naturalistic processes (to do so would be to fall into the naturalistic fallacy, as Sellars called it) because the set of rules governing conceptual behaviour is different *in kind* from those laws that govern the logical space of nature. However, the way in which the logical space of nature is described immediately fixes the game, such that the only kind of naturalism capable of appeasing the force of second nature (the space of reasons) is empirical explanation. I believe, however, that Schelling's naturalism escapes the above restrictions placed on naturalism generally, since, it is not a bald naturalism as McDowell would put it; rather, given Schelling's speculative concept of nature, his naturalism questions the descriptive ground put in place by the Pittsburgh Hegelians (as well as that of Fichte).

Put otherwise: if naturalism is the strand of thought that fundamentally describes laws and their empirical ambit, such a formulation presupposes the efficacy of description, already grounded, as the boundary of the space of nature. Such a formulation dismisses outright the varieties of naturalism, as well as all of the speculative tools they wield, whether in Hegel, Schelling, or otherwise. While one can overemphasise the speculative, one can also, perhaps not quite as easily, erase the speculative tools of philosophy (as well as those of the physical sciences), which pushes past the immediacy of the practical via the risk-taking move of generating a hypothesis.[19] While I will address the Pittsburgh Hegelians at length in Chapter 6, I bring them up briefly here in order to suggest that their articulation of Hegel, particularly their jettisoning all talk of nature in Hegel for the sake of reason's power, makes him similar to Fichte. Schelling's break from Fichte over the problem of nature potentially explains the dismissal of, or simply silence regarding, Schelling in contemporary analytic philosophy that is sympathetic to German Idealism.

Schelling's concept of nature appears at its most critical when it is taken as a naturalism in the form of speculative physics (an expression he explicitly attaches to his philosophy of nature in the *Introduction to the First Outline* of 1799). Though initially uncertain as to the efficacy of speculation in his earliest texts, Schelling later pushes speculation as the necessary means by which thought can begin to ascertain, however indirectly, what nature *has to be* in order for something like us to exist at all. Schelling begins these speculations through a naturalisation of Kantian formalisms (via an appeal to Plato's nature-as-forming in the *Timaeus*, Aristotle's proto-ethology, and a decentralising of Fichtean thought-as-activity), thereby making naturalism dynamic as opposed to substantive, and idealism derivative and natural.

This naturalisation of Kant's transcendental in Schelling has been most expertly fleshed out in the work of Iain Hamilton Grant. Whereas Kant is concerned with how experience is possible (as a synthesis of impressions, which, in an empirical register, must be *of nature*), Schelling asks himself how nature must be in order for us to exist and to be able to think of something like nature. The first point – the question of how nature must be in order for us to exist – assumes, as a ground, that nature pre-exists us (or more generally that being precedes thinking). Schelling does not at all dispute the starting point of Kantian critical philosophy; he even claims that Kant should not be lambasted for peeking through the door at the in-itself illegitimately, and yet he insists that this peeking (through our speculative capacities) can only ever be grounded in a continuum between the space of nature and the space of reasons. In so doing, Schelling claims that Kant did not go *far enough*, where 'going far enough' would mean making things-in-themselves into forces-in-themselves or activity in itself in order to make them into an object of 'higher realism'. In this sense, on a formal level, Schelling appears to go in a direction opposite to Fichte who, in order to shore up Kant's idealism against its critics, denied the noumenal realm *tout court*, replacing it with an internalised not-I.[20] Fichte's very project of the science of knowing (*die Wissenschaftslehre*) is a project of internal critique taken to an impressive extreme.[21] Seemingly paradoxically, Schelling's fascination with Fichte's I as the form of philosophy, the I as endless doing, is not taken by Schelling as a seed for a rampant idealism (at least for a subjective idealism, as it would be construed by Kant) but as a stepping stone in arguing that the activity of being-as-self can only be grounded in an existence outside of it, namely, in the speculatively determined dynamics of nature.

As Dieter Sturma puts it:

> As far as Schelling is concerned, it is an unshakable fact of finite existence that the latter does not simply possess the external and inner conditions of its own 'coming to self awareness' at its own disposal. Our various forms of theoretical and practical dependence upon inner and outer nature impose narrow limits

on the possibility of self-knowledge. By virtue of the naturalist incorporation of subjectivity, these forms of dependency continue to exercise their effects and do not simply lose their influence when rational individuals enter into the domain of explicit consciousness and self-consciousness.[22]

That is, whereas Fichte took nature (as not-I) to be an internalised and formal constraint on which the activity of the I operates, Schelling sees this activity of nature, as well as its appearing in our minds, as our own activity (as intentionality), and as only possible as one form of self-inhibiting activity (viewed as cognition) in order for anything resembling reason to even be possible. Put otherwise: the activity of thought weighs itself down with the not-I (as constraint) in order to think cogently, and not, as Fichte would have it, to exceed this not-I. While on the one hand this can be read as Fichte simply arguing for the irreducibility of conscious experience, the degree to which he claims that existence, and not merely thinkability, depends upon the I obscures the reality of external beings.[23] In *Ideas for a Philosophy of Nature* Schelling writes:

> Fichte's philosophy was the first to restore validity to the universal form of subject-objectivity, as the one and all of philosophy; but the more it developed, the more it seemed to restrict that very identity, again as a special feature, to the subjective consciousness; yet as absolute and in itself, to make it the *object* of an endless task, an absolute *demand*, and in this way after extracting all substance from speculation, to abandon it as just empty froth, while proceeding, on the other hand, like the Kantian theory, to reconnect absoluteness with the deepest subjectivity, through action and faith.[24]

Fichte's error, according to Schelling, is to locate such activity in the consciousness alone while at the same time bringing in objective constraints (in terms of Kantian schemata) in order to ground the consciousness-as-activity in the world.[25] In other words, Fichte abandons all of nature, because all activity and all constraint are internal to thought itself. Fichte does not set out to eradicate nature, but to ground philosophy in what he sees as really living.[26] Fichte argues that other post-Kantian thinkers (Schelling no doubt being the one he has in mind) have held too close to the thing-in-itself 'as a dead being', instead of focusing on the absorption of the thing-in-itself into consciousness.[27] For Fichte, it is not even possible to conceive of an unprethinkable realm, as thingness must be always already thinkable.[28]

This core dimension of Fichte's thought can be construed as either identifying the ground of consciousness as *a posteriori*, rooted in a self-evident *factum*, or as locating it in an absolute beyond facticity as such. Paul Franks argues for the former, stating that Fichte, following Niethammer's critique of Reinhold, got around the problem of thought as self-grounding by taking it as a self-evident feature of consciousness.[29] Allen Wood argues, *contra* Franks, that Fichte fundamentally agreed with Reinhold but simply amplified Reinhold's principle of consciousness into an absolute subjectification of the subject-object (by turning it into I and Not-I).[30]

Given Fichte's influence on Schelling, how is it even possible for the latter that we can think something like a nature outside of us? Schelling's alternative is to place activity provisionally within the noumenal realm, turning the form and constraints of the subject into a self-inhibition of such activity. Again, the functional constraints of consciousness that allow the activity of thought to recognise itself as thought would be at least partially inaccessible to the mind as self-constraining (hence the importance of Schelling's assertion that only nature is *a priori*). As Schelling put it in the 'Stuttgart Seminars', quoted above in the introduction, the cosmos existed before any system created by human thought. Thus, in Schelling's view, mental powers such as reflection and judgement become second-order functions – powers exercising themselves only after the activity of the mind had been restricted to give itself form and to thereby relate to the exterior world. Schelling writes in the *System of Transcendental Idealism*:

> The self *senses* when it finds in itself something opposed to it, namely, since the self is mere activity, a real negation of activity, or state of being affected. But to be that which senses, for itself, the (ideal) self must posit *in itself* that passivity which till now has been present only in the real; and this can undoubtedly occur only through *activity*.[31]

For Schelling, the real (the logical space of nature) interferes with the space of reasons in such a way that the space of reasons must limit itself (posit something like nature, some outer field or manifold) in order to recognise its own capacity to act. For Schelling, nature comes to be thought simultaneously with thought recognising that there is nature, since thought would never operate without assuming the reality of that which is ideal in it. The difference between Fichte and Schelling here is apparently slim, yet far reaching. While Fichte recognises some level of inaccessibility of the root of consciousness for consciousness, this obscure activity must still be *in* consciousness. For Schelling, this 'in' functions only as an ideal copy of the actual natural activity from the outside passing though, and constituting, interiority.

Thought as dynamic nature: Schelling via Spinoza

To address nature appropriately, Schelling found himself faced with the task of constructing a species of monism that circumvented the limitations and purported dangers of traditional monisms proposed and criticised within the pantheism controversy – that controversy which, centring upon the figure of Spinoza, spurred German Idealism forward, at least partially. Following Paul Franks, if the central tenet of German Idealism is what he refers to as heterogeneous monism (of systematising difference within continuity), Schelling is able to accomplish this construction via a system of philosophy (or, perhaps more accurately, a series of systems) that is disseminative in its structure and is comprised of forces (not substances).[32] Furthermore, in such a monism, which for many implied determinism, Schelling articulates a notion of the transcendental as the very movement of abstract form to abstract form, thereby granting an *abstract heterogeneity* to his thought while maintaining a meontological (non-being, or power-based) continuity.

Schelling's general position regarding the relation of thought and nature should be viewed not merely as a repetition of Spinoza's, or of the reformulations of Spinoza coming out of the controversy (namely Lessing's, Jacobi's or Mendelsohn's), but as a reformulation of the role of subjectivity-without-subject following a synthesis of Kant, Fichte and Spinoza in the light of the dynamics of Schelling's time. While, like Kant, Schelling is wary of making space merely real in accepting Spinozistic substance, he does not wish to make it as ideal as either Kant or Fichte would have it. It is how Schelling handles the integration of the absolute-as-concept into his thinking of space and motion that interests us here. However, it will be of benefit to rehearse the pantheism controversy's general contours to get a general grasp of the role that Spinoza, and Spinozism, played at the time.

The controversy, which raged for over a decade, saw the numerous pivotal minds of Germany deadlocked in a battle over the importance and reach of reason *vis-à-vis* faith. The debate was not couched in terms of philosophy versus religion, but was made internal to the structure of philosophy itself. It was a debate that centred on the limits or non-limits of reason as a power and the ground of such power. In this respect, it was asked whether such a power could be self-grounding or grounded in nature, or whether it was necessarily grounded in divine calculations.

The controversy erupted between Friedrich Heinrich Jacobi and Moses Mendelssohn, who were both friends of and commentators on the late Gotthold Ephraim Lessing. When Jacobi revealed that Lessing was an avowed Spinozist, debate ensued over what kind of Spinozism Lessing had subscribed to (since Spinoza's teachings in any form were tantamount to heresy at the time), and whether reason (without faith) could lead to anywhere but nihilistic ruin. Jacobi claimed that since, for Spinoza, everything was extended substance, his dogmatic system necessarily excluded God and faith. Mendelssohn's shocking response was that theism and pantheism were essentially the same, and that reintroducing faith or belief into philosophy was exactly what the Enlightenment had attempted to do away with in the first place.

In a sense the pantheism controversy, which Kant attempted to stay out of as long as possible, repeated the debate for which he had supposedly thrown down the gauntlet, and which ended with the advent of his critical system – namely the debate between dogmatism and empiricism, in which his postulation of the transcendental was intended to put a stop to endless scepticism. Following the basic plot of the *Critique of Pure Reason*, Kant denied both the dogmatist's claim that reason could construct knowledge purely and speculatively, that is, apart from reality (most notably referring to Spinoza and Leibniz), and the empiricist's claim that experience could ground its own justifications without appealing to the non-empirical constructions of reason (referring to Hume).

Kant's great legacy, as is well known, was to create a neutral zone between the camps – a zone in which we utilise reason, so as to retroactively construct only that which is necessary to make sense of the experiential world with which we are always already in contact. In essence, the pantheism controversy posed the question: 'What is the realm or domain of this critical middle ground in terms of reason or belief?' That is, if the middle ground is a mixture of reason and experience, what is the basis for the very possibility of this mixture? On one side of the controversy, the middle ground was construed like the schemata in Kant's philosophy, so that the argument for the retroactive construction of schemata via reason to make experience coherent could be applied to the very possibility of this middle ground. This led to accusations of Spinozism which, in turn, meant nihilism and atheism. On the other side, Jacobi argued that a belief in God, whether the ontological proof could be wagered in its favour or not (Kant had decidedly argued that it could not), is necessary in order to have a critical system that avoids falling into godless speculation. Whereas Kant famously left room for faith, but argued that reason could not prove God's existence, the pantheism controversy demonstrated an attempt to force the issue regarding the consequences of the separation of reason and God, that is, to ask: at what point does faith step in to function with and/or against, reason?

To sum up, the pantheism controversy was troubled by whether the ground of reason (however carefully delimited by Kant) was a self-grounding function of reason itself or an externally gifted and ultimately unknowable ground that was itself unreasonable. In addition, the controversy being a crisis of meaning, I would argue that it was actually a crisis of location, of reason in space (and, subsequently, of the space of reason itself). Jacobi, in recounting Lessing's initial revelation of his Spinozism to him, writes:

> *Jacobi*: Whoever does not want to explain what is inconceivable but only wants to know the borderline where it begins: he will gain the largest space for human truth.
> *Lessing*: Words, dear Jacobi, mere words! The borderline you want to fix cannot be determined. And on the other side of it you give free rein to dreaming, nonsense and blindness.
> *Jacobi*: I believe that the borderline can be determined. I want not to draw it, but only to recognize what is already there.[33]

Whereas Schelling would assert that the answer to the question 'Where is reason?' is 'in nature', he would also acknowledge the unsatisfactory character of this reply. As Grant has discussed in recent lectures, this epitomises the novel, yet limited, capacity of transcendental thinking to relocate the tensions within nature and to re-describe them, but in a way that deadens them.[34] Or, for Schelling, the transcendental should not be a cognitive reappropriation of nature, but a demonstration of how nature passes through consciousness, determining it. Hence, the Kantian advent of the transcendental disavows any ontological responsbility by submitting it to the practical or ethical as ground – a project that Jacobi initiated, brandishing nihilism as the punishing spectre should the project fail. Against this, Schelling sees Spinoza's mechanistic view of nature, in its immanent form, as too limiting in that it decides, from the beginning, what the borderline mentioned by Lessing and Jacobi above is, and where it is. That is, while Spinoza's construction of the singular substance of God in nature, and nature in God, brought down accusations of heresy and eventual banishment on the modern thinker, Schelling is able to avoid such threats by striking against Spinoza's monism and opening up the productivity of nature (and incidentally divinity), processual in the sense that the transcendental serves as an irrecoverable motion of forms-making-forms and not merely as the engine of reason's *schematic* form.

While the pantheism controversy set Fichte, Mendelsohn and others afire with the flames of nihilism (as they made claims for reason's self-sufficiency, thereby eschewing the need for faith or belief), Schelling remains above the fray as his articulation of the transcendental is not beholden to reason as such, but merely makes possible the emergence of reason out of the unreasonable on the one hand, while disturbing the facticity of reason, as we are born into it as unavoidable schema, on the other. In other words, Schelling changes the problem from 'along what lines do we divide the territory of reason from the territory of faith?' into 'how do we best discover the way in which the apparently unreasonable feeds and forges the reasonable?'

This shift of terrain allows Schelling to critique Kant for metaphysically separating freedom (or what I will argue is better described as dynamics) from the noumenal realm (the posited realm of things in themselves existing outside of human experience). As Schelling makes clear in a lengthy footnote in his lectures on *The History of Modern Philosophy*, Kant obliterates the possibility for a 'higher realism' when he denies the thing-in-itself its properly dynamic character:

> If one had to distinguish a *Prius* and *Posterius* in sensuous representation, then the true *Prius* in it would be what Kant calls 'thing in itself'; those concepts of the understanding which it shows itself as affected by in my thinking are, according to Kant himself, precisely that by which it first becomes object of my thinking, thus is able to be experienced by me; the true *Posterius* is, then, not as he assumes, that element which remains after the concepts of the understanding have been removed, for rather, if I take these way then this is the being which is unthinkable, *before* Seyende and outside the representation, it is thus the absolute *Prius* of the representation, but the true *Posterius* is precisely this Unknown (which he himself compares with the X of mathematics).[35]

In this same text Schelling charges Spinoza with *a priori* extracting freedom from nature. He writes: 'Spinozism is really the doctrine which sends thought into retirement, into complete quiescence; in its highest conclusions it is the system of perfect theoretical and practical quietism, which can appear beneficent in the tempestuousness of a thought which never rests and always moves.'[36] Thus, for Schelling, thought is a form of activity or real movement, but one that is necessary but not sufficient to explain thought's efficacy. In contrast to figures such as Deleuze, Schelling's naturalisation of thought-as-activity, following a combination of Kant, Fichte and Spinoza, requires a dynamic rethinking of nature and not merely an application of the model of thought on to nature in general. If the latter were the case, Schelling would not require the caveats listed above in relation to Kant; namely, he would not need to be concerned with how thought affects reality and how reality affects thought, or replace the notions of origin and end with *Prius* and *Posterius*.

Despite such passages, there remains an attempt to simultaneously claim that Schelling is a pre-critical Spinozist through and through, a thinker who merely ignores the Copernican turn of the critical revolution. A particularly acerbic example can be found in Adrian Johnston's *Adventures in Transcendental Materialism* (2014). Engaging with Johnston's text will be helpful in exhibiting not only the constant misunderstandings of Schelling's relation to Spinoza, but also the dominant mode of understanding the transcendental between Kant, Fichte, Schelling and Hegel in microcosm. In a chapter entitled ' "Off with their thistle-heads!": Against Neo-Spinozism', Johnston aligns the *Naturphilosophical* Schelling and some of his commentators, particularly Iain Hamilton Grant in *Philosophies of Nature after Schelling*, with a contemporary group of neo-Spinozists – a group that includes Jane Bennett, William Connolly and Michael Hardt, to name a few.[37] Johnston claims that Deleuzianism is the 'master-matrix' behind Grant's text, and yet fails to mention Grant's critiques of Deleuze, via Schelling, in the closing two chapters.[38] Johnston implies that Grant unjustifiably argues that Schelling's work over time has general consistency and claims that Grant's book overwhelmingly focuses on Schelling's work between 1794 and 1804.[39] Johnston claims that the *Freedom Essay*, as well as other 'later work', does not feature in Grant's account, remarking that this work is more dialectical and speculative.[40]

Here, I would like to make some remarks *contra* Johnston. For one, referring to Schelling's work after 1809 as 'later' is not particularly helpful, since Schelling's texts continue for longer after 1809 than they do before.[41] Next, Johnston implies that Schelling became more Hegelian after 1809 and hence that the 'later' work is supposedly missing from Grant's book – due to Deleuze's anti-Hegelianism.[42] In essence, Johnston is claiming that Grant's 'unacknowledged' Deleuzianism (though a relation to Deleuze is acknowledged and Deleuzianism is critiqued within the book) means that he is anti-Hegelian and must hide Schelling's later 'Hegelian' texts. Moreover, given that Schelling is increasingly critical of Hegel at least from his introduction to a text of Victor Cousin (1834) as well as in *The History of Modern Philosophy* and *The Berlin Lectures*, it is difficult to discern the basis for Johnston's claim.[43] Despite the young Schelling's claim that he had become a Spinozist in a letter to Hegel in 1795, it is not at all established in Schelling scholarship that he was deeply Spinozistic. While Dalia Nassar has expertly pointed out how Schelling utilised Spinoza to escape Kant and, by association, Fichte, Schelling was consistently critical of the limitations of Spinoza's notion of immanence, as well as of his inadequate definition of the place of thinking within his system. This complex relation to Spinozism has been highlighted by Allan White as well as Andrew Bowie, Dale Snow and, recently, Bruce Matthews.

One of the best antidotes to strong Hegelian-Žižekian responses such as Johnston's, which seem to paint Schelling as a mere dogmatic Spinozist, is to note the more recent attempts at analysing the appeals to nature's form that Schelling makes before, during and after his utilisation of Spinoza through his use of a combination of Platonic cosmological realism and Aristotelian biologically focused naturalism. But would this not constitute an admission of Johnston's critique, that is, an acceptance that Schelling is merely pre-critical after all? As I hope to show, this is not the case, because Schelling views the problems of philosophy as cosmological. In essence, he does not believe that the adoption of methodologies closes problems; it only re-spatialises, relocates them.

As is evident in Schelling's reading of Plato's *Timaeus*, a one-world dynamics allows him to give idealism a physical utility: since the ideal is part of the real, continuity is not reduced to an abstract geometrical artefact, but reorients thought as part of a continuum with nature (this, as I will argue, also naturalises geometry). Whereas Spinoza's immanence and substance left monist philosophy a lifeless realism, Leibniz gives Schelling an overly lively idealism, but one that, despite its errors (which for Schelling culminate in Leibniz's reliance upon God's morals to explain physical necessity), demonstrates the power of idealism as a means of navigating and speculating as to what the forms of nature *might be* in order to explain how nature proceeds as a self-lacerating form, always giving rise to new forms while still remaining physically continuous.[44]

It is here that Schelling's Identity philosophy appears inseparable from his discussions of nature. Although there is a continuity between thinking and nature, transcendental systems (what Schelling takes from Fichte and Kant and transforms in the Identity philosophy) appear to behave according to their own rules and problems. Given a dynamically productive nature, transcendental philosophy, for Schelling, does not determine the inner workings of this nature, but only ever how our own thinking can take in and think those workings through the mediation of experiment (through the detour of the actual). While our thinking is caused, however strangely and indirectly, by nature, the way thought functions is to recapitulate and copy nature according to its own terms. Whereas Kant's systematic constraints were directed fundamentally to make sense of how we have experience at all, for Schelling the constraints on nature are sceptically constructed in order to explain how it is that there are things at all, given a nature which seems endlessly productive. That is, while Kant's combinations of sense experience and intuition to create experiment do not sound far afield from Schelling's view just outlined, it is the authority of reason to reclassify these combinations that separates Kant and Schelling: Kant views the reclassification as to be decided by reason alone. Put otherwise, Schelling sees limits to the conceptual in the face of nature, while for Kant those limits manifest only as a failure of reason. According to Schelling, reason, as a juridical function, is insufficient to investigate the depths of nature. This has been interpreted as an irrationalist position, which is a hasty declaration. It is not that Schelling doubts reason's importance or the importance of the form of the transcendental for Kant, but only that, for Schelling, thinking (in the form of reason or otherwise) is more intimately bound to a dynamic nature that Kant's philosophy can allow.

In *Ideas for a Philosophy of Nature*, Schelling writes:

> What then is that secret bond which couples our mind to Nature, or that hidden organ through which Nature speaks to our mind or our mind to Nature? We grant you in advance all your explanations of how such a purposive Nature has come to be actual *outside us*. For to explain this purposiveness by the fact that a divine intelligence is its author is not to philosophize, but to propound pious opinions [. . .] For the existence of such a Nature *outside me* is still far from explaining the existence of such a Nature *in me*; for if you assume that a predetermined harmony occurs between the two, indeed that is just the object of our question [. . .] Nature should be Mind made visible, Mind the invisible Nature.[45]

Schelling's assertion that mind is invisible nature and nature is visible mind is thus not an adherence to a form of either crude realism or crude idealism. It is rather a manoeuvre that addresses the continuity or identity of both (on a natural level or according to nature), while admitting that a methodological or descriptive split exists between then. That is, while reduction is explanation (at the level of nature), the ideal as description has an efficacy (or a power, following Schelling's language) because of the natural realm in which it has emerged.

The strangeness of this claim can be reduced if one takes for granted the justificational impenetrability of the empirical as Kant's starting point. Kant, fully absorbing the fear of Hume's scepticism, begins by accepting that our cognition has no external ground, which allows him to justify reason's self-originary state as following from the capacity of the always-already conceptual, that is, of empirically recognising the appearances we encounter, although those seemingly have no final supersensible ground beneath them. Reason must, for Kant, be able to draw final conclusions about all other forms of thought. As Iain Hamilton Grant describes it, such a procedure, whether in Kant, Fichte, Hegel or Brandom, can only seem to be so much immaterial rational bootstrapping.[46] Such a paranoid fear of the groundless can of course be covered over, again following Grant's lead, by appealing to the practical. Another trajectory for avoiding the problematic of groundlessness is that of Johnston and Žižek, which is to transcendentally, in a Kantian sense, privilege the form of the human subject as a symbolic rupture or gap in the world.[47] In both cases, nature is excluded. In the first case, the necessity of the practical stops the creeping advance of scepticism at the expense of nature. In the second, the inexplicability of human capacities means we represent the 'weakness' of nature, in other words, human freedom is *the* expression of the gaps in the natural world structure.

The missing gesture: Plato and Aristotle via Schelling

> Suppose that the nurslings of Cronos, having this boundless leisure, and the power of holding intercourse, not only with men, but with the brute creation, had used all these advantages with a view to philosophy, conversing with the brutes as well as with one another, and learning of every nature which was gifted with any special power, and was able to contribute some special experience to the store of wisdom, there would be no difficulty in deciding that they would be a thousand times happier than the men of our own day. Or, again, if they had merely eaten and drunk until they were full, and told stories to one another and to the animals – such stories as are now attributed to them – in this case also, as I should imagine, the answer would be easy. But until some satisfactory witness can be found of the love of that age for knowledge and discussion, we had better let the matter drop, and give the reason why we have unearthed this tale, and then we shall be able to get on. In the fullness of time, when the change was to take place, and the earth-born race had all perished, and every soul had completed its proper cycle of births and been sown in the earth her appointed number of times, the pilot of the universe let the helm go, and retired to his place of view; and then Fate and innate desire reversed the motion of the world.[48]

> Some things are only actually, some potentially, some potentially and actually, what they are, viz. in one case a particular reality, in another, characterized by a particular quantity, or the like. There is no movement apart from things; for change is always according to the categories of being, and there is nothing common to these and in no one category. But each of the categories belongs to all its subjects in either of two ways (e.g. 'this-ness' for one kind of it is 'positive form', and the other is 'privation'; and as regards quality one kind is 'white' and the other 'black', and as regards quantity one kind is 'complete' and the other 'incomplete', and as regards spatial movement one is 'upwards' and the other 'downwards', or one thing is 'light' and another 'heavy'); so that there are as many kinds of movement and change as of being. There being a distinction in each class of things between the potential and the completely real, I call the actuality of the potential as such, movement.[49]

> The best course for a life devoted to philosophy is to have begun with Plato and to end with Aristotle.[50]

Schelling's transcendental naturalism, a naturalism that takes thought and ideas to be within nature, can be pictured broadly in his augmentation of Plato with Aristotle and of Aristotle with Plato. This augmentation allows for an unorthodox reading of both thinkers. For Schelling, Plato's treatment of the idea only makes sense when Platonic cosmology is set within one world, a world composed of small naturalistic motions such as described by Aristotle. In a parallel fashion, Aristotle's treatment of activity or motion denies any notion of perfection to close or contain the collection of actions that compose and direct the world. Thus, the movement of the idea is one example of a motion that seems uncontainable, as the very notion of containment moves beyond any notion of closure. How can this picture be articulated?

In *The Philosophy of Art* Schelling writes:

> A picture is symbolic whose subject not only signifies or means the idea, but is itself the idea. You can see yourself that in this way the symbolic painting coincides completely with the so-called historical painting and actually designates the higher potence of the latter. Here again we encounter distinctions according to the object, which can either be something universally human that perpetually recurs and renews itself in life, or refer to completely spiritual and intellectual ideas. The latter is represented by Raphael's *Parnassus* and *The School of Athens*, which symbolically portray the entirety of philosophy.[51]

We can illustrate the Platonic–Aristotelian tension from within this very image. The reason why Platonic images can exist in this world and need not exist in their own ideal realm, as well as the reason why naturalistically explained animal motion must exceed its roots and its future containment, lies in the nature of potencies, powers that exponentially create and yet are inexistent. Inexistence here denotes the constructive amphiboly of being and becoming as that which is already but may never be, in a way that we recognise as either being or becoming, and powers function by having the qualities of being and becoming, but not necessarily the status of things.[52]

Consequently, the inexistent can be taken as the unpainted movement in Raphael's *The School of Athens*: the unseen fall of the hand from Plato's ideal-upwards finger, to Aristotle's actual-emphasising downward palm. Motion (here as gesture) is the continuum by which Schelling can make the claim that Platonic abstraction and Aristotelian concretion are contiguous rather than oppositional. One begins with Plato because thinking (for us) begins in abstraction, and it is only through abstraction that we can burrow down to the concrete. Yet abstractions are the result of an augmentative procedure of compounded actualities best understood in an Aristotelian vein. It is this open-endedness of thought, focused through the locality of the concrete, in which Schelling's emphasis on motion highlights the tension between the mobile and the immobile – the tension of explaining the seemingly unlimited power of thought via the unavoidable

problems of localised action. The problem here is not simply one of applying or transforming thought into action, but of asking how thought and
all motion are localised at all.

To put this in Schelling's terms: how do we pass from the Platonic first
motion, the world-soul, to isolated forms of activity, thereby allowing them
to be animated, yet perform their own motions? Or, how does one move
from Plato's account of the abstract as universality arising from nature's
potencies to Aristotle's exploration of the actual in terms of the accretion
of dimensionality consequent on animality? In addressing motion and
subsequently space through the question of world in the ancient sense,
Schelling is able to reintroduce nature as a problem since the Greek notion
of world is congruent with that of our modern cosmos, or the all, or nature
in its fully creative sense.

Plato

For Schelling, the *Timaeus* functions as a philosophical Proteus, a form
that he couples with the assertion that only nature can be said to be
a priori, thereby suggesting that philosophy is the attempt to think the
unconditioned all. In other words, against the parochial view of Plato
as driving a wedge between idea and physical existence, Schelling argues
for a Platonic nature (however thinly constructed in the *Timaeus*) as that
which must be capable of genetically producing both thought and thing.
In always being mindful of this ur-form of philosophy (nature as radical
continuity without purely thinkable unity), the question becomes: what is
the presumed first motion of the world an abstraction from? As the young
Schelling pointed out in his essay on the *Timaeus* (1794), the motion that
seems to be in matter, in the possibility of an internal alteration of the
world, is the *notion* of motion or change – it requires cognition and thus
is not original.[53]

It may appear anathema to claim that the world-soul, one of the most
abstract and ideal components of Plato's system, should be considered
an important part of a naturalistic view. Yet if physics is taken as a basic,
if abstract, component of naturalism, the non-total absolutisation of
motion appears less curious given a non-totalised or open-ended world.[54]
Or, put otherwise, absolute motion is the assumption that allows a naturalism to occur and occur in a world with no fixed beginning or end in
time or space.

Taking the world-soul of the *Timaeus* as a one-world physics, nevertheless treated methodologically as two,[55] we can derive from it basic
categories of sameness and difference – categories that can exist in relation

to each other in periods of rest and motion around an axis. Thus, for Schelling, existence is the mystery, whereas essence is a determination that leaves the residue of ground as remainder. The non-totality of the world is not justified solely by the insufficiency of classificatory knowledge, but by the errancy of production or the fact that motion is recursively added to itself. If the *Timaeus* provides the ur-form of philosophy itself, and if this form is central to Schelling's *Naturphilosophie*, then speculative physics, in its present rudimentariness outlined thus far in this chapter, must apply to Schelling's own way of forming philosophy as such. Taking our afore-mentioned themes in stride (dynamics, motion, space), we can say that Schelling's own practice of philosophising is a self-destructive or, more accurately, as already mentioned in the introduction, an ablative one.

While he is often himself seen as being too protean a thinker due to internal inconsistencies, it can be readily argued that Schelling is in fact committed to a protean form of philosophy as such. This is not to say that Schelling is consistently inconsistent. It rather means that since thought, as a part of nature, is dynamic motion in a continuous space, one can only ever hope to construct local meta-stable constructions.[56] In other words, there can only ever be systems and not one system. If there is a personal motivation to this mode of philosophising for Schelling, it is not manic inconsistency, but melancholy. As seen in one of the epigraphs from the introduction above, Schelling wrote, already at an early age, that nothing saddens the philosopher more than seeing their own system completed. This opposition to totality is also indicative of the concerns levelled at Schelling, via the charge of Spinozism addressed above, namely, that Schelling absorbs pre-critical metaphysical systems in terms of their demands and not their forms nor their methods. To ignore the desire and motives for metaphysics is to be less critical than to accept Kant's system wholeheartedly.

Yet the functions of the categorical and the mobile are not divorced. The Platonic dialogue most attentive to motion (after the *Timaeus*) is *The Statesman*, which attempts to flesh out the logic of classification in how abstract or theoretical knowledge relates to practical knowledge. The Eleatic Stranger, one of the *dramatis personae* in the dialogue and arguably a stand-in for Parmenides of Elea, demonstrates the seemingly unending variety of classes before arguing that a certain fiction needs to be enter-tained – that of the universe in motion, a motion that at times in the past has retrograded, so that the material of the world is recycled.[57] At its root, this illustration functions to say that there is a material at stake in motion, which interferes at the level of the concrete in terms of 'the due measure. Or, no formal measurement can function without some stability to substrate being measured.'[58] That is, the determination of a particular pragmatic skill (a knowledge coupled with a local motion) is required to make order out of the spinning chaos of the world. In addition, the art of measure (or determination) is especially important for hunting or tracking (as the Stranger describes it) those movements that are not readily visible. This claim thereby points to the importance of the being of non-being, or the being of the inexistent, or the motion of the world-soul demonstrated in its products. Schelling's utilisation of the world-soul is due to the abstraction (or de-potentiation) of thought itself as an activity. But this activity is consequent upon its discovery in thought, which in turn is consequent on animal motion.

The immediate problem for a philosophy of nature that Schelling recognises is the following tension: the unconditioned cannot lie in a particular product of nature, and yet analysis can only work with products. Transcendental philosophy, under Schelling's transformations, takes up the unconditioned of nature as the process of speculative construction, thereby ungrounding the form of the transcendental put forth by Kant. But, following Aristotle, this speculation has an ontologically naturalistic ground. Yet, and as will be articulated in the chapters that follow, idealism is not a philosophy concerned with thinking forces above the world, but an inexistent guarantee that the naturalistic world can function immanently without being bound to a closed form of immanence.

Aristotle

> That is, just as the human reason represents the world only according to a certain form, whose visible expression is .the human organization, so every organism is the expression of a certain schematism of the intuition of the world. Just as we surely see that our intuition of the world is determined through our original limitation, without our being able to explain why we are precisely limited in this way, and why our intuition of the world is precisely this and no other, so too the life and the intelligence of animals can be just a peculiar (although inconceivable) kind of original limitation, and only their mode of limitation would distinguish them from us.[59]

Schelling's 21st lecture from the *Presentation of Pure Rational Philosophy* cycle begins with a critique of Kant's utilisation of Copernican imagery and ends with the corpses of frozen mammoths. Why? Schelling notes that Kepler, following Copernicus, wanted to end 'the ineffable celerity of the world', to bring things to a calm. Taking this as the motor for knowledge, as Kant famously did, has, according to Schelling, the result of erasing the activity of nature (as well as the tension between motion and rest) by placing it within reason.[60] Schelling finds in the palaeontological work of Georges Cuvier the opposite gesture, that of saying that extinction is to be found in materiality alone. Yet Cuvier's geological and palaeontological catastrophism threatens to erase the realm of movement of forces. Schelling writes: 'From matter alone the Invisible that is relentless and as it were knows no other principle that nothing possible remains, that in the place of the disappeared, the now living ever more similar kinds constantly change.'[61]

Neither an internal idealisation of absolute motion nor a complete externalisation of motion as material contingency can do justice to nature – that nature which, according to Schelling, functions by the law of the world: that all possibilities are self-fulfilling and everything deploys in equal measure to the extent that something does not make creation or generating of others impossible. Yet, given this, how do we move in a well-spring of motion that is doubled (as both seemingly external and seemingly internal)? That is, how do we come to reason as a compass, a ground of dimensions, caught in (at least two) series of motions? Iain Grant addresses this in his text 'How Nature Comes to be Thought':

> The 'ground of dimensionality' can only be thought consequently upon dimensionality, or, in other words, dimensionality is emergent, if it is at all, from what is not dimensional. This does not mean that there *are no dimensions prior to their thought*, but that there are none prior to the operation of dimensions such that only such a thought is capable of thinking the emergence of dimensionality from non-dimensionality as such [. . .] since thought is that dimension of motion that causes the problem of the ground of dimensionality to be a problem, it is clear that thought is amongst the dimensions of the motions of bodies, or better, is precisely the totality of motions of which bodies are capable.[62]

Not only does Grant's point re-emphasise the importance of motion in Kantian and post-Kantian thought, it also points to a place for physics in terms of grounding reason beyond establishing the physical conditions for the limitation of the senses. Physics as speculation in this sense becomes more closely aligned with the way in which naturalism is utilised to probe the conditions for producing reasons. It also introduces the importance of locality in addressing the relation of thought to nature. In focusing on animal-centric movement (locomotion), we can begin to construct the relation between the abstract local account of motion in the previous section and a speculative theory of the numerous kinds of thought rising from basic animal navigations.

In his 19th lecture from the *Presentation of Pure Rational Philosophy* Schelling investigates these basic navigations via Aristotle. Schelling points out that Aristotle goes against his own philosophy in indexing a form (namely perfection) rather than attempting to derive animal dimension from the progression of line, surface and body.[63] The progression of organic forms is a development of trajectories, both in an embodied sense and in the way in which this very embodiment allows for the ramifications of dimensionality and engenders them. While external definition of dimensionality (length, width, breadth, etc.) is anchorless, Schelling points out that the ground of dimensionality is one internal to species. The difficulty, which Aristotle attempts to avoid through an uncharacteristic appeal to perfection (or, for our purposes here, totality), is that of deciding which bonded pair or dialectic is first – back–forward or right–left. This indecision valorises the inexistent, or relative-non-being, of ground (this is, again, the reason why the presumed first motion is consequent but operates as absolute), which is both origin and the past.[64]

Bemoaning both Aristotle's and Plato's obscure notions of matter, Schelling writes: 'The first natural motion of what sinks into proto-materiality is to re-emerge as principles, by which means dimensions in fact arise.'[65] From this motion, which we understand as length, a negative ground, a ground to move away from, is posited – hence motion is the test of its own potential escape from its abstracted origin. The voluntary production of movement, however, requires a mapping of direction. It is the capacity to map and to place, via dimensionality and direction, that Schelling takes to be the fundamental meaning of soul in Aristotle's work.[66] Rationality is consequent upon an augmented series of motions built upon a further series of motions – sentience (the ability to track motion and map dimensions) feeds into sapience, which pushes sentience behind it as a ground, but persists in exploring the consequences of sentience for itself (the visual line of navigation becomes the mathematical line of construction).

In order to construct entities such as the abstract line, I will now move on to the relation of thought and sense as it is constructed in late Kant and Maimon, as well as to the way in which Schelling's work follows indirectly from these figures.

Notes

1. In this regard my initial starting point is similar to Thomas Nagel's, as exemplified in his book *Mind and Cosmos: Why the Materialist Neo-Darwinian Concept of Nature is Almost Certainly False* (Oxford: Oxford University Press, 2012). However, as I will argue in the latter chapters of this book, Nagel suffers from a narrow reading of reductionism. As an alternative to Nagel, I believe that Schelling's concept of depotentiation preserves the capacities of thought without overdetermining the cosmos with the structure of thought.

2. F. W. J. von Schelling, 'Of the I as a Principle of Philosophy', in *The Unconditional in Human Knowledge: Four Early Essays (1794–1796)*, trans. F. Marti (Lewisburg, PA: Bucknell University Press, 1980), 126–7.

3. For an extensive account of this unease, see Joan Steigerwald, 'Natural Purposes and the Purposiveness of Nature: The Antinomy of the Teleological Power of Judgment', in *Romanticism and Modernity*, ed. Robert Mitchell and Thomas Pfau (New York: Routledge, 2011), 29–46.

4. F. W. J. von Schelling, *On the History of Modern Philosophy*, trans. Andrew Bowie (Cambridge: Cambridge University Press, 1994), 107–8.

5. Immanuel Kant, *Critique of the Power of Judgment*, trans. Paul Guyer and Eric Matthews (Cambridge: Cambridge University Press, 2000), 143–4 (5:260–1). I follow the standard citation of Kant's work where notations in parentheses refer to Kant's *Gesammelte Schriften* (Berlin: de Gruyter, 1902), while references to the *Critique of Pure Reason* have the standard A and B versions referenced as well.

6. Ibid., 3–5 (20:196–8).

7. Ibid., 8 (20:202).

8. Ibid., 19 (20:216).

9. Immanuel Kant, 'Concerning the Ultimate Ground of the Differentiation of Directions in Space', in *Theoretical Philosophy 1775–1780*, trans. and ed. David Walford (Cambridge: Cambridge University Press, 2003), 365 (2:377).

10. Ibid., 366 (2:378).

11. Ibid., 369 (2:381).

12. Christian Kerslake, *Immanence and the Vertigo of Philosophy* (Edinburgh: Edinburgh University Press, 2009), 133.

13. The texts I am working with are lectures translated by Iain Hamilton Grant from Schelling's *Philosophische Einleitung in die Philosophie der Mythologie oder Darstellung der Reinrationalen Philosophie*, in F. W. J. Schelling, *Sämmtliche Werke*, ed. K. F. A. Schelling (Stuttgart: J. G. Cotta, 1856), Vol. XI. Throughout I will refer to them as the *Darstellung* following Grant and Daniel Whistler's usage.

14. F. W. J. von Schelling, *First Outline of a System of the Philosophy of Nature*, trans. K. R. Petersen (Albany, NY: SUNY Press, 2004), 14–15.

15. Immanuel Kant, *Opus Postumum*, trans. Eckhart Förster and Michael Rosen (Cambridge: Cambridge University Press, 1993), 240 (21:41).

16. F. W. J. von Schelling, *Darstellung Lecture 19*, trans. Iain Hamilton Grant (unpublished manuscript, 2013), 2. Translated excerpt from Schelling, *Sämmtliche Werke*, Vol. XI, 433–56.

17. See Slavoj Žižek, *Tarrying with the Negative: Kant, Hegel, and the Critique of Ideology* (Durham, NC: Duke University Press, 1993).

18. A kind of historical irony is at work here, since several thinkers attempted to defend Kant from idealist interpretation against Fichte and Schelling. These pre-neo-Kantians (including Fries, Herbart and Beneke) paved the way for the neo-Kantianism of the 1860s which would, in many ways, open the door for analytic philosophy. These figures would, however, be rejected for being 'too mired in psychology', thereby moving thought back towards a kind of idealism.

19. The relation of the speculative and the pragmatic against the restrictions of the practical will be the focus of Chapter 6.

20. By 'internalised I', I am referring to the notion of projection that is the focus of Fichte's 14th lecture in the 1804 *Wissenschaftslehre*. This projection can be taken as the outside world influencing pre-intentional consciousness, or it can be viewed as simply the capacity to be objective within the realm of consciousness.

21. J. G. Fichte, *The Science of Knowing: J.G. Fichte's 1804 Lectures on the Wissenschaftslehre*, trans. Walter Wright (Albany, NY: SUNY Press, 2005), 39.

22. Dieter Sturma, 'The Nature of Subjectivity: The Critical and Systematic Function of Schelling's Philosophy of Nature', in *The Reception of Kant's Critical Philosophy: Fichte, Schelling, and Hegel*, ed. Sally Sedgwick (Edinburgh: Edinburgh University Press, 2007), 227.

23. This is tied to Fichte's notion of facticity, namely, that facticity applies to how sense functions for the natural sciences as well as to the so-called facticity of the individual. Or, in other words, the trouble for Schelling is whether Fichte's notion of fact has more to do with a form of subjective-objectivity of the senses, or whether it is rather a proto-phenomenological form of intentionality when it comes to the topic of nature, or externality more generally.

24. F. W. J. Schelling, *Ideas for a Philosophy of Nature*, trans. E. Harris and P. Heath (Cambridge: Cambridge University Press, 1988), 54.

25. The concern is where does the Fichtean act reside? Is it formal in the same way as Kant's schema as being neither here nor there, as neither intuition nor concept purely?

26. Fichte, *The Science of Knowing*, 21.

27. Ibid., 25.

28. Ibid., 25.

29. Paul Franks, 'Transcendental Arguments, Reason, and Skepticism', in *Transcendental Arguments: Problems and Prospects*, ed. Robert Stern (Oxford: Oxford University Press, 2000), 129.

30. Allen Wood, 'The "I" as Principle of Practical Philosophy', in *The Reception of Kant's Critical Philosophy: Fichte, Schelling, and Hegel*, ed. Sally Sedgwick (Edinburgh: Edinburgh University Press, 2007), 94.

31. F. W. J. von Schelling, *System of Transcendental Idealism*, trans. Peter Heath (Charlottesville, VA: University of Virginia Press, 1978), 61.

32. Franks, *All or Nothing*.

33. Jacobi quoted in Frederick Beiser, *The Fate of Reason: German Philosophy from Kant to Fichte* (Cambridge, MA: Harvard University Press, 1993), 67.

34. Iain Hamilton Grant, presentation at '*Naturphilosophie*' Summer School, Pittsburgh, PA, 5–9 August 2013.

35. Schelling, *On the History of Modern Philosophy*, 104.

36. Ibid., 66.

37. Adrian Johnston, *Adventures in Transcendental Materialism: Dialogues with Contemporary Thinkers* (Edinburgh: Edinburgh University Press, 2014), 50–65. Johnston is suspiciously silent on the fact that all the neo-Spinozists he cites have largely political motivations for their adherence to Deleuze and/or Spinoza, while Grant does not.

38. Ibid., 52.

39. Ibid., 52.

40. Ibid., 52.

41. Grant's book references texts from after 1809 63 times by my count, which, in a book of just over 200 pages, is quite a substantial number.

42. Johnston, *Adventures in Transcendental Materialism*, 53.

43. Ibid., 53. Also it is important to note that *The Berlin Lectures* are a selection of Schelling's *Philosophie der Offenbarung*.

44. I will address Schelling's emphasis on God's personality, as between Spinoza's and Leibniz's, via the work of Edward Beach in Chapter 4.

45. Schelling, *Ideas for a Philosophy of Nature*, 41–2.

46. Iain Hamilton Grant, 'The Movements of the World: The Sources of Transcendental Philosophy', *Analecta Hermeneutica*, 3 (2011): 6.

47. Žižek has consistently maintained this position from at least as early as *The Sublime Object of Ideology* (London: Verso, 1989). For a recent formulation, see *Less than Nothing: Hegel and the Shadow of Dialectical Materialism* (New York: Verso, 2012), 266–7.

48. Plato, *The Statesman*, in *Plato: Complete Works*, ed. John Cooper (Indianapolis, IN: Hackett Publishing, 1997), 314.

49. Aristotle, *Metaphysics*, in *The Basic Works of Aristotle*, ed. Richard McKeon (New York: Modern Library, 2001), 759.

50. F. W. J. von Schelling, *Darstellung Lecture 16*, trans. Iain Hamilton Grant (unpublished manuscript, 2013), 5. Translated excerpt from Schelling, *Sämmtliche Werke*, Vol. IX, 361–3.

51. F. W. J. von Schelling, *The Philosophy of Art*, trans. Douglass Stott and David Simpson (Minneapolis, MN: University of Minnesota Press, 2008), 151.

52. For an extended treatment of the concept of inexistence related to Schelling's notion of powers, see Iain Hamilton Grant, 'The Law of Insuperable Environment: What is Exhibited in the Exhibition of the Process of Nature?', *Analecta Hermeneutica*, 5 (2013): 1–12.

53. F. W. J. von Schelling, *Timaeus*, trans. Adam Arola, Jenna Jolissaint and Peter Warnek, *Epoche*, 12.2 (2008): 210–11.

54. While it has become almost commonplace to lean on Cantorian set theory to emphasise the non-existence of a set of all sets, Schelling's mathematical interests lie in proto-intuitionist geometry and, particularly, in the importance of the trans – an emphasis that the mathematician Fernando Zalamea has recently pointed out was typical of Romantic era thinkers. In this sense Schelling's interests lean more towards the categorical than the set-theoretical, more towards transformation (or motion) than in belonging. I discuss Zalamea in Chapter 3.

55. This was an open debate between specialists in Plato as late as the 1940s and it seems to have been closed after Arthur Lovejoy's *The Great Chain of Being* (Cambridge, MA: Harvard University Press, 1936). For an opposed Platonic realist view, see Constantin Ritter, *The Essence of Plato's Philosophy* (Mcmphis, TN: Jackson Press, 2007).

56. In *Schelling's Organic Form of Philosophy*, Bruce Matthews suggests a similar problem with Schelling's thought, but in hermeneutic not physical terms: Matthews suggests that Schelling's proclaimed strategy for discovering the singular thought of a given philosopher is a strategy that is difficult, if not impossible, to apply to Schelling himself.

57. As the Eleatic Stranger says: 'Remaining permanently in the same state and condition, and being permanently the same, belongs only to the most divine things of all, and by its nature body is not of this order. Now the thing to which we have given the name of "heaven" and "cosmos" certainly has a portion of many blessed things from its progenitor, but on the other hand it also has its share of body. In consequence it is impossible for it to be altogether exempt from change, although as far as is possible, given its capacities, it moves in the same place, in the same way, with a single motion; and this is why it has reverse rotation as its lot, which is the smallest variation of its movement.' Plato, *The Statesman*, 311.

58. Ibid., 327.

59. Schelling, *First Outline*, 132.

60. Schelling, *Darstellung Lecture 21*, trans. Iain Hamilton Grant (unpublished manuscript, 2013), 3. Translated excerpt from Schelling, *Sämmtliche Werke*, Vol. XI, 490–515.

61. Ibid., 8–9.

62. Iain Hamilton Grant, 'How Nature Comes to be Thought: Schelling's Paradox and the Problem of Location', *Journal of the British Society for Phenomenology*, 44.1 (2013): 25–44.

63. Schelling, *Darstellung Lecture 19*, 1–2.

64. Ibid., 7.

65. Ibid., 9.

66. Ibid., 9.

Chapter 2

Castles of Ether and Asymptotic Bridges: Kant, Maimon, Schelling and the Relation of Inner and Outer Sense

If, as we saw in the last chapter, Kant's *Critique of the Power of Judgment* (1790) showed some possible escape routes from the critical system, routes which the German Idealists later explored, the *Opus Postumum* (1804) is a work that appears to simultaneously break with, and yet shore up, the speculative reach of the critical project. While one could engage *The Metaphysical Foundations of Natural Science* (1786) as Kant's definitive and sophisticated engagement with the physical sciences, fully determining the relation of inner and outer sense, I will address the far more controversial *Opus Postumum* for several reasons.[1] Centrally, the *Opus Postumum* is Kant at his seemingly least critical and most metaphysical, following the much-vaunted Copernican turn. Kant's Copernican turn, as has been widely discussed, placed the subject-as-observer at the centre of the epistemological cosmos. In other words, for Kant, the forces and dynamics detected in outer sense are made possible by the forms of inner sense in order for us to speak about the world at all. Whether this placement is a necessary assumption for a modest epistemological stance, or whether it amounts to a form of anthropocentrism in thinking, remains a much-debated issue. Confusion over the nature of Kant's revolution, I argue, stems largely from collapsing a position (*where* we know from) and subject–object relation (what has the final say on the judgement of the knower on the known, or the known's effects on the knower). While Schelling would be critical of Kant on the later point, he would fully appreciate the uprooting of humanity's fixed place in the cosmos coextensively actual and epistemological.[2]

In the *Opus*, Kant touches upon Schelling's work (albeit slightly) and, more extensively, engages with numerous Schellingian themes close to our project here: the importance of motion, the continuity of nature and the division between speculative metaphysics and empirical physics.[3] More specifically, while in the *Critique of Pure Reason* Kant moved away from absolutising space to relying on an internal and ideal space of observation, he appears to swing back towards something more like absolute space in the *Opus*.

The first two above themes are addressed in the *Opus* through the notions of the ether and matter, both of which are connected with, and brought to bear on, the metaphysical/physical divide through a lengthy discussion of space.[4] Before discussing the *Opus*, however, I wish to examine a precise treatment of space in Kant's critical thought. Kant's remarkable 'What Does It Mean to Orient Oneself in Thinking?' (1786), which additionally addresses the pragmatic/navigational terms that we will tackle towards the end of this book, gives some clue as to the relation of inner (intensive) to outer (or extensive) conceptual space in practical navigation. I use the term navigation as shorthand for the synthesis of motion and space, between the numerous capacities of inner navigation (experience, intuition, reason, speculation) and that of outer structure (space, horizon, direction, magnitude, etc.). Furthermore, navigation, as it is described in Kant, can be taken as a measure of the tensions between the inner and outer rooting of space and motion and a machinery for constructing the bridge between the inner and outer. It can be considered either analytic (as self-evidently external) or synthetic (as provisionally internal). Or, put otherwise, the analytic are those concepts true by definition (a bachelor is an unmarried man), whereas the synthetic requires some 'work' on the part of the observer (a red chair is a combination of redness and chairness).

Following this, I will then address how Salomon Maimon's critique of the *a priori* synthetic activity, supported by his discussions of mathematics, suggests that speculation breaks the critical system, allowing for a synthesis of the natural and mental in a fashion that inspires Schelling's dynamic treatment of nature, which I explore in the last two sections of this chapter. Maimon's work, as we will see, pushes the tentative dynamism of Kant's thoughts on nature (from the *Critique of Judgment*), on which Schelling indirectly expands.[5] This dynamic push centres on the problematic relation of the qualitative to the quantitative primarily in terms of magnitude, which interlaces construction (understood genetically) and intensity (understood as polarity). Maimon's law of determinability, in what appears to be a proto-Schellingian fashion, attempts to combine a genetic or asymmetrical creation of objectivity on the one hand, with a polarity between intuition and conceptualisation on the other. The notion of the genetic, which accompanies that of determination, is imperative for maintaining difference in any case where dualisms (mind and nature, inner and outer) are questioned and treated as magnitudes.

I wish to argue ultimately that a physicalisation of Kant's perspectival mode, conjoined with Maimon's discussion of magnitudes, creates a historically indirect, but conceptually fertile, ground for Schelling's reconstruction of nature via powers. That construction will be the focus of Chapters 3 and 4.

Kant's 'What Does It Mean to Orient Oneself in Thinking?'

Kant's essay 'What Does It Mean to Orient Oneself in Thinking?', which shares its general theme with the far better known 'What is Enlightenment?' essay written two years previously (focusing on the Enlightenment as thinking for oneself), is his answer to the pressure to speak to the pantheism controversy raging in Germany at the time. In both texts Kant argues that reason must subject itself to its own law unless it wishes to be yoked to external law. But, unlike 'What is Enlightenment?', Kant's orientation essay works with the terms of geography and horizons, and seems more willing to admit the possible pitfalls of reason, specifically of reason as being potentially dangerous in its somewhat arbitrary selection of a horizon and the subsequent navigation towards it. Kant writes:

> In the proper meaning of the word, to orient oneself [*Bedeutung*] means to use a given direction (when we divide the horizon into four of them) in order to find the others – literally, to fix the sunrise. Now if I see the sun in the sky and know it is now midday, then I know how to find south, west, north, and east. For this, however, I also need the feeling of a difference in my own subject, namely, the difference between my right and left hands. I call this a feeling because these two sides outwardly display no designatable difference in intuition. If I did not have this faculty of distinguishing, without the need of any difference in the external objects, then in describing a circle I would not know whether west was right or left of the southernmost point of the horizon, or whether I should complete the circle by moving north and east and thus back to south. Thus even with all the objective data of the sky, I orient myself geographically only through a subjective ground of differentiation; and if all the constellations, though keeping the same shape and position relative to one another, were one day by a miracle to be reversed in their direction, so that what was east now became west, no human eye would notice the slightest alteration on the next bright Starlit night, and even the astronomer – if he pays attention only to what he sees and not at the same time to what he feels – would inevitably become disoriented.[6]

At first glance, the question of position and horizon suggests that the spatiality of Kant's orientation is (unsurprisingly) neither purely empirical nor purely dogmatic. The insistence on 'a subjective ground of differentiation' reasserts the apparent (though tautological) formalism of the critical system. As Schelling argues in *The Grounding of Positive Philosophy*, the transcendental ideal that motivates Kant's critical philosophy only ever leads to a negative philosophy in that it can only critique from essentially nowhere, or only from the non-location of its own conditions as the functioning of reason outside experience. At the same time, 'What Does It Mean to Orient Oneself in Thinking?' demonstrates the shift in emphasis, suggested by Peg Rawes, regarding the relation of inner and outer sense to the conceptualisation of space. She writes:

> Thus, in the development from the first to the third Critique, the relationship between experience and space undergoes a dramatic shift in which external or transcendental understandings of spatial relations become internalised into the powers of the sensing and reflective subject. Space and time are transformed from limited transcendental forms into indeterminate cognitions or judgments that are constituted by the thinking subject: cognizing geometry and space become embodied aesthetic judgments so that disembodied reason is transformed into a perceiving and embodied sense-reason.[7]

This transition is evident in the above passage from Kant, as it becomes somewhat dubious whether the notion of the transcendental from the *Critique of Pure Reason* can account for the articulation of 'feeling' in the embodied sense it immediately invokes. An internal sense of space referring to external objects (the sun, Kant's hands) allows one to retroactively accept 'a given direction' as analytically valid (the sun is there, so that is west). The act of extrapolating from chirality (or handedness) to an objective division of the horizon may appear to be slightly more synthetic than Kant might feel comfortable with, given the subsequent self-judging responsibility of reason. Rawes argues that whereas in 'Concerning the Ultimate Ground' Kant keeps sense and reason closely related, by the time of the *Critique of Judgment*, and as already suggested in 'What Does It Mean to Orient Oneself in Thinking?', they have become more and more alienated from each other while, somewhat paradoxically, the synthetic power of orientation has become more internalised.

A whole nexus of issues can be investigated here, all of which are too large for this book. It is, however, important to note that Kant's uprooting of the subject, which risks falling into a crude idealism, is in fact is coupled with an emphasis on navigation and locality. Inner sense, in this regard, becomes obscure, since Kant chooses to localise it, but arguably without emphasising any notion of embodiment. It is for this reason, and to return to the present stakes of this chapter, that so much ink has been spilled regarding the status of space, and the relation of sense to space, in the *Critique of Pure Reason*. While in 'Concerning the Ultimate Ground', Kant seems to rely on some notion of embodiment, in the first *Critique* he makes internality abstract or ideal, all by carefully dividing kinds of thinking, and by relying on the separation of faculties and careful categorisation.[8]

Beyond this reading, can the Kantian view of sense as orientation suggest an attention to perspective, one that de-emphasises the groundedness of the empirical subject, and puts in its place a more aimless or abstract navigator? The tension, and one which I will explore both through Kant's wrestling with nature in the *Critique of Judgment* and the *Opus*, is brought into the open most directly by Salomon Maimon. Maimon 'out-Kants' Kant in asserting that the judgements Kant sees as analytic are in fact already synthetic. Maimon's emphasis on mathematics is particularly crucial here since, whereas Kant downplayed the constructive power of mathematics (according to Maimon), the internalisation of the power of navigation in a more and more abstract subject requires an extension of the descriptive power of geometry, as Rawes suggests.[9] But before engaging Maimon's critique, as well as Kant's turn towards the physics of the sensible (and arguably to Spinoza in the *Opus Postumum*), we must ask: what can we make of Kant's use of orientation? It would be easy to dismiss the potentially non-critical aspects of the piece as simply adventures in metaphor, but the very opening line of Kant's essay seriously limits, if not completely obliterates, such a possibility. Kant opens the essay with the following: 'However exalted the application of our concepts, and however far up from sensibility we may abstract them, still they will always be appended to *image* representations, whose proper function is to make these concepts, which are not otherwise derived from experience, serviceable for *experiential use.*'[10] Kant goes on to argue in 'What is Orientation' that image representations in thinking are unavoidable, since we could have not given flesh to the bones of inner sense as logical argument otherwise. This point is, of course, important for Kant as the universality of logics comes about from articulating the universal appeal of concepts with their contingently attached intuitionistic (or imagistic) content. It is not difficult to ascertain why Kant appeals to a practical image, such as orientation, in order to avoid falling into what seems to be a vicious circle on the one hand, and to valorise his project of immanent critique on the other. Images, as a conceptual gatekeeper, guarantee swift passage from apparently external objects (horizons) to our already established intuitions about them ('this is my left hand') and allow us to move back out to extrapolate further about the visible horizon. But the status of synthesis between these moments is the central question here. Both Maimon's critique and Kant's fleshing out of space-as-sense in the *Opus* demonstrate that the act of synthesis cannot be as internalisable as Kant suggests in the first *Critique*; but the critical Kant must reject this conclusion out of hand given reason's (normative) responsibility to itself.

Kant argues that neither the vaunted power of speculation, nor religious faith, can be charged with assigning the location of human cognition; only reason, as a formalised aspect of cognition's capacity to judge itself, can accomplish this.[11] Following the passage quoted above, Kant argues that, in the last instance, what allows for orientation is a conditional ground, or understanding's feeling for where it is.[12] Kant writes:

> it will be a concern of pure reason to guide its use when it wants to leave familiar objects (of experience) behind, extending itself beyond all the bounds of experience and finding no object of intuition at all, but merely space for intuition; for then it is no longer in a position to bring its judgments under a determinate maxim according to objective grounds of cognition.[13]

Yet what does Kant mean by *objective* ground here? If objective ground is a solidification of cognition by understanding in relation to intuition, as a feeling supplied by the external need to get from A to B for instance, then how does such a ground hold firm? While fixing the sunrise, for instance, points to the arbitrariness yet necessity of moving into the visual field in order to orient oneself, Kant ends his essay by reinscribing the necessity of following reason's *internal* rules in order to avoid getting swept up in otherwise unbridled and reckless intellectual enthusiasm. Here I do not mean to critique the oscillation between the external force of intuition and that of reason's functional rigidification, but to point out that even here, in the last instance, Kant calls in the normative cavalry to cut down the sheer possibility of infinite regress resulting from an orientation affected by nature.[14] Although Kant's warning against enthusiasm is warranted to avoid getting 'the authorities mixed up in the game', that is, in that normative claims are important to avoid inviting meta-norms, such as state laws, to impinge on intellectual freedom, this precaution does not seem to justify the means by which he limits the ramifications of naturalistic analysis.[15]

The contemporary philosopher Reza Negarestani has a different take on Kant's Copernican navigator as being an advancement towards an imaginary and futural point of scientific observation.[16] As Negarestani puts it:

> Rather than heralding the abolishment of the subject, the perspective operator cuts the subject loose from its immediate foundation by mapping it from one domain to another. Once the subject's reference point to any privileged

instance or position (first or last, particular or generic) is removed, it is finally possible to draw a non-trivial passage from the local subject to the global structure, in effect realizing a continuity that defines an absolutized nature as a universal continuum.[17]

While ostensibly operating within Peircean language, Negarestani goes on to engage Gabriel Catren's Schellingian argument in stating that this passage of self to nature incurs a thesis that reflections, judgements and other forms of thinking can be taken to be cases of nature relating to itself. As he goes on to state: 'If the subject is now immersed in a continuous global structure, the separation of the subject from nature is a required epistemological distinction, not an inherent ontological severance. And if such separation is not ontological, then instantiations of the absolutised nature cannot be measured, or scaled against, the subject.'[18]

In Negarestani's functionalist reading, the structural or formal interiority of Kant-as-judge is nature unfolding itself in the particularity of a generic subject. Yet what remains in question is the status of the valences of the formal, and why particular forms or fields of the subject, and not others, can be articulated as nature relating to itself. But do Kant's normative worries not sabotage this radicality? That is, if the normative or navigational mode of reason is continually set up as not ontological, as merely a local or convenient determination, then this negative condition of normativity becomes, whether intentionally or unintentionally, a blank cheque that absorbs all future consequences of normative actions back into the normative space, back into the domain of inner sense's control.[19] While the degree to which Kant is willing to unmoor the subject remains in question, more at stake, for our purposes here, is the ideality of space-as-space in Kant's thought. While the *Opus Postumum* to which we now move ends with an incomplete doctrine of the self, most of its pages comprise a transformation of Kant's views on space (and time) and, in particular, how they relate to sense and the role of the subject.

The ether proofs: crystallising space or concretising ideality?

The question now raised is that of whether Kant's late work supports or undoes the suggestions made in the last section concerning the radicality of epistemological orientation with regard to the interior and exterior construction of horizons. Specifically, does the *Opus* physicalise space as an external medium *for* sense through which synthesis can occur, or does the text only highlight the physical side of the already present imagistic and intuitional aspects of Kant's treatment of space in the critical system and in the 'Orientation Essay' discussed above?

In some respects, Kant's *Opus Postumum* appears as a kind of panic, or perhaps more fairly a regretful worry, in which he becomes concerned with philosophically reconnecting his critical system, critiqued at large for being 'too distant' from reality, with the physical world by addressing Spinoza's legacy in particular. However, this view is complicated by several factors. For one, it does not take into account Kant's pre-critical views in which nature also seems to operate non-mechanically, if not outright dynamically.[20] While these issues are arguably clearer with regard to the notions of biological life, as Kant separates life and freedom from nature at the opening of the *Critique of Judgment*, and stays with this separation to the end pages of the *Opus Postumum*, it remains somewhat unclear how exactly dynamics fits into nature, as translated into sensible magnitudes. The central issue for the moment, however, is whether the role of representation in the *Opus*, whether drawing on Spinoza and/or the physical sciences, especially in the so-called ether proofs, amounts to a fundamental reworking of the critical system or not. The question here is: does Kant move to embody or otherwise materialise sense, or does he further abstract the subject *vis-à-vis* the sensible outside of nature?

Setting aside the extensive problems with treating the *Opus Postumum* as a coherent text, Kant, in the last work of his life, sets out to finish the critical work, to correct the failings of *The Metaphysical Foundations of Natural Science*, and to make the transition from a philosophy of nature to physics proper. As Förster argues, Kant begins by critiquing the *Metaphysical Foundations*' inability to address the non-empirical *a priori* dimensions of physics in order to systematise physics' empirical endeavours.[21] Kant's endeavour in constructing a physical bridge between the metaphysical and physical worlds is immediately problematic according to the Schellingian view constructed thus far, as the separation between those worlds (in Kant's terms) transforms physics into merely empirical observation justifying *a priori* conditions in a Newtownian language, obfuscating the very nature of hypothesis-construction based on the import of physical data. In other words, the speculative content of the hypothesis is kept at a distance in Kant's *Opus*. That is, as I will attempt to investigate further, Kant appears more comfortable with the notion of construction in the *Opus*, but only to the degree that the powers of such construction are inversely proportional to the embodiment of the subject in a relatively unchangeable net of transcendnetal conditions.

However, while this follows the letter of Kant's work, its spirit is troubled in at least two aspects. First, Kant's bridge-building between the metaphysical science of nature and physics, as a systematised collection of empirical facts,[22] relies upon a theory of the ether (or caloric matter) which Kant argues penetrates all of space, and is the basis for the very possibility of representation.[23] While Kant entertains a similar line of argumentation in the opening pages of the *Critique of Judgment*, there he focuses on reflection and the unity of experience for the subject, whereas, throughout the *Opus*, he goes to even greater lengths to discuss intuition and its importance in probing the admixture of matter and experience. In the *Opus*, Kant seems to physically 'concretise' the field of sense via the ether, while still leaving the subject attached to it (via intuition).

The physical status of this caloric matter is questionable, as it is not only material and all-penetrative, but also described, in more idealistic terms, as a hypostatisation of space itself.[24] Thus, in the *Opus*, it is hard to distinguish the critical, that is, representational need for the ether from its physical necessity (as the possibility of all things to appear). While Schelling, as we will see below, weighs heavily on the side of physical necessity, he is able to do this by leaning on a dynamical physicality over and against Kant's reliance on mechanics and kinematics, thereby keeping the dynamic philosophy separate from Kant's physics (such as under the name of phoronomy, or the *a priori* study of movement).[25] This difference could be ultimately reduced to Kant's and Schelling's respective use of form. Schelling is far more sceptical about the degree to which humans contribute to the forms they find in nature, and yet acknowledges that these forms make their way into our very thinking. Kant, on the other hand, has a far more participatory model, since forms are indispensable for us to engage in acts of cognition and understanding at all, but his views on their subsistence beyond cognition position him too close to dogmatic idealism.

It is not surprising that many commentators have zeroed-in on Kant's apparent physicalisation of sense and argued that he is either falling back into dogmatism (particularly of the Spinozistic variety) or simply expanding the perspectival aspect of the critical enterprise to physics. That is, in the former case Kant would be supplanting schema with sense and in the latter, 'perspectivising' matter itself. Paul Guyer in 'The Unity of Nature and Freedom' argues that Kant's *Opus* is a return to Spinoza in that, for Kant: 'Spinozism is right in its general form of seeing both nature or the order of causes and thought or the order of reasons as modes of an underlying substance, but wrong in identifying God as that substratum.'[26] Jeffrey Edwards, in the same volume as Guyer, disagrees and argues that the substance of the ether (as a continuum of material forces) is only the object of intuition and nothing more.[27] However, Edwards admits that Kant's text presents a serious roadblock to the separation of causality and freedom.[28] This separation, from which Kant sets off in the *Critique of the*

Power of Judgment, is particularly foggy given the somewhat ambiguous use of both dynamics and of the relation between forces of movement and their translation into the motion of bodies. That is, while Schelling fully entangles freedom and dynamics, in that freedom is a human mode of nature's dynamics, Kant maintains that the capacity for movement is separate from any expression of that movement's deeper underlying dynamism. These problems point to Kant's stake in the noumenal, a stake which Schelling, alone among the German Idealists, complicated.[29] While we will engage Schelling in this regard, for the moment it is important to fully explore the ramifications of Kant's final work.

While sense is a central term here, I will not address it directly in relation to the ether proofs but, in keeping with the theme of this book, I will focus on the terms of motion and space. Furthermore, I will address how sense functions as the ground of epistemology in detail in Chapter 5. For now, I will attempt to place the *Opus* (and specifically the ether proofs) in relation to the physical sciences on the one hand, and the capacities of reason on the other. In doing so, it is helpful to examine Eckhart Förster's *Kant's Final Synthesis* and Beth Lord's *Kant and Spinozism*.

Förster argues, in the closing of *Kant's Final Synthesis*, that the *Opus* justifies a reordering of the relation between understanding and reason; he claims that whereas the latter appears, at least in the first *Critique*, as a ramified version of the understanding, it becomes more creative or constructive in the *Opus*, with its creativity constructively constrained in the forms of understanding.[30] In such an articulation, reason becomes more like an ungrounded force and less like a development of well-organised, pre-existing cognitive systems. Yet Kant's reliance on sense to articulate this power troubles reason's creative relation (or lack thereof) to schematicism (in terms of the necessary categories of cognition) or formalism (in terms of generating abstract frameworks), as such. This is most apparent with regard to mathematics and in particular in relation to the work of Salomon Maimon, which I will address below.

Largely in agreement with Förster, Lord sees the *Opus* as a continuation of the critical project and not its undoing. But rather than putting it in terms of shifting the relations of understanding and reason, Lord argues that the *Opus* was 'an attempt to incorporate a principle of immanent genesis into transcendental idealism'.[31] Placing the text in a lineage that includes Maimon and stretches all the way to Gilles Deleuze, Lord argues that the *Opus* was an ambitious, albeit unsuccessful and incomplete, attempt at incorporating difference into Kant's brand of idealism. Lord does an impressive job of demonstrating why she believes this is the case given Kant's diagonal relation to Spinoza. Complicating the accounts outlined above by Guyer and Edwards, Lord argues that Kant's knowledge

of Spinoza should be viewed as second-hand, passing through the interpretation of Jacobi.[32] Kant, in attempting to distance himself from Jacobi's
project to combine the critical philosophy with Spinozistic dogmatism,
does not engage Spinoza directly, but only Jacobi's presentation of him.
The *Opus* is particularly interesting in this regard, as Kant appears to be
softening his view of Spinoza to some extent.

Lord argues that in the *Opus* Kant needs to explain how particular bodies could arise from the tension of forces and hence why the ether appears
as both a material stratum and a condition, or 'a single continuum filling
cosmic space through the oscillation of force'.[33] Lord also argues that Kant
introduces the ether as more of a condition (of sense), but it becomes more
and more substantialised over time.[34] For our purposes here, the most
striking feature of Lord's account of the ether proofs is that it demonstrates
Kant's admission, however slight, that a material unity, or continuum,
must be asserted in order to have even the most basic account of thought.
Whereas the central key of the critical project is often the much-lauded
transcendental ideal – the distributive unity of experience that is achieved
by reason, or the fact that it is our thought that holds the world together
– in the *Opus* the object of the collective unity of experience is *given* prior
to the distributive unity of experience.[35]

The ether, as a simultaneously material and transcendental condition,
seems to disturb not only the normative dismissal of first nature for the sake
of second nature (normativity), but also the very attempt to posit the ether
as a universal condition from a local place (that of the human subject), one
that moreover falls into the logic of orientation already outlined. The ether
becomes the ocean of that navigational project as well as the very capacity
for a 'dynamical horizon' to be detected as such.[36] Again, and to follow
Rawes's suggestion about the internalising of space-making capacities, why
would the ether need to function, even abstractly, as a medium for images,
if the projective capacity of space were located in the powers of the subject,
if inner sense were the final judge?

Lord ends her book with a somewhat critical account of Kant: 'Kant's
transcendental and genetic condition for the real is positioned alongside a
transcendent subject that must still overlay it with those "external" concepts
not to be found in the ether itself.'[37] In this regard, Kant fails to recognise
the limit of the subject, a failure that Lord opposes to the identity thinkers
of German Idealism as well as to Deleuze, who 'truly' appreciated difference. Yet Lord's account of German Idealism is too unitary and assumes
that collectively the Idealists have no concern for difference, particularly
the difference between thought and being. This is not at all the case for
German Idealism writ large and especially not in the case of Schelling. The
suggestion that Kant's use of the ether could be read as keeping nature

separate from thought more so than Schelling's concept of nature and nature's asymmetrical production of thought appears nonsensical.

In his *Philosophies of Nature after Schelling* Grant addresses Kant's ether proofs, arguing that Kant makes the ether, as an insubstantial body, into a broad notion of materiality.[38] In other words, Grant argues that the ether proofs *are* the transition from metaphysics to physics that Kant sought in his twilight years.[39] Rather than follow Lord's emphasis on the ether as having to do with assigning a substratum of material cause, Grant argues, following Schelling's critique of teleological judgement (to be addressed below), that Kant's ether is endemic of the ontologisation of access itself.[40] Grant's account is convincing given, on the one hand, Kant's indirect return to metaphysical concerns in the *Opus* and, on the other, his continuous empowering and desubstantialising of the notion of subject. Arguably, Kant can avoid appearing to fall back into dogmatic metaphysics, as well as maintain his emphasis on the subject as a free and self-regulating agent, by increasing the uprootedness (and abstract definition) of the subject. This he does in the final pages of the *Opus*, while strengthening the tether of sensibility between the subject and the manifold above which it floats. Yet this simultaneous abstraction and empowerment causes difficulties when those theoretical moves include acts of construction such as mathematics, since, in Kant's time and thereafter, the grounds of mathematics began to point to and necessitate greater and greater acts of free creation.

In the *Opus* – and this is already suggested in the Orientation essay – reason's self-policing has to determine sense's externality in order to know the very borders that it is meant to police. There are at least two recognised alternatives to naturalising sense for thought, as Kant does: one is Schelling's naturalisation of thought as that nature which is only subsequently, and methodologically, accessible to us, while the other is Maimon's synthetisation of Kant's analytic realm. This does not mean that Maimon simply absorbs Kant's category of the analytic into the synthetic, but that Maimon thinks that construction plays a slightly more active role in determining the real objects of thought (which might be said to replace the analytic). The self-evidence of these determinations for Maimon is based on a construction, but one that slowly proceeds by a hierarchy of rules. Important for our project here is whether, or how, this project connects to the influence of empirical data for Maimon, or the influence of the non-cognitive on the acts of rule construction.

As we will begin to develop at length in the next chapter, it is Schelling's insistence on naturalising thought, and on arguing that the difference between thought and nature is one of degree, a degree that requires methodological recognition, that harbours the greatest capacity for difference (or genetic construction) as such, and hence has most potential for philosophy. Claiming that an ontological distinction between the ground of the subject and the ground of the real preserves difference is false – such a distinction only preserves the capacity to decide difference at the cost of nature.

I will now move on to the work of Maimon to address how the synthetic power of determination complicates the Kantian appeal to the given in the form of the ether as physicalised sense, as that which makes space as such for us. This critique lies, generally, in Maimon demonstrating that Kant cannot adequately articulate the synthetic *a priori* – judgements that are universally and necessarily true, and that require the connection of concepts to pure *a priori* intuitions (such as Kant's notion of space). Thus, for Maimon, judgement is far more modest in terms of its authority; it can only make determinations in a cautious and piecemeal sense via a rule construction more generic than Kant's, and cannot rely on reason's self-certainty in the same way. It is for this reason, most importantly, that Maimon's emphasis on mathematics is critically different from Kant's.

Magnitudes and determination: Maimon's polarised ideality

> Although mathematics is not a canon for the science of nature, it is, nevertheless, a potent instrument (*organon*), when dealing with motion and its laws.[41]

> [W]e should take into account the fact that mathematical concepts are not copies of anything, so that we would have to compare them with their originals to determine their completeness; rather they are themselves the originals produced by the understanding out of itself *a priori*. From this it follows that the completeness of mathematical concepts can be judged only relatively, with respect to the consequences to be drawn from them.[42]

Before jumping into Maimon's particular critique of Kant's synthesis *vis-à-vis* mathematics, it is necessary to introduce him generally, since, unfortunately, he remains a somewhat obscure figure. Maimon's *Essay on Transcendental Idealism* (1790) was recognised by many Kantians, and Kant himself, as one of the sharper critiques of the Kantian enterprise. Maimon suffered from relative obscurity partially because of his economic hardships and also because of his style of writing and use of language (purportedly due to his Lithuanian and Jewish background). Maimon's self-taught philosophical knowledge and reputedly bohemian existence caused problems for him until Kant openly praised him after receiving his work from Markus Herz. The central and fundamental aspect of Maimon's critique, one that will reappear, albeit in different form, in Chapters 5 and 6, is that, for Maimon, the formal constraints discoverable by cognition did not consist in objects to be articulated through sharper forms of outer sense, but were only ever the results of construction, or synthesis affected by the empirical genesis of ideas, carried out by the investigator. This asymptotic form of investigation, which is central to algebra and geometry, involves endlessly approaching one's investigative goal without ever reaching it *per se*.[43] Now we move on to Maimon's more specific critique.

Maimon's emphasis on relation and difference (via mathematics) makes a dynamic, yet non-dogmatic, articulation of nature possible – an articulation that indirectly opens the way for Schelling, specifically by sharpening the concepts of determination and derivation, which both follow from Maimon's attention to magnitudes. It is with these tools, and by focusing on magnitudes, that Maimon addresses the problematic status of nature in Kant's thought. This indirect approach to nature occurs through Maimon's focus on the notion of the synthetic *a priori*. Maimon's challenging of this notion arguably makes a combination of transcendentalism and naturalism possible in thinking after Kant. Maimon manages this by stating that the analytic and the synthetic stem from a single root, but one whose origin cannot be discovered. Thus, Maimon doubts the existence of things lying outside the mind as absolutely separate from it, but at the same time argues that the manifold of experience is only possible if a minimal difference exists between two things co-determining one another structurally via Maimon's use of the infinitesimal.[44] Paul Franks's excellent essay 'From Quine to Hegel' addresses how this logic of determination leads to a form of methodological naturalism.[45] Franks argues that this methodological naturalism cuts Kant so deeply because Maimon argues that Kant's rejection of naturalism, via his critique of Hume, does not adequately separate explanation from justification.[46] That is, for Maimon, Kant cannot justify his anti-Humean stance from within thought, that is, that causality must hold in order for cognition to properly function. Maimon instead claims that naturalism implies that the relation we perceive must be *more than* we perceive, but not necessarily correspond to a form *for the sake of our cognition*. Fundamentally, whereas Kant builds magnitudes from within human conceptualisation, Maimon argues that magnitudes are discovered asymptotically by taking apart human experience.

Here we can take a look back at 'What Does It Mean to Orient Oneself in Thinking?' On one level Kant appears as dualist with regard to thinking and sense (or, as he puts it, feeling) – a step he undertakes in order to find the subject's orientation. While this explanation functions in the practical 'go of things', the ground by which this occurs would seem to beg naturalistic explanation (hence our argument regarding Kant's late appeal to the ether and his attempt at bridge-building in the *Opus*). It is when explanation (always potentially speculative) encroaches upon rational justification that Kant can be accused of violating, or otherwise leaving behind, the critical project (as he routinely is by readers of the *Opus*).

It is for these reasons that Maimon adeptly latches on to mathematics as existing in the pivot, or hinge, between inner sense and outer sense. As Meir Buzaglo has pointed out, it is important to notice how Maimon is concerned most precisely with the relation of pure intuitions (and not empirical or sensorial intuitions) to *a priori* material and, furthermore, how Maimon's emphasis on the division between pure cognition and *a priori* cognition is collapsed into the question 'How is synthetic *a priori* knowledge possible?'[47] Maimon questions the operational utility of Kant's axiomatic definition of the co-synthesis of sense and understanding.[48] The form of the question does not imply that Maimon is disputing the connection between inner sense and outer sense or between intuition and concept, but that he does not believe that the interactive dualism is self-explanatory. In order to combat this apparently seamless connection, Maimon challenges the formal character of space-time in Kant (arguing that they cannot be *mere* intuitions). At the same time, and as we saw in the *Opus* and 'What Does It Mean to Orient Oneself in Thinking?', Kant, like Maimon, believes that the thinker as navigator can simply 'carry' space-time relations with them. For Maimon, however, difference and relation must dynamically constitute objects (difference and relation are pressures which co-create, or construct) and are less categorically certain.

Whereas Kant remains agnostic as to construction's abstract functioning (at least beyond that which can be schematically or, we might say, visually demonstrated), Maimon suggests that a degree of speculation is necessary in order to maintain the possibility of difference (and, following Schelling, we could say that of nature as dynamic productivity). Maimon attempts this through his discussion of magnitudes. For instance, in order to say that 1 is bigger than 2, or that 3 is less than 5, Maimon argues that difference and relativity construct number. The very operations of 'more than' or 'less than' suggest that numbers are co-constituting and that there is nothing in the numbers themselves that indicates that 2 is bigger than 1. So whereas co-constituting relations can be carried on in the mind of the thinker for Kant, for Maimon such relations construct the very objects of thought.[49] These relations are composed of differentials as the ultimate real unities,[50] and hence are not real or noumenal objects, as in the case of Leibniz's monads. Furthermore, whereas Kant is content to remain within the bounds of Aristotelian logic as explanation, Maimon argues that the differentials, that derivation as such, is more primal than logic, as logic is only manipulation of objects after the fact and not their production or construction.[51] Because of this fact, the operation of synthesis carried out in Maimon is an amplification and not an equation, or an operation at the same level as the mathematical operations.[52] Logical identity, taken in the view of the differentials or magnitudes, means that a statement of identity, a chain of subject and predicate, is one of amplification and not logical equation.

How is it then that Franks ends his aforementioned essay by arguing that mathematics, which was the central focus of Maimon, proves a 'hard case' for methodological naturalism?[53] As argued in Chapter 1, if the pantheism controversy can be taken as a question of the boundary and location of reason, then mathematical diagnosis, in its various means, can be skilfully manipulated to speak to basic ontological conditions, that is, nature as movement, as the engine of derivation on which thought obtains but does not exhaust. While Maimon was himself uncertain as to the ultimate ontological status of number, he convincingly showed that the demonstrative aspect of mathematical practices demonstrates that intuition and conceptualisation can be treated as polarisations flowing from one cognition. Whether or not there are real objects outside of consciousness misses the method by which Maimon determines objectivity: the objective (as a concept) is objective because it has been intuited singularly and collectively, as a widely shared and thus stable object of interrogation. In this regard, its reality depends upon the hierarchy of rules for thought upon which it has been built, and is not connected to any notion of the thing in itself but more to an empirical influx of a world of sense.

To take a geometrical example: whereas the concept of line can serve as the formal ground of the circle, that is, the circle can be taken as the consequent of the line through the act of bending it, this does not explain the *particularity* of the circle whatsoever.[54] This is because the understanding finds the use of the line as ground for the circle only when the line is taken as having a direction of movement.[55] Here we can see that the notion of amplification (as touching on magnitudes) has both qualitative and quantitative valences.[56] Or, put another way, whereas Fichte's groundless ground for the subject is a qualitatively postulated magic circle, for Schelling, following Maimon against Fichte, the quantitative, all too often taken as an abstraction or reduction of the qualitative, is in fact more constructively viewed the other way around. For Maimon, quantities simply are, and qualities, such as redness, are abstractions or extensions of existing differentials.[57] The language that Maimon utilises to describe differentials matches Schelling's description of actants as limit concepts in the *First*

Outline. In terms of magnitude, Maimon is claiming that what appears as vague qualitative expanses, whether extensive (plurality thought as unity) or intensive (unity thought as plurality), is in fact an abstraction of an expression of differences which, while only accessible synthetically, are not themselves solely synthetic.[58]

How does Maimon claim that synthesis is a part of this process of differentiation, yet is neither only in thought nor completely alien to it? He does this by giving determination, as an ideal operation, a naturalistic slant (*contra* Franks cited above). Determination or determinability is the notion of asymmetry that Maimon introduces into the ideal reversibility of subject and predicate, or, as Oded Schechter refers to them, determinable and determinant.[59] The subject (or the determinable), according to Schechter, is that which stands on its own.[60] The asymmetry of the determinable speaks to metaphysical necessity in Maimon, in that only in formal logic can the predicate 'float freely' away from the subject, that is, stand apart from it.[61] To return to a geometrical example, the line determines the circle but only when the action of the line's creation (such as the moving pencil) remains in motion.

This ideal reversibility of Maimon between determinable and determinant, while still maintaining a granulation of the real, is where he seems more rationalist than empiricist. These limits are, however, not intrinsic; they are not due to noumenal withdrawal nor to inherent human finitude, but to the very fact that knowledge, as a picturing or spacing, allows Maimon to transform the schematic, making these limits into an outside.[62] It is in this regard that synthesis (or construction) is the generation of new syntheses. The consequence of this transformation is that the status of the noumenal is deprived of its rationally objective status.[63] That is, a synthesis produces more syntheses and is itself due to a deeper process: nature, not as a world of inaccessible things, but as a process that makes any notion of thing or world possible (hence Maimon's minimal naturalism).

Immediately, one can see how Maimon's synthesis, in league with the measurement of magnitudes, speaks to a mode of thought that is concerned with trajectories rather than objects, with the use of concepts and with how far they can be taken. As Schechter puts it, Maimon's notion of reduction is a pendular motion: synthesis creates new concepts which move from the general to the particular, while analysis creates new judgements in the move from the particular to the general.[64] Yet Elhanan Yakira claims that subject and predicate cannot be equated with 'general' and 'particular' for Maimon, since he maintains a scepticism that effectively exteriorises knowledge from things themselves.[65] Thus, it becomes difficult at times to determine the degree to which the synthetic is exterior or interior. In this regard we may see ourselves approaching Kant's navigator again, staring at her hands and then outwards towards the horizon. But while Maimon is critiquing Kant for often not admitting the complexity of the synthesis regarding which aspects of mind must already be synthetic in relation to the empirical, it is more difficult to ascertain how this maps on to problems of location, that is, in what sense the degree of construction relates to its proximity to immediate sensory surroundings with regard to interiority and exteriority as separate conditions. Hence, for Maimon, unlike Kant, the analytic cannot be self-constructing but must be 'picked up along the way', in the very course of thinking it.[66]

Yet the difficulty for us here is how this imaginative transference of limitations to the outside is different from the speculations of the German Idealists, from whom Maimon apparently distanced himself.[67] This transference seems to rest upon the degree to which the outside for Maimon is to be read as an internal limit to thought; if the empirical outside is the limit of thought, as Peter Thielke seems to suggest.[68] Or, as Franks puts it, the question becomes whether Maimon sees himself as committed to merely formal distinctions, whereas Kant's distinctions, such as that between sense and understanding, are real.[69] For Thielke these distinctions are taken as formal, thereby aligning Maimon with the likes of McDowell.[70]

Furthermore, this issue is complicated by the apparently huge role that Maimon played in inspiring Fichte. As Frederick Beiser argues, the power of the imagination as the privileged engine of the synthetic is what Fichte adopts and transforms into the formal distinction of I and not-I, a distinction that Beiser claims is not merely ideal.[71] In order to dispute Beiser's claim, and to clarify the naturalistic tendency of Maimon's thinking, I will demonstrate that one must return to nature and, specifically, to the notion of dynamics in Kant, to show how the negative account of nature (as not-I or as something inert only to be discovered as law) in Kant and subsequently Fichte is problematic.

Furthermore, I believe that Schelling extends Maimon's notion of determination to nature itself in terms of the relation between spatiality and the purported immediacy of intuition. I will begin to develop this thought in the following section, although it will be addressed head-on in the closing chapters. Schelling's emphasis on Kant's third *Critique* forms the basis of his philosophy as it becomes that which must ground the first and second *Critiques*. That is, the schematic or normative space of reasons that Kant's constructions in the first two critiques require is, for Schelling, the dynamic ground that Kant provides in his later critical work. But, whereas Kant combines these dynamics with a notion of teleology, Schelling relies upon the middle grounds of mediation within which we find ourselves caught in any analysis. Or, as begins to become clear in Schelling's *Essay on Human Freedom*, and remains central to all his work after that point, logic, or predication, is the becoming-of-being; it is how nature functions and not a synthetic add-on. This problem leads to the question of how natural sense or imagination, as a middle ground, behaves in Kant's *Opus*.

Schelling's dynamisation of the *Critique of the Power of Judgment*

Kant's project in the *Opus Postumum* can be read as an attempt to make thought as natural as it can be, without abandoning the explanatory power of the transcendental method. As Grant puts it, Kant's unsolved problem is 'How, if at all, is a non-dogmatic account of the relation of reason to nature possible?'[72] Through mathematics, Maimon demonstrates not only the possibility but also the necessity of approaching the dangerous territory of dogmatic speculation, but Kant will not yet give mathematics the power to tightly lace sense and intuition that Maimon does. As we saw in our analysis of the ether proofs, Kant may instead make conceptualisation more developmentally primitive (following Eckhart Förster's reading) in order to grant reason more synthesising powers. If this is the case, the question I wish to engage in this final section is the question of what happens to Kant's attempt to quarantine nature in the *Critique of Judgment* if we read his augmentation of sense from the *Opus* back into it.[73]

To begin, it will serve us to return to what it is that Schelling does with (or to) Kant regarding the latter's dynamic theory of matter. Simply put, whereas for Kant the connection between experience and matter is a regulative unity, for Schelling unity is better rendered as productive continuity, and is the producer of problems, namely in terms of nature as *Prius* – as something behind which thought always lags.[74] Schelling's continuity is not a homogeneous continuity, but a dynamic one. A dynamic continuum produces actual things because nature itself is polarised between being and becoming, between creative expansion and productive contraction.

One methodological consequence here is that Schelling can be seen as reversing Kant's critiques – in that through recognising the power of nature in the *Critique of the Power of Judgment* one should restructure the apparatuses of the *Critique of Pure Reason*. The dynamic or de-substanialising possibility, which lies in the *Critique of Judgment* (against the stratifications of the ether proofs), is that of Kant's ascribing teleology to nature. Schelling expands this teleological aspect to all of nature as such, and by doing so he effectively argues for the decomposability of all things, and asserts, as we saw in the introduction, the primacy of movement, or the *Prius* of motion in nature.[75] Here, for Schelling, teleology is less about the setting up of definite beginnings and ends for nature, and more about arguing that while nature is purposefully creative, that is, it creates particular things, we cannot ascertain why this is *in a fundamental way.* Just as modality only partially captures the ramifications of potency, teleology only partially captures nature's punctuated stability in the incalculable volition of its creativity.

Whether or not nature functions teleologically is central to Kant's second *Critique*, as its initial and broadest concern lies in the separability of freedom from nature (or in the terms we have been utilising, the importance of demonstrating that our motions are our own). This is complicated by Kant as he insists that, though nature behaves mechanically (an assertion that Schelling will destroy), it *appears* to act intentionally.[76] It is especially at the level of the organic, or of biological plasticity, that Kant argues that nature appears to have something akin to a dynamic freedom (putting it in Schellingian terms for the sake of comparison).[77] Beth Lord argues that Kant's main motion here, in supplanting nature's force with judgement's power, is to counter the philosophical moves of Herder's speculative thesis that nature had organic powers.[78]

However, dynamics is not only a biological concern for Schelling since, as early as the *First Outline*, he is critical of overdetermining biological life as conceived by vitalism. Dynamics, expressed by both physics and chemistry, have grounds that must affect everything from inorganic formations to human freedom. The reason for mathematics' importance here, despite Schelling's scant explicit treatment of it, lies in the fact that the kind of abstract dynamism he discusses, both outside the domain of human knowledge and within it, is best represented by the exponential model of the potencies, a concept that is as mathematical (through its being diagrammatic) for Schelling as it is organic. Thus, Schelling wishes to avoid both merely taming nature with understanding's stability (via Kant) and giving nature, or particular parts of nature, inexplicable creative or vitalist tendencies (à la Herder).

Furthermore, the movements on which Kant so heavily relies in 'What is Called Orientation in Thinking?' appear strait-jacketed in the *Critique of Judgment*. This is due largely to the fact that the degree of mental movement, particularly that of self-isolation, takes precedence in order to separate the horrible from the sublime.[79] Kant describes the distinction between mathematical and dynamic sublimity in terms of a 'movement of the mind'.[80] This movement must be both of and from the mind for Kant, yet in a way that is not ungrounded by the mind in its movement, whereas for Maimon, the depth of the synthetic reach cannot be erased. That is, the assertion that reason can separate itself from the events of nature is what allows for the sublime feeling to coincide with otherwise horrible events. Again, Kant translates the depth of synthesis into the language of the aesthetic in that nature, as an external power, must be fearfully rejected or have its infinity recognised as one inferior to the infinite capacity of reason.[81] To return to our opening section, and to Peg Rawes's suggestion that Kant focuses the projective power of space starting with 'Concerning the Ultimate Ground' and moving until the *Critique of Judgment*, the analytic is an exterior space of self-evident law that emerges prior to any sense or act, and the act of finding or creating such laws is subject to reason, yet analytic and therefore self-evident. One ramification of this is that any substratum is an idealistic instrument for directing the activity of thought and cannot be objectified as part of nature or as a necessary condition itself not revisable by nature's forces. It is this worry that leads Maimon to rely upon the 'fiction' of infinite mind, thereby highlighting the impossibility of trying to self-ground the ideal, as well as that of simultaneously grounding the real, or nature, as removable from the space of reasons.[82]

In his remarkable 'Universal Deduction of the Dynamic Process' (1800), Schelling argues that Kant illegitimately attempts to assert a purity of forces by subsuming forces to logical rule, a rule which, following the articulation of nature grounding logic, is only possible because of nature. Kant must rely on forces, Schelling argues, even to construct the very notion of synthesis. Schelling writes:

> A great deal of the incomprehensibility of Kant's dynamics has its ground principally in the fact that he thinks them as pure so long as he constructs only logically, but as soon as it comes to real construction (to an encounter) he always takes them bound up with matter which of course for the substrate-seeking imagination power which finds it difficult to think a force without something to inhere in, can be quite comfortable, but which constantly distorts the speculative outlook.[83]

It is here that the various themes of this chapter can be brought to a head. On the one hand, Kant seems to argue that the abstract subject must have the capacity of determining the time-space relation (as a kind of navigator), in that, if we follow Förster, reason must be a projective capacity prior to the synthesising of the understanding. But the sensible must be of a matter following the ether of the *Opus*, and thus a tension must remain in order for Kant not to fall into absolute idealism. Maimon complicates this picture by inserting movement into nature (or, more cautiously, we could say into space-time) as well as the asymmetry of determinability, but, at the end of the *Essay*, he also holds on to some notion of substantiality. At least, he does so insofar as objectivity is constantly, yet asymptotically, approached by the infinite Intellect. The infinite intellect, as Buzaglo argues, is itself nothing but a fictional propellant for the act of thinking.[84] The opening lines of Maimon's *Essay* are telling in this regard:

> If it is true that every being strives as much as it can to persist in its existence, and if it is true that the existence of a thinking being consists in thinking (in accordance with the Cartesian identity claim [*identischer Satz*], cogito, ergo sum): then it quite naturally follows from this that every thinking being must strive as much as it can to think. It is not difficult to prove that all human drives (in so far as they are human drives) can be resolved into the single drive to think; but I shall save this for another opportunity. Even those who despise thinking must admit this truth, if they would only pay careful attention to themselves. All human activities are, as such, simply more or less thinking.[85]

So what is the middle ground of mediation and how to properly create a space for the relation of space, intuition and thought, if there is no ether and if space is not merely dead or formal matter? Given a seemingly overly formal notion of matter, what becomes of the substantiality of Schelling's determinations after Maimon? Or, put otherwise, if reason (or thought more generally) is an exploratory procedure, what is the place of nature if we are to avoid lapsing into the Fichtean–McDowellian isolation of the practical and its derivations (or explicit giving of reasons following Brandom)? Furthermore, if we can never 'leave' nature, as, according to my suggestion in the previous chapter, is argued throughout Schelling's work, then what is to become of judgement?

Judgement, for Schelling, becomes more like Maimon's determination through the ideal isolation of experiment, in that judgement is always-already occurring in terms of predication in an intentional sense, and as spatial intuition in an immediate sense. The determinability of an intuition's concreteness can be exported to a community of other thinking beings in a normative sense but, particularly with regard to the sciences, this must have some adherence to a logic (or we might better say a geometry) of immediate physical invariants. Whereas Maimon *appears* more of an idealist than Kant, in that determinability is a product of the activity of the mind (behaving under the auspices of the fiction of the infinite intellect), the limitations of thought are less *a priori* decided and more pragmatically *discovered*. Pragmatism, for the purposes of this project, will be construed through and through as practical thought with speculation built in. In order to further elaborate the pragmatic yet speculative nature of Schelling's thought, I will, in the following chapter, pursue a Schellingian philosophy of mathematics, particularly geometry, in order to move towards a more focused engagement between Schelling, the formalisation of nature and the nature of formalisation, as it applies to space.

Through his abstract utilisation of geometry and the exponents of algebra, Schelling is able to present a notion of difference (or quality) that is neither against formalisation, nor without it. While Kant required greater and greater powers to be located in more and more abstract, or disembodied, notions of the subject, as a mere 'X' in the *Opus*, Schelling instead elaborates what subjectivity is both for us and without us. Judgement becomes a diagrammatic and experimental tracing and working out of aspects of nature that have invaded our minds, and not, as it was for Kant, an attempt to isolate the rigour of our capacities from the increasingly unstable grounds on which they rest and navigate.

Notes

1. While the tension of inner and outer sense may not be central to the *Metaphysical Foundations*, it appears in the text in relation to the degree to which Kant wishes to avoid relying upon construction in relation to nature and to notions of matter. While Kant's hesitancy stems from attempting to avoid Cartesian Idealism, he appears to box himself in regarding nature's dynamism *vis-à-vis* the non-ideal dynamism of the I, or the subject. For an exposition of this problem, see Michael Freidman, *Kant's Construction of Nature: A Reading of the Metaphysical Foundations of Natural Science* (Cambridge: Cambridge University Press, 2013), 223.
2. Quentin Meillassoux (in *After Finitude*) stands in a long line of thinkers who claim that Kant's turn is actually Ptolemaic, and not Copernican. Thinkers such as Norman Kemp Smith, Bertrand Russell and Roy Wood Sellars, to name a few, have made similar claims throughout the twentieth century.
3. As far as I can tell, while Schelling knew that the *Opus* existed following Kant's death, I can find no sign that he was aware of, or had read, its contents. Its sole mention lies in Schelling's obituary of Kant written in 1804. See *Sämmtliche Werke*, Vol. VI, 8.
4. This is, of course, already evident in Kant's connection between sensation and matter at the beginning of the 'Transcendental Aesthetic' sections A19/B34 in Immanuel Kant, *The Critique of Pure Reason*, trans. Norman Kemp Smith (Basingstoke: Palgrave Macmillan, 2007 [1929]).
5. As far as I can tell, Maimon had no direct influence on Schelling's work. However, Schelling's later focus on empiricism appears very similar to Maimon's general approach to Kant.
6. Immanuel Kant, 'What Does It Mean to Orient Oneself in Thinking?', in *Religion and Rational Theology*, trans. and ed. Allen Wood (Cambridge: Cambridge University Press, 1996), 7 (8:133–4).
7. Peg Rawes, *Space, Geometry, and Aesthetics* (New York: Palgrave Macmillan, 2008), 20.
8. For an expert analysis of these kinds of issues in Kant, see Angelica Nuzzo, *Ideal Embodiment: Kant's Theory of Sensibility* (Bloomington, IN: Indiana University Press, 2008).
9. Rawes, *Space, Geometry, and Aesthetics*, 20–5.
10. Kant, 'What Does It Mean to Orient Oneself in Thinking?', 7 (8:133).
11. Ibid., 8 (8:135).
12. Ibid., 9 (8:136).

13. Ibid., 9 (8:136).
14. See also Stephen Palmquist, *Kant's System of Perspectives: An Architectonic Interpretation of the Critical Philosophy* (Lanham, MD: University Press of America, 1993).
15. In separate texts, both Hegel and Schelling take issue with Fichte's musings on passports in *On the Foundation of Natural Right*. For Hegel and Schelling, Fichte falls exactly into the error that Kant warns about – of overly solidifying the norms of thought into state-sanctioned rules. On this latter point, see Gregorie Chamayou, 'Fichte's Passport: A Philosophy of the Police', trans. Kieron Aarons, *Theory and Event*, 16.2 (2013): 16.
16. Reza Negarestani, 'Synechistic Critique of Aesthetic Judgment', in *Realism, Materialism, Art*, ed. Christopher Cox, Jenny Jaskey and Suhail Malik (Annandale-on-Hudson, NY/Berlin: Bard College/Sternberg Press, 2015), 333.
17. Ibid., 333.
18. Ibid., 333.
19. It is telling that not long after the text cited was presented as a talk, Negarestani began to turn more towards a Brandomian position. I will address the consequences of this turn in the final two chapters of this book. See, for instance, Reza Negarestani, 'The Labor of the Inhuman', in *#Accelerate: The Accelerationist Reader*, ed. Robin McKay (Falmouth: Urbanomic, 2014), 425–66.
20. In particular, see Immanuel Kant, 'On Creation in the Total Extent of Its Infinity in Both Space and Time', trans. Martin Schonfeld, *Collapse: Philosophical Research and Development*, 5 (2012): 379–414. In this pre-critical text, Kant entertains the possibility of cosmological models that resemble contemporary ones such as the 'Big Crunch'. This kind of speculation is not permitted following the *Critique of Pure Reason*.
21. Kant, *Opus Postumum*, xxxiv.
22. Ibid., 13 (21:387–8).
23. Ibid., xl.
24. Ibid., 71 (21:222).
25. In this sense, the sublime, as a kind of formless object (operating in the matter-experience role of the *Opus*), shifts between the mathematical and the dynamic, whereas these domains are brought arguably closer together in the *Opus*. See Kant, *Critique of the Power of Judgment*, 128–34 (5:244–51).
26. Paul Guyer, 'The Unity of Nature and Freedom', in *The Reception of Kant's Critical Philosophy: Fichte, Schelling, Hegel*, ed. Sally Sedgwick (Cambridge: Cambridge University Press, 2007), 45.
27. Jeffrey Edwards, 'Spinozism, Freedom, and Transcendental Dynamics in Kant's Final System of Transcendental Idealism', in *The Reception of Kant's Critical Philosophy: Fichte, Schelling, Hegel*, ed. Sally Sedgwick (Cambridge: Cambridge University Press, 2007), 59.
28. Ibid., 70.
29. Sturma, 'The Nature of Subjectivity', 220.
30. Eckart Förster, *Kant's Final Synthesis* (Cambridge, MA: Harvard University Press, 2000), 148.
31. Beth Lord, *Kant and Spinozism: Transcendental Idealism and Immanence from Jacobi to Deleuze* (Basingstoke: Palgrave Macmillan, 2011), 3.
32. Ibid., 16.
33. Ibid., 155, 158.
34. Ibid., 159.
35. Ibid., 162.

36. Ibid., 166.
37. Ibid., 174.
38. Iain Hamilton Grant, *Philosophies of Nature after Schelling* (London: Continuum, 2006), 75.
39. Ibid., 76.
40. Grant emphasises that Kant's last work marks a return to his earlier Leibnizan roots found in *The Metaphysical Foundations of Natural Science*, rather than, as indicated often by the critiques above, a return to Spinoza, or at least a version of Spinozism. But what seems more likely, given Förster's evidence, is that Kant recognised the critiques of Maimon and of the then nascent movements of German Idealism as valid not in terms of their different grounds but in that the directions they wanted to take reason's limitations into pointed to territories that Kant had ineffectively explored.
41. Kant, *Opus Postumum*, 63 (21:208–9).
42. Salomon Maimon, *Essay on Transcendental Idealism*, trans. Nick Midgley, Henry Somers-Hall, Alistair Welchman and Merten Reglitz (London: Continuum, 2010), 46.
43. Maimon focuses on this in Chapter 5 of his *Essay*. For a discussion of asymptotic analysis in the broader context of German philosophy of the time, see John H. Smith, 'Friedrich Schlegel's Romantic Calculus: Reflections on the Mathematical Infinite around 1800', in *The Relevance of Romanticism: Essays on German Romantic Philosophy*, ed. Dalia Nassar (Oxford: Oxford University Press, 2014), 239–57.
44. Maimon, *Essay*, 114–15.
45. Paul Franks, 'From Quine to Hegel', in *German Idealism: Contemporary Perspectives*, ed. Espen Hammer (London: Routledge, 2007), 51–3.
46. Ibid., 53.
47. Meir Buzaglo, *Salomon Maimon: Monism, Skepticism, and Mathematics* (Pittsburgh, PA: University of Pittsburgh Press, 2002), 31, 44–5.
48. As we shall investigate in the final chapters, McDowell, following Sellars, argues that intuitions and sense must always already be conceptual by the time we can operate upon them. This relies upon a mediating third thing which, for Kant, is that of the aesthetic dimension of judgement which we will address in the following section.
49. Although, at the same time, Maimon does not abandon the navigational model of epistemology totally, as he argues that there must be some permanence or unity to the I to explain our consistent relation to the shoreline. Maimon, *Essay*, 86.
50. Ibid., 15.
51. Buzaglo, *Salomon Maimon*, 40.
52. Maimon, *Essay*, 14–15.
53. Franks, 'From Quine to Hegel', 65.
54. Maimon, *Essay*, 60.
55. Maimon discusses this relation in terms of asymptotics, which we will approach in the last two chapters.
56. For more on this, see David Wood, *Mathesis of the Mind: A Study of Fichte's Wissenschaftslehre and Geometry* (Amsterdam: Rodopi, 2012).
57. Maimon, *Essay*, 16.
58. Ibid., 68.
59. Oded Schechter, 'The Logic of Speculative Philosophy and Skepticism in Maimon's Philosophy: *Satz der Bestimmbarkeit* and the Role of Synthesis', in *Solomon Maimon: Rational Dogmatist, Empirical Skeptic: Critical Assessments*, ed. Gideon Freudenthal (New York: Springer, 2003), 20.
60. Ibid., 22.

61. Ibid., 22.

62. Buzaglo, *Salomon Maimon*, 23, 107.

63. Schechter, 'The Logic of Speculative Philosophy', 24.

64. Ibid., 27.

65. Elhanan Yakira, 'From Kant to Leibniz? Salomon Maimon and the Question of Predication', in *Salomon Maimon: Rational Dogmatist, Empirical Skeptic: Critical Assessments*, ed. Gideon Freudenthal (New York: Springer, 2003), 79.

66. Schechter, 'The Logic of Speculative Philosophy', 37.

67. In his introduction, Gideon Freudenthal notes that while Maimon influenced the German Idealists, they represent the opposite of his thinking. Gideon Freudenthal, 'A Philosopher between Two Cultures', in *Salomon Maimon: Rational Dogmatist, Empirical Skeptic: Critical Assessments*, ed. Gideon Freudenthal (New York: Springer, 2003), 16.

68. Peter Thielke, 'Intuition and Diversity: Kant and Maimon on Space and Time', in *Salomon Maimon: Rational Dogmatist, Empirical Skeptic: Critical Assessments*, ed. Gideon Freudenthal (New York: Springer, 2003), 90.

69. Paul Franks, 'What Should Kantians Learn from Maimon's Skepticism?', in *Salomon Maimon: Rational Dogmatist, Empirical Skeptic: Critical Assessments*, ed. Gideon Freudenthal (New York: Springer, 2003), 207.

70. Thielke, 'Intuition and Diversity', 119.

71. Frederick Beiser, 'Maimon and Fichte', in *Salomon Maimon: Rational Dogmatist, Empirical Skeptic: Critical Assessments*, ed. Gideon Freudenthal (New York: Springer, 2003), 241.

72. Grant, 'Prospects for Post-Copernican Dogmatism', 421.

73. Here I am extending even further a suggestion made by Iain Hamilton Grant at the '*Naturphilosophie*' Summer School in Pittsburgh in August 2013, where it was suggested that, for Schelling, Kant's critiques should be carried out in reverse order. Here I am stating that the *Opus* should even precede the *Critique of Judgment* as attempting to discover the emergence of conceptual sense.

74. Dalia Nassar makes this clear in distancing Kant's regulative unity from the non-substantial yet not strictly regulative concept of the absolute in German Idealism writ large. See Dalia Nassar, 'The Absolute in German Idealism', in *Edinburgh Critical History of 19th Century Philosophy*, ed. Alison Stone (Edinburgh: Edinburgh University Press, 2011), 29–46.

75. This is not a cut and dried issue, as some have argued that Kant argues against teleology here.

76. Kant, *Critique of the Power of Judgment*, 20–2 (20:217–20).

77. Ibid., 36 (20:235).

78. Lord, *Deleuze and Spinozism*, 78.

79. Kant, *Critique of the Power of Judgment*, 128–9 (5:244–5).

80. Ibid., 131 (5:248).

81. Ibid., 144–5 (5:261–2).

82. The problem becomes one of measure; the quantitative appears completely arbitrary in relation to quality. One attempted solution, as Iain Hamilton Grant has shown, is to attempt to substantialise the number, as was done in the work of Lorenz Oken. I will investigate this treatment of number in relation to Schelling's utilisation of algebra in Chapter 3.

83. F. W. J. von Schelling, 'Universal Deduction of the Dynamic Process of the Categories of Physics', trans. Iain Hamilton Grant (unpublished manuscript, 2013), 16–17.

84. In some ways this demonstrates the connections between Fichte's 'magic circle of consciousness' and Maimon's infinite mind, in that both serve as justification for the conceptualisation of thought itself as a closed circuit of investigation. But while Fichte's circle emphasises the non-being of the not-I, Maimon's infinite mind emphasises the consistency of determination.
85. Maimon, *Essay*, 5.

Chapter 3

The Force of the Continuous: Schelling's Naturalisation of Mathematics

While much attention has been paid to Kant's, Fichte's, Hegel's and even Maimon's philosophies of mathematics, little to no attention to has been given to the function (and importance) of mathematics in the work of Schelling. In the following, I argue that Schelling's flirtations with geometry, in conjunction with his utilisation of K. A. Eschenmayer's notion of *Potenz* as algebraic exponential, speak to an early form of intuitionist mathematics[1] which is important to Schelling's thought in (at least) two areas: first, in discussing the relation of quantity to quality, and second, in constructing and describing thought as a species of motion. These pursuits, in different but related ways, illustrate the complex form that Schelling uses to integrate human thought into nature, naturalising that which seems most artificial: the synthetic creations of mathematical intuition.

Furthermore, by focusing on the quantity–quality relation, one can demonstrate Schelling's difference from Fichte and the later Kant, while also pointing out Schelling's importance for contemporary thought and, subsequently, for the renewed significance of *Naturphilosophie*. Schelling's Identity philosophy, which concerns the mathematical through its focus on the logical form so important to Fichte (A = A), expands one concept from his *Naturphilosophie*, namely how the addition of quantities and qualities is to be understood and, subsequently, how this aritthmetic connects to the deeper issue of the continuity of nature *vis-à-vis* the continuity of thought.

Schelling's Identity philosophy, which is often considered only slightly less of a dead dog than his *Naturphilosophie*, is commonly viewed as nestled in the shadow of Fichte's influence while simultaneously attempting to break free from it. In Schelling's *Presentation of My System* (1801) and *Further Presentations of My System* (1802), the themes of both motion and quantity/quality are evident, as Schelling writes in a Spinozistic (but also Fichtean) style (one of geometrical proofs, lemmas, postulates), while pushing beyond the strict activity of the I. Yet to regard these writings as simply amateurish, or as attempting to keep up with Fichte's demonstrable mathematical prowess, does a great disservice to Schelling's thought even at a relatively early stage.[2] Such critiques often rely upon the well-worn thesis that Schelling's protean nature led to his thought being a series of unrelated systems and scattered approaches. These critiques risk making the claim that Schelling was inconsistent, which, in my view, damages the very subject of one's study to an unhelpful degree. If we take seriously the aforementioned continuity thesis, which Iain Hamilton Grant has convincingly articulated, that is, if we accept that Schelling's work is continuous yet varied, then we can view the Identity system as 'de-isolated' from the *Naturphilosophie* and from the later work on freedom, myth and beyond.[3] In relation to this, if the continuity thesis is accepted, the mathematical themes of Schelling's work become amplified, I would argue, because they concern the very notion of continuity as such, a notion that appears from his earliest diary writings to the very end of his life. The general form of this continuity, however, can be read differently, whether it be a productive model of nature, the form of myth, or Schelling's theological concerns. This general sense of continuity is indicated in Schelling's particular form of monism discussed in the Introduction and in Chapter 1. For the project at hand, this continuity has to do with the inability to separate mind from nature ontologically while indicating the difficult necessity of creating methodological islands within that monism from which thought can coherently operate.

As we will see below, Schelling's 'trajectorialisation' of algebraic powers, that diagramming of powers to equate qualitative change with the trajectory of a geometric line, functions to strike this balance. Before addressing the *Presentations* and *Further Presentations* in detail it will be helpful to examine Schelling's explicit comments on mathematics and particularly geometry in his other texts.

Schelling on mathematics in general

> Mathematics is not the rigid and uninspiring schematism which the layman is so apt to see in it; on the contrary, we stand in mathematics precisely at that point of intersection of limitation and freedom which is the essence of man himself.[4]

Setting aside Schelling's pursuit of geometry in the *Presentations* for the following section, I will here address the question of his general view of the science of mathematics. Schelling studied mathematics in Jena in 1796 and then in Leipzig until 1798, while also delving into examinations of physics and medicine. Concerns about the mathematical appear, albeit somewhat obliquely, in his early work 'Of the I as a Principle of Philosophy' (1795), in which he makes reference to mathematical properties as only ever following from dynamic categories particularly in reference to magnitudes. However, the degree to which Schelling is discussing the mathematical in terms of judgements raises the question of whether this relates to mathematics proper.[5] Schelling argues that qualities are prior to mathematical categories and different in kind from them. This early foray is not altogether promising and lends itself to a reading of Schelling's approach in the *Ideas for a Philosophy of Nature* (1797) as anti-scientific or, at least, as against the mathematisation of nature as it appeared to him at the time in the form of Newtonian mechanics. But Schelling's attitude towards mathematics is anything but naïve. It can be mistakenly perceived as such because in 'Of the I as a Principle of Philosophy', he does not thoroughly define dynamics in a scientific context, and his claim that *some* notion of dynamics defines the contents of mathematical categories may therefore appear as idealist excess.

In an attempt to clarify Schelling's particular approach here, one could see his appeal to dynamics and trajectories as an attempt to cut across Kant's division between the aesthetic and the mathematical treatment of magnitudes in the *Critique of the Power of Judgment*. While Kant states that mathematics can measure the greatness of a magnitude to an infinite degree, it cannot grasp the *feeling* of the sublime, the overwhelming of a subjective aesthetic dimension reflecting upon the object of nature.[6] Here it should already be clear that Schelling cannot share this separation between natural and subjective intensity, since the activity of the I cannot be *a priori* separable from the dynamics of nature. And, as we saw with Maimon in Chapter 2, the removal of this separation in turn affects the analytic–synthetic distinction, calling for a more exploratory approach to the very notion of construction, that is, an approach acknowledging that any kind of thinking's capacity to build, whether through reason, intuition or the understanding, never constructs from mental material *only*, but also from extra-conceptual sources. Thus, whereas certain mathematical devices for Kant are *a priori*, mathematics' true power lies in its construction of construction, in how enacting what appears as a self-stable measurement of the exterior is itself an effect of exterior powers moving through the purportedly interior I or self that is thinking.

This does not mean that one abandons all divisions, but that one accepts the consequences of exactly making and maintaining such divisions and constructions. This is immediately evident in how Schelling attempts to relate philosophy, as that which attempts to construct construction, to the natural sciences. Throughout the *Ideas* Schelling tries not only to make room for philosophy among the natural sciences, but also to keep open a place for nature's productivity within both domains. Schelling critiques and builds on Kant's *Metaphysical Foundations of Natural Science* following his concerns with Kant's bracketing off of teleology.

Schelling closes the preface of the *Ideas* in the following manner: 'It is true that chemistry teaches us to *read* the *letters*, physics the *syllables*, mathematics *Nature*; but it ought not to be forgotten that it remains for philosophy to interpret what is read.'[7] The majority of Schelling's early comments on mathematics generally appear in the 1803 supplements to various chapters in the *Ideas*. In the supplement to the introduction, he connects the equation of the absolute real and the absolute ideal to the necessary ground for any science, singling out mathematics and specifically geometry.[8] Put directly, any science or practice that centres on the generation of abstracta must, in the gesture of that generation, sublate the difference of real and ideal. The production of a line, or the production of a concept is, on the face of it, a demonstration of that generation's own capacity.

This equation of ideality and reality in the 1803 *Ideas*, as we will see, exemplifies Schelling's particular notion of identity borrowed from Fichte in the logical form of A = A. To say that absolute reality = absolute ideality is not to say that there is no difference between them, but to say that the one follows from the other, that is, that the two are bound as variables, that they are in an equation. They follow in the structure of the equation and are thus only differentiated by their sequence. To say 'this A' equals 'that A' notes a difference of location between two things, things that are not absolutely separated since they are connected by the bridge of equation, and since the first and the second terms are related through a certain determination, whereas they may or may not be absolutely first and second. It is only by understanding identity in such a manner that Schelling can insist that absolute ideality and absolute reality must have a dependency if the construction of the geometer is to have any effect in the world. As is clear in the supplement to the introduction, the validity of such an equation is itself constructed: it must be *posited* as a necessity, albeit as a consequent necessity. Relating this fact to mathematics more broadly, Schelling writes:

> In the Philosophy of Nature, explanations take place as little as they do in mathematics; it proceeds from principles certain in themselves, without any direction prescribed to it, as it were, by the phenomena. Its direction lies in itself, and the more faithful it remains to this, the more certainly do the phenomena step of their own accord into that place in which alone they can be seen as necessary, and this place in the system is the only explanation of them that there is.[9]

I will address the way in which *direction* can be read quite literally below, but for now it is important to see how Schelling celebrates the pure rationality of mathematics as *the model* of demonstrative systematised construction. While the very structure of finding causes and effects is an endless circular game,[10] Schelling advocates for a peculiar form of constructive reduction in which one can reduce a phenomenon to a placeholder, but a placeholder that is an ideal foothold for explanation. That is, in the context of the quote above, any thing is an act of creation, but the consequences of this creation have to be ideally traced in its consequences in the actual world. Or, in other words, the certainty of principles is a wager, a foothold, and what they make possible, in the form of direction or trajectory, is the ongoing proof *of that certainty*. The systematisation of creative acts and consequences is locked into place, but only temporarily, by its location in relation to other principles and consequences.

It is this logic that motivates Schelling's critique of Le Sage's usage of particles. Schelling celebrates Le Sage's ingenious use of the mathematical to move beyond experience, but argues that such a supposition is threatened by an appeal to body or substance, which thereby undermines such speculation: an appeal to body or substance necessitates an explanation for the emergence of that body or substance.[11] In other words, and in a logic that will reappear in Schelling's adoption, yet alteration, of Kant's physical monadology via the actants in the *First Outline*, atomistic thinking lies at the bleeding edge between introducing an explanatory entity and a reliance upon substance as universal *explanans*.[12] The constructed real-ideality of number in Schelling's work most intensely illustrates this critique of substance while also distancing Schelling from a purely or naïvely Platonic take on mathematics.[13] This position can be made clear in reading Schelling's fellow *Naturphilosoph* Lorenz Oken, who argued that number was constituted by the very accretion of substance, where base substance is represented by zero. Oken's 'organification' of number can be read as one alternative that makes Schelling's position clearer in comparison and in relief.

This difference, regarding the Okenian thesis concerning the substantive nature of number, can be detected in Schelling's *First Outline of a System of the Philosophy of Nature*. Like Oken, Schelling begins with an unconditioned nature and argues that adopting polarity as a principle for speculation about nature can best explain the complexity of nature's products from the simplest or most basal – that is, that nature is polarised. Iain Hamilton Grant argues that Oken's substantialised zero amounts to a proto-field theory whereby antecedents and consequents (or the higher and lower forms of nature) become regionalised and relative to one another.[14] The zero, on the line of a tracing of a power, becomes a hinge (or indifference region), where different intensities or polarities cancel each other out. However, whereas Schelling's actants of the *First Outline* are logical footholds, Oken's slime-points are, as Grant argues, fundamentally substantive.

Grant demonstrates in his essay 'Being and Slime' that Oken's thought follows a path by which logical or rational forms (such as numbers) entail ontological consequences.[15] More specifically, Oken is concerned with how something derived its existence from nothing,[16] a derivation which Oken illustrates as the repetition of zero. The question, Grant argues, is as follows: to what degree is this repeated zero substantive or formal? Phrased otherwise, the question asks about the degree to which substance only makes sense as a logical foothold, therein pointing again to the copulation of the real and ideal.[17] Although Oken relies on the zero as the point of indifference (which could be aligned to the copula or equals sign in Schelling), this zero of Oken's is endowed with substance.[18] As Oken puts it on the first page of his *Elements of Physiophilosophy* (1809), mathematics describes the spirit of the cosmos while nature exhibits its material manifestation.[19] Or, as he puts it a few pages later, physiophilosophy is mathematics endowed with substance.[20]

A non-obvious and somewhat controversial aspect of Grant's reading is that slime (or mucus) is the proper name for all of substance in Oken's work generally and in his *Elements* specifically. Grant argues that Oken's clear alignment of the biological with the process of individuation of matter as such contributes to his 'organification' or 'animalisation' of the cosmos in general.[21] This is evident in Oken's *Elements* when he discusses the processes of the cosmos as occurring within 'an aetherial globe of mucus'.[22] Furthermore, while Oken distinguishes inorganic from organic in a classificatory sense, he subsumes all forms of creation, regardless of their category, under the notion of life.[23] How, and to what extent, the inorganic and the organic are both considered life is somewhat unclear, but both are subject to motion and comprised of the repetition of zero. And because mathesis is best at simply schematising the motion and creativity of life, Oken argues that science must be a materialised arithmetic. However, since Oken emphasises the biological sciences as the central organisational paradigm, it is difficult to discern how biological or material mathesis as such exists in a context-independent manner.

As Grant points out, Oken equivocates between zero or substance (as slime) as having priority – mathematics is a description of the agglomeration of substance and yet its formal power pre-exists humanity. But how does one explain human access to mathematical capacities in a non-trivial manner? Either substances accreted to the point of mathesis or mathesis was, from the start, potentially accessible by creatures capable of thought.

From this Oken argues that numbers represent the direction and motion of zero – zero is a primary act and numbers are its repetitions.[24] The zero is the impossible respite between the polarities of nature whereby the expansive and contractive tendencies (which correspond to positive and negative integers) fight against one another endlessly. Nature, including human thought, is the repetition of this combat as substance. Thus, the lateness of human thought implies its evolutionary greatness for Oken and explains our ability to discover the mathesis implicit in all of nature's working. But Oken's emphasis on the domain of life is not situated properly methodologically, and neither does he justify how non-biological entities and processes benefit from being described in biological terms (other than appealing to common-sense experience in that biological ontogenesis is more recognisable to us).

Oken's zero is an act of creation; it names the points that move and congeal into materiality (as an original mathesis we discover after the fact). Furthermore, it names a place that must be assumed in order to measure the motions and intensities of these creations (as the zero on the number line). While at the end of his *Elements* Oken asserts that spirit and mind are merely blossoms of nature, the act of speculating that mathesis is, in a *material sense*, that which pre-exists the emergence of mind can appear to over-idealise the initial *Naturphilosophical* move of naturalising zero as a slimy building block. So while zero precedes slime or the primordial ooze from which all life sprang, the question remains: how does one argue that mathematics is thoroughly material without overly, and retroactively, biologising mathematics or number? Following Grant's account further, Oken's mathesis is akin to the repetition of identity in Schelling's system; it is a repetition of the logical copula (*das Band*) in a logical sense, or the tension of potencies between direction or dimension in the geometrical sense, whereby form leads to neither dead formalism nor to naïve idealism.[25]

In both logic and geometry for Schelling, the involved concepts (dimension, direction) or the involved terms (subject and predicate) have motions and behaviours that cause the link between them to generate space relative to the domain in which one thinks them. Thus the intermixture of real and ideal is again highlighted: the boundedness or logical connectivity found in the world cannot be merely ideal if its discovery tests the very limits of thought and ideality. Yet at the same time, Oken's emphasis on arithmetic and on the anchoring aspect of zero points to how the zero as an act demonstrates, in equal measure, its self-sufficiency as zero (as a point of indifference in fields of intensity, difference, magnitude, etc.), and the cost of any given demonstration. Oken's zero is thus a *more complex* account of the traditional philosophical decision, of the philosophical starting point consisting of the subject–object or mind–world division – all since this act, retroactively recognised, was already occurring and, in the particularity being recognised by cognition, produced the problem of materiality (in terms of the location of this traditional decision in the world). For Oken then, ideal and real correspond to intensity and extensity (or contraction and expansion for Schelling) of the number series.[26]

Here again intensity is connected to temporal experience and to arithmetic, addition as the counting of time with extensity, connected to the outer intuition of space, being connected to geometry and the diverse capacites of space. Thus, the zero and the copula approach one another, in that Oken's use of the former and Schelling's use of the latter both refuse the absolute separation of real and ideal while necessitating an act that appears to enact such a separation. However, as I will attempt to argue below, Schelling differs from Oken in that the difference between the qualitative and quantitative orders for Schelling is greater than Oken would allow.

While Oken's polarisation of the zero introduces fields within an otherwise immanent nature, Schelling seems to argue that the exponential (or contractive and expansive) status of the *Potenz* is not adequate to explain the arithmetic of dimensionality within a pre-established space defined physically. This requires a brief summary. For Oken, mathesis occurs materially, which requires treating zero as both building block of and observational post between intensities or magnitudes. Because of this, movement or activity for Oken is captured through acts that are more or less intense from where they are measured while being fully materially constituted.

However, for Schelling, using the zero as notion and anchor is a powerful case of the demonstrative capacity of mathematics, but it over-biologises these determinations. Thus, every determination of zero, whether as building block or indifference point of magnitudinal observation, is always-already within the restraint of life as Oken understands it. Because of this, the organic or slimy point appears too close to functioning as an explanatory substratum, itself unexplained and thus mysterious. This is why, for Schelling, the *Potenz*, emphatically not a substance, functions as the least assuming meontological solution to the emergence of things and the position from which one thinks them.

That is, whereas Oken's mathesis explains the *intra-Potenz* logic, Schelling argues in his *Presentations of My Philosophy* that the accumulation of dimensions demonstrates a qualitative change *of a different order*. While the zero for Oken, or exponential nature of the *Potenz* for Schelling, demonstrate how the direction of the real and the ideal can be reversed (in terms of what is contained within what, and what can explain what through the recapitulation of forces), the arithmetic of dimensions or directions appears to reinforce the asymmetry of being preceding thinking. Or, put another way, Oken's exponential model, without a corresponding diagrammatic one, can tend towards a materially immanent model of the cosmos, since for him the exponent is merely a repetition of zero, and so is just more of the same, however ontologically changed through accretion. Or, to relate more specifically to mathematics, the generative formalism within mathematics has yet to be grasped by the mathematical navigations of human brains, which leaves room for further discoveries about mathematics, as well as about the real ramifications (consequents) of mathematical knowledge.

Schelling keeps mathematics close to philosophy in his *System of Transcendental Idealism* (1800), where he reasserts the one-sidedness of knowledge (read: that the ideal does not dominate the real) in that 'the lamp of knowledge only points forward'.[27] Since knowledge cannot properly uncover the past, but can only extend what little we know of it outwards, mathematics as a formal science of demonstrative abstracta remains imperative. Schelling discusses the difference between mathematics and philosophical knowledge as the difference between the knowledge of the act of construction as intuition – philosophy only trumps mathematics as a form of pure reasoning by investigating the act of construction itself, and treating mathematics as the more pure, albeit unreflective, form of this construction.[28] Yet this distinction becomes harder to maintain given the fact that for Schelling, unlike Kant, mathematical intuition cannot be said to be contained only within the mind, given Schelling's naturalistic account of thinking. This naturalistic account appears in relation to intuition later in the *System*.

It may be worth pausing here to examine how exactly Schelling's notion of construction relates to all of naturalism, the naturalisation of cognition, mathematics and the naturalisation of the schemata. For Kant, the schemata function to link non-empirical concepts with sense impressions. In this regard, and to point back to the Orientation essay, Kant emphasises the difference between schemata and images within the domain of mathematics. Whereas concepts in the Orientation essay are connected to sense impressions, constructed with reliance upon them, and are *a posteriori*, mathematical schemata are always incompletely captured by sense impressions and are therefore *a priori*. For example, any triangle one encounters will fail to live up to the concept of a triangle.[29] Much ado has been made about how cognition generates schemata, particularly as their generation appears to erode Kant's already mentioned apprehension regarding the limits of construction and those of intuition. That is, the power and necessity of schemata, for Kant, undermine his general claim that intuition is limited in how it can construct or be productive, using the material of sense. Schelling, in naturalising cognition, can offer an evolutionary explanation for the generation of diagrams, schemata, postulates and the like, by arguing that they stem from basic capacities of motion and perception, beginning with bodily motions and subsequently genetically informing thought as various species of motion. Michael Vater, in his introduction to Schelling's *System of Transcendental Idealism*, suggests that Schelling saves Kant's notion of the schema by attaching it to the importance of time in the development of consciousness via a stronger appeal to naturalism and the concept of naturalised cognition.[30]

For Schelling, the schema is a basal form of intuition that draws the border between concept and object in thought, thereby allowing the activity of thought to reflect upon itself, to divide the internal and the external.[31] It is basal, or particularly abstract, because it does not directly bring forth an object, but merely embodies a rule. Schelling emphasises, however, that this embodiment of a rule is bound to the very act of bringing an object into existence, as in the example of a craftsman. Intuition, in the sense of the function of the schema, is necessarily productive, and tied to actual generation.

Following the embodied nature of productive intuition, which is necessary for the self to recognise its own activity, and what appears as almost a nod to the qualitative difference of a different order (*contra* Oken, for whom all difference seems to be an augmentation of the same), Schelling argues that mathematics does not need to recognise the difference between absolute and relative negation.[32] While the schema informs material production, it becomes difficult to separate the function of higher level abstracta, such as that of magnitudes or forces, from the models we generate of them. This confusion is a risk in the very form of an equation. In the equation, there is no recognition of whether the equals sign means a return to a balance of forces, a previous capture of one force by the other, or the annihilation of those forces. For Schelling, philosophy and physics recognise that the sequence of positivities and negativities says something about the underlying tendencies, tendencies that he believes are erased in the operations of mathematical formulas. Yet mathematical progress allows for the light of knowledge to be extended ever forward as the advent of decimal fractions allows for better approximations, for instance, of the movements of the stars.[33]

Setting aside *Presentation of My System*, to which we will soon move, Schelling's treatment of mathematics seems to largely disappear, only to emerge later in life in the *Darstellung* lectures (1847–52), particularly in the form of a geometry of motions, or a geometry of dimensionality. But I have saved, for the end of this section, Schelling's most direct commentary on mathematics as a science. In 1803 he gave a series of lectures on the method of university study in which he devotes a lecture to the purely rational science of mathematics. In his *On University Studies*, Schelling appears to reiterate the sentiments about the role and place of mathematics *vis-à-vis* philosophy that he expressed in 1800 – namely that philosophy is almost as adept at setting the conceptual stage for mathematics as it is at pure rational thought. In his fourth lecture, Schelling rehearses the identity between absolute ideality and absolute reality in order to move to discussing space as the intuition of the negation of activity (or, as we might say for our purposes here, negation of trajectory or dimension).[34] Space is both activity and the arresting of activity, just as a dimension or trajectory is a movement in space (as activity) and a measurement of that movement (as actuality). Following this, Schelling argues that mathematics presupposes the intuitions of pure space and pure time as reflections of a deeper unified being – a being which, following Schelling's divide between philosophy and mathematics, must be being as self-inhibiting becoming. In other words: in order for mathematics to be a demonstrative science of abstraction, it needs to presuppose a continuum in which its demonstrations can occur with proper impact.

Mathematics, for Schelling, rests its laurels on surpassing the law of causality[35] in that it intuits the idea as such by equating construction and demonstration (again, only philosophy peers into the act of construction itself). Perhaps hedging his earlier statements about the use of mathematics in astronomy, Schelling argues that pure rational mathematics can abuse evidence, and create empirical laws as if they were absolute laws.[36] It is worth quoting Schelling at length as he closes the lecture:

> Philosophy and mathematics are alike in that both are founded upon the absolute identity of the universal and the particular. Hence, both are purely intuitive, since every relationship of this type is perceived through intuition. But whereas mathematical intuition is a reflected one, philosophical intuition is rational or intellectual intuition and identical with its object – with primordial knowledge itself. Philosophical construction interprets what is grasped in intellectual intuition. The particular identities, which like the universal identity, express absolute primordial knowledge can be grasped only in intellectual intuition, and in this sense are Ideas. Philosophy is therefore the science of Ideas or the eternal archetypes of things. Without intellectual intuition no philosophy![37]

It is worth briefly articulating a broader account of Schelling's notion of intellectual intuition. Following from the outline of Schelling's methodology as construction, productive intuition is construction embodied in a sensate and mobile subjectivity. This model of intuition has very particular consequences for construction in that, according to it, mobility conditions and localises intuition, but in a sense that is initially and continually apprehended in higher or more abstract forms such as intellectual intuition. In so many words, intuition is a guess from immediate surroundings about the potential deeper connectivity of nature and mind. The intellectual form of intuition comes from an indifference point, or a *seemingly* unconditioned place. Yet as soon as that intuition encounters any form, its testing of that form's extensity will demonstrate the locality of any given happening of intuition.

Setting aside the more specific role of intuition to be fully addressed later on, it is nevertheless important here to emphasise that mathematics can reconnect to its more primordial roots, a project that I believe Schelling himself pursues in the *Pure Rational Philosophy* lectures. Before proceeding to those lectures and then to intuitionist mathematics, the continuity of Schelling's concern with mathematics should be demonstrated in terms of the centrality of the distinction between quantity and quality. To reach that point, however, one must re-examine the possibilities that lie in the purported limits of mathematics' diagrammatic inventions.

Schelling's extensity/intensity relation

> There is one absolute magnitude (= 1) which, though continually annihilated in this series, continuously recurs, and by this recurrence produces, not itself, but the mean between itself and nothing. – Nature, as object, is that which comes to pass in such an infinite series.[38]

While Schelling repeatedly noted the interchangeability of analytic and geometrical thinking, he appears to prefer the latter over the former.[39] Formally, the two are compatible: triangularity, for instance, is taken to be the diagrammatic expression of the interrelation and (relative or consequent) totality of those dynamic processes of nature that correspond to the triplicity (or, as we might somewhat oddly say, to the temporal triangularity) of the copula and its bonded antecedents and consequents. Or, simply put, the labelling of the geometrical with a, b and c allows for a translation between the figure and the formula. Yet, as I have argued, it would appear that the repetition of number as intensive difference cannot be simply mapped on to the addition, multiplication or 'exponentialisation' of trajectories. Hence, determining the point from which intensities are measured is not a trivial issue, as it is not only a question of perspective, but also of the potentiality of different materials and actualities in a particular horizon. Qualities, or excessive intensities, cannot usefully be said to be intense for their own sake but only to better articulate the limits of knowing and navigating.

Previously I mentioned that Schelling's interest in mathematics seemed to wane after 1803, yet one can argue that Schelling moves away from the geometrical and simply focuses on the logical structure of predication. This is evidenced in his increasing attention to temporality and the form of the copula in the language of unground and ground. Temporality allows Schelling to demonstrate the logic of unground and ground in that the generation of any thing is dependent on its ground, but the thing only becomes what it is in ungrounding its own point of genesis. In terms of space, Schelling complicates the notion of determination by always construing it as a co-determination, as always occurring in a web of co-determining entities. Ground and unground thus become fundamental to deciding the boundaries between things. As Oken will subsequently argue, Schelling attempts to naturalise formal structures, but whereas Oken attempts to attach mathematics to the generation of substance as such, Schelling attempts to explain mathematics as a second-order form of intuition, one that demonstrates and formalises how abstracta behave given a continuous space and time as established by philosophy. This occurs across Schelling's work, but is most evident in *Presentation of My System of Philosophy* and *Further Presentations of My System of Philosophy*.

While the reflective delay of mathematical intuition can be taken as a weakness, I believe that it is mathematics' strong suit to act as the engineer of conceptual isolation. Throughout Schelling's texts, but particularly in the *First Outline*, he points out the necessity of isolating a product of nature to think it. This operation renders the object inert and disconnects it (in an ideal sense) from nature. This isolation is necessary, however, in order to perform experiments, in order to test how many antecedents and how many consequents this singularity *may* highlight. In effect, isolation makes the product into an abstract entity whereby its production and productivity can be held in temporal and spatial isolation. It is logic that speaks to the former, whereas geometry speaks to the latter. This would, however, assume that logic is over and above the geometrical, as the copula connects the object to logical forms over geometrical ones. Or, in other words, the very notion of Schelling's connection is logical, not geometrical. However, I would argue that this imbalance is undone by the geometrical nature of trajectory. Whereas the extensity test is one of temporal stretching, it is equally an intensity test in the object's field-theoretical gravity (where it tends to go, and what is drawn to it), referring to the relation of ground and unground mentioned above. This form of experiment is clarified in the relation of quantity (usually associated with the extensive) to quality (usually associated with the intensive).

If this is the real dimension of mathematical intuition, one could argue that it is reversible as an ideal series: the extensive as spatial, and the intensive as temporal (both thought in organicity – the possibilities of the body in the former, and the particular temporality belonging to the form of life in the latter). To refer back to Oken once more: whereas in his work, the material reality of mathematics appeared in different biological forms from those it took in Schelling, for Schelling those forms and limitations alter the sense and perception of dimensions that inform and contaminate their mathematical codification. We could tentatively say that, for Schelling, logic approximates the cause–effect relation complicated as a naturalised transcendentalism, whereas geometry is the attempt to diagram the horizons of co-determining things in a given field. This can be brought back again to the division of quantities and qualities.

In *Presentation of My System of Philosophy* Schelling makes a striking statement about the relation of geometry to arithmetic and quantity to quality. Arguing diagrammatically, he states that the triangle is the formal character that represents the totality of the dynamic processes (being composed of the line and the angle, which represent magnetism and electricity respectively). Rather than a pure formalism, Schelling's demonstration of the triangle is one of the co-dependence of motions of otherwise unrepresentable potencies. As mentioned above, this demonstration seems to suggest a difference in kind between quantity and quality, or that the difference *between* the potencies is different than those *within* a single potency. The extension of a shape in space is, on the face of it, radically different from the creation of an altogether different form. Schelling writes:

> The schema of the three basic forms of the dynamic processes is, as is known, the line, the angle, and the triangle, or in addition, these three processes are equated with the first three prime numbers of the arithmetic series. Just as 2 results only from the addition of 1 + 1, and three from the joining of 1 to 2 (so therefore these numbers are not *powers* of 1), so too, therefore, the three stages of the dynamic process [result from successive addition].[40]

An immediate concern is raised: how are the potencies (whether formulaic as a, b, c or geometrically as line, angle, triangle) themselves isolated non-arbitrarily within the ideal? Or, how are the stages of the dynamic process themselves not merely ideal footholds? We could say that Schelling's considerations here appear close, at first glance, to Fichte's infinitesimal calculus (as a form of practical worlding).[41] For Fichte, the I is an auto-positing force that sets itself against the inert materiality of nature (which, since it is internalised, is merely seen as the non-I) by introducing smaller and smaller cuts (as infinitesimal calculus) into the material of the world. While I investigate this connection in more depth below, it is here that the continuous nature of Schelling's work is the central theme around which quantity and quality interrelate without eliminating or supplanting one another. In the *Introduction to the First Outline* (1799) Schelling argues that nature must be continuous since it is neither mere being nor mere becoming, but the ongoing attempt to be both, something that cannot be ascertained *vis-à-vis* the practical (*contra* Fichte).[42] Schelling writes:

> As long as we only know the totality of objects as the sum total of all being, this totality is a mere world, that is, a mere product for us. It would certainly be impossible in the science of nature to rise a higher idea than that of being if all permanence (which is thought in the idea of being) were not deceptive, and really a continuous and uniform reproduction.[43]

The substantial difference between Fichte and Schelling here is that the continuity of intuition for Fichte can only come from the source of thought, which itself must be cut out of and isolated from nature. This, for Schelling, is highly objectionable. While Fichte leaves the connection between thought and world intact, in that the world must be 'out there' for the actions and speech of the I to hold together, it is not at all clear how this notion of world relates to nature. From a Schellingian standpoint, there is no quarter wherein thought can isolate itself from nature. Furthermore, the positing of activity in the act of positing (I = I) cannot be formal-practical as there would be no motor (no productive difference) by which thought would come to be thought at all.[44]

To return to the mathematical, that is, to quality and quantity: Schelling's articulation of the productivity of thought speaks to why the second-order status of mathematics as a form of productive intuition must be reflective to the extent that it recognises, and can artificially construct, the heterogeneous from the homogeneous, or to how mathematics makes the composite out of the continuous. If mathematics divides the continuous in an ideal sense, because of the reversibility of the copula in the equation 'ideal = real', we could say that it is through qualities as trajectories (expressed through the geometrical) that the arithmetic of qualities makes the heterogeneous out of the homogeneous in a non-trivial sense, a process by which the transcendental obtains its naturalised status despite and through a symmetry 'break' within nature. Furthermore, the spatial exploration of the exponential is a navigational exploration, whereas every trace of expansion and contraction is registered in the real as condition, and in the ideal as possible ground for future consequent (in the form of speculation).

It is due to the spatial character of conceptual exploration that Schelling spends so much time foregrounding his discussion of mathematics with a sense of space as absolutely real and absolutely ideal. The divisibility of space is highlighted in both the *First Outline* and the *Ideas*. The unconditioned, the purported *Ungrund* of all qualities, is both the intensity by which the procedure of ungrounding, or isolation, could take place (this, once more, points to how Schelling's notion of derivation and determination differs from Fichte's) and the intensity that produces qualities. Or, in other words, the unground is the engine of both nature's productions and our constructions since '[b]eyond space only pure intensity is thought'.[45] Qualities cannot be constructed due to the fact that they are pure *action*.[46]

This statement reinforces the two-plied duality of thought and world suggested by Oken. One can state that there is an unground, or that there is pure action, but this statement, as mere statement, would only introduce the stated concept without potential consequences. But as soon as a thinker begins to pursue the consequences, she begins to move on the spectrum of ideality and reality. To state that 'the unground ungrounds' is thus not mere definitional tautology, when the antecedent (or ground) is so abstract as to transform following the thinnest occurrence of instantiation. Thus, the quality of qualities as pure action noted above is not explanatory *per se* but forces the thinker to pursue other means in order to understand qualities – to decompose or de-potentiate them.

Schelling highlights the importance of decomposition (at least in mathematics) in the *Ideas*:

> For mathematics proceeds, for that reason [the inability to physically ground particles], to dwell upon the infinite divisibility of space, and philosophy, though it may be wary of saying that *matter* (considered in itself) *consists* of infinitely many parts, does not cease, on that account, to insist upon an infinite *divisibility*, i.e., the *impossibility* of any *completed* division.[47]

As Schelling emphasises a few pages later, connecting this problematic to physics, such divisibility is an ideal procedure which cannot rely upon a physical substratum if that substratum is exempted from physical explanation.[48] Schelling's very notion of ideality and construction contribute to a naturalism and are far afield from a naïve idealism. To quote at length once more:

> Space is conceptless intuiting, and thus in no way a concept that might have been first abstracted, say, from the relationships of things, for although space arises for me through abstraction, it is still no abstract concept either in the sense that categories are, or in the sense that empirical or specific concepts are; for if there was a specific concept of space, there would have to be many spaces, instead of which there is but one infinite space [. . .] space is merely an intuiting throughout.[49]

To take Schelling at his word in saying that space = intuiting means that since being precedes thinking, since nature is intuiting through us, then intuition, in this productive regard, is space. Here, in contrast to Kant's disallowing of intellectual intuition because of its temporal immediacy, we might say that intuition, in Schelling's sense, can be taken as a *spatial* immediacy, a snapshot of the proximal territory.

It is difficult, for these reasons, to define space. On the one hand it seems to be an effortless production of conceptless intuiting and yet, following Kant, space is prior to conceptualisation in that it cannot be conceptually differentiated in an abstract sense, but is also purely constructed by our moving in it.

Philosophy and mathematics both gain ground as they maximise the degree to which ideal construction obtains upon real production. While philosophy and mathematics are not substantively different, they are different in their methods due to the transcendental symmetry break that nature endures before producing the organ of human thought. But this break is not pursued by merely testing a correspondence, since the very nature of nature is to invade thought (in addition to producing it). Nature constructs products through thought, products with varying degrees of impact in the world due to the freedom of logical modality, which is a simulation of nature's actual potencies.

Finally, we can proceed to the meaning of a quality's trajectory. Pursuant to this is how Schelling, in his later work, approaches a so-called lived, or positive, philosophy. However, this philosophy is lived not in Fichte's sense, whereby life must be given productive autonomy from nature to guarantee the construction of its own ethical stability, but a philosophy in which only by testing the bonds of the real's relation to the ideal do we get some sense of the law of the world and the capacities of our own thought as a peculiar form of dimensionality.

Potencies and trajectories

A thought experiment does not set out to predict a fact or to transform this or that object, but rather to stage the physicist himself grappling with his mental habits, and above all to lay bare the imagery that he uses when he claims to be merely 'commenting on' or 'verbalizing' the operative power that is supposed to be buried in the calculations. We know that Einstein liked to imagine himself being dragged along in a chariot at the speed of light or totally isolated in a lift: to have shown that there is no innocence of intuition is certainly one of his most decisive contributions to the community of physicists.[50]

The *interlacing of romanticism and transmodernity* is perhaps surprising at first, but less so when we notice that many great romantics – Novalis, Schelling and Goethe in particular – have taken up, with technical instruments far less robust than the contemporary ones, extensive studies of the *trans-*.[51]

If the potencies are the addition of different trajectories, then quantitative difference appears in between two operations of qualitative difference – the original ground of qualities, or the unknowable number of the potenices, which can only ever be ideally posited (and never constructed) and the symmetry-breaks, which result from the non-merging addition of direction, and kinds in motion. Here again we see why space is so important for Schelling – while space is 'conceptless intuiting', this does not mean that intuition creates space in itself, but that intuition constitutes a space and moves through it, as intuition is one of nature's intensities. It is only when such intensity is turned on itself (as when nature thinks itself through us) that space is occupied *by intuition*: 'What *occupies* space is not matter, for matter is the occupied space itself.'[52] Furthermore, whereas absolute quality may exist, we only experience relative quality, quality as forces acting between those sites of self-investigation (the entities which, by their very nature as entities, are experiments).[53] But these experiments have trajectories of their own, and so how are we to map the space of the experimental as well as the space of our own navigation?[54]

One can re-examine not only the *Ideas* and the *First Outline* but also, with an eye to specific treatments of mathematics, take Schelling's discussions of dimensionality into account. By taking dimensionality seriously in these earlier texts, as well as noting Schelling's attention to it in his later work in the *Darstellung der Reinrationalen Philosophie*, one can see how the intuitive and constructive aspects of geometry are ramified as a lived (or navigational) philosophy. But whereas for Fichte this lived philosophy is taken in predominantly practico-ethical directions, for Schelling it results in a focus on a form of pragmatics, or what we might call a mechanics or kinematics of reason.

What is ultimately at stake is whether, by addressing the embodied nature of dimensionality, Schelling is softening his critique of somaticism or of substance (pointing back to Oken's zero), or whether the reflective or second-order status of geometry is undone by the embodiment of animal dimensionality or of viewing thought as a species of motion. Furthermore, if quantity is a result of quality's auto-affection as opposed to a Fichtean auto-positing (that of the I extracted from nature), then how is one to account for the plethora of trajectories in the world? Or, put another way, if the apparent difference across different trajectories is one of quantitative increase in motion, then how can one account for the conditions specific to species that determine the kinds of motions of which they are capable?

Against Fichte's divisional derivation, Schelling's naturalistic derivation attaches to the evolutionary status of human thought. This move, while initially stemming from his earliest investigations of the *Timaeus*, is later accelerated by his interest in Aristotle's *De Anima*. According to this investigation into the ancients, mathematics appears as the demonstration of the free construction of reason, of thought playing openly in the constructed space of intuition which is itself then traversed by intuition. It then seems sensible to tie the naturalistic derivation of mathematical capacity to movement. How does this map back on to Schelling's geometrical reading of the quantity/quality relation?

In his remarkable *Les Enjeux des mobiles* (translated as *Figuring Space*), Gilles Châtelet takes up Schelling's focus on the indifference point (earlier examined via Oken's kin concept of the zero) as itself the producer of two symmetries.[55] In attempting to avoid both the ineffective calm of Spinozism and the overly confident idealism of Leibniz, Schelling sees indifference as a point of analysis between two operating powers or polarities. The indifference point is less about nullifying difference, and rather about simply establishing an intuitive place from which differences in kind can be recognised.

Schelling's productive intuition is what makes possible the description of the universe as polarities that can only be adequately described in the diagrammatic register. The productive intuition is also made possible by this very description, albeit on a different scale. Where Schelling's concept of the *Potenzen* is often reduced (such as by Beach) to Spinozistic power and nothing more, Châtelet recognises that it speaks to an original tension of powers in Schelling that exponentially produce and spin out of control, producing more and more stages of being (*Stufenfolge*).[56] Or, as we have already put it, the arithmetic of qualities gives rise to a different order of quantity (or fields). This is why power(s), just as identity, must be plural, yet univocal. Powers amplify qualities in such a way that not only are magnitudes (or intensities) equally extensive and intensive, but the manifestation of intensities functions as the metric for measuring the difference between intensities of different types.[57] An intensification can, at the same time, be a new intensity, but both of these measures must be related to the continuum of nature that the various powers constitute. Châtelet's description of the *Naturphilosophical* project as 'feeding on the specificity of the singular to reach the plane where the intuitive and the discursive are born synchronously' illustrates this keenly.[58]

The inhabiting of an exponential or a potentiated being, as in the thought experiment of Einstein imagining himself riding a photon, becoming the photon, creates a productive tension (or delirium, as Châtelet has it) between the quantitative and the qualitative, as this intuitive inhabiting produces a potentiation of both, as well as an intensification of the unknowability of the relation between them. This unthinkable qualitative change again points to the unreflective nature of mathematics regarding the act of construction as a positive condition. It also speaks to the asymmetrical difference of one's own sense of motion detected in the intuitionistic move to another potentiated body (a photon).

To put it more directly, intuition allows us to put ourselves in the place of another kind of intensity to try and imagine what moving, and operating, according to that intensity would be like. This is not a foolproof action, however, as the very act of intuition, and its aforementioned lack of innocence, skews the setting down of oneself into another place. But by taking up the potential motions of another intensity, the very capacity of intuition itself becomes contaminated by those potential alien movements. It is with regard to this later point that Schelling's focus on dimensionality is fundamental, particularly in the *Darstellung* lectures.

To quote Iain Hamilton Grant again from his essay 'How Nature Comes to be Thought':

> The 'ground of dimensionality' can only be thought consequently upon dimensionality, or, in other words, dimensionality is emergent, if it is at all, from what is not dimensional. This does not mean that there *are no dimensions prior to their thought*, but that there are none prior to the operation of dimensions such that only such a thought is capable of thinking the emergence of dimensionality from non-dimensionality as such [. . .] Since thought is that dimension of motion that causes the problem of the ground of dimensionality to be a problem, it is clear that thought is amongst the dimensions of the motions of bodies, or better, is precisely the totality of motions of which bodies are capable.[59]

Thought, taken as motion, creates for us the problem of dimension. Or put otherwise, if thought is a seemingly open-ended motion, then it presents us with an enormous version of 'Where do we go?' Here Zalamea's point in the above epigraph is taken seriously: Schelling's approach to the mathematical is one whereby he attempts to understand how the isolation of a field of space is related to motion; or, put otherwise, Schelling's mathematical interests are proto-category theoretical (concerned with transformation) rather than proto-set theoretical (or concerned with belonging).

In the 13th *Darstellung* lecture, Schelling notes that Kant's inability to move beyond Aristotelian logic bears two interconnected positive aspects – that of assuming the simultaneity of time in the idea, and that number is the temporal designation of moment; numericity (measurement) co-evolves

with dimensionality (direction).[60] In the 16th lecture, he engages the primordial nature of science, a primordiality that numerous forms of mathematics
always point to, if only indirectly, through the formation of diagrams. This
primordial nature is 'the movement resting in what has being[, which] is also
a movement of reason'.[61] Movement is an arithmetic of qualities where the
polarised is not negated, but added as different potentialities in the actual,
thereby appearing as different trajectories. This marked polarisation guarantees that 'the antecedent has its actuality in the consequent' as this antecedent
is what science separates (or, in the language we have been using, isolates) as
Potenz. Following this ideal reversibility, Schelling argues that mathematics
is a potential science that demonstrates the conditional necessity of space-
time's interrelation.[62] Or, in other words, mathematics is the potential science that diagrams the capacities of being, whereas philosophy looks one
step deeper into the *possibility* of such a potentiality. In Schelling's 19th
Darstellung lecture, he addresses the ground of dimensionality mentioned
above by Grant. Schelling attempts to demonstrate how dimensionality, as a
problem, exists in the non-living world, or how it is that dimensionality can
be derived at all.[63]

In one sense, dimensionality is the result of the polarity of nature
manifested in organic beings (the arbitrariness of right and left, for
instance) which is species-specific. For instance, Schelling celebrates the
utility of height for human experience over breadth, whereas breadth
dominates in inorganic nature, for instance in the layering of the geological strata.[64] In order to explain voluntary movement, Schelling argues
that one must invoke some notion of drive (or the Aristotelian soul) as a
cause of movement in particular directions according to species' embodiment.[65] Schelling traces the development of animal life to the successive
addition of the manipulation of dimensions.[66] Again, what results is an
arithmetic of qualitative change whereby trajectories give rise to more
than mere dimensions; they produce an altogether different law of worlding within nature. That is, the sum total of the capacities of motion of a
species constitutes a consequent universal, an abstract range of motion.
Consequently, thought is that species of movement that condenses all
antecedent and material dimensions.

Dimensionality offers a more concrete, yet still abstract, form to thought
than intentionality or other phenomenological tools. However, the organic
capacity for motion is not a necessary and indelible mark on the world, nor
a domain of infinite freedom, but that which tests avenues of dimensional,
and environmental, exploration, often failing and/or going extinct. But
in their constrained freedom, life-forms change their environments; they
redraw, albeit superficially (in the context of the depths of nature), that
which conditions their embodied freedom. At the same time, the gestures

that discover dimensionality and are discovered by it suggest that the synthetic capacities of reason are loosely bounded, in a productive (or we might say copulating) sense, as in the very form of synthesis, or in Schellingian identity (A = A).[67]

(Re)Constructing continuity or folding mathematics into nature

The question with which I would like to close, to fold the mathematical back into the philosophical, is as follows: what happens to mathematics if its productive blind-spot (of its incapacity to look into the act of its own construction) is revealed by philosophy; that is, what happens once you apply Schellingian *Naturphilosophie* to mathematics? This problem is compounded by the fact that, if we take the continuity thesis seriously, the philosophy of mathematics is a species of *Naturphilosophie*. And furthermore, if Schelling subcribes to neither a strictly Platonic (or Okenian) substantialisation, nor an instrumental approach to number, what exactly is the status of mathematical synthesis such that it is not purely ideal? Or, simply put, how do we situate, and measure, the consequences of mathematics in nature?

Mathematics' limited sense of self-reflection is a positive constraint that consequently produces the capacity of simulation – of feeding constraints forward as apparently unbridled construction, or ideal synthesis. As a consequence, productive intuition is not a revelatory immediacy that conceals such synthesis, but its jumps and leaps highlight the qualitative differences that location and navigation engender. Mathematics is closest to its intuitionist philosophical roots when it recognises a limit and attempts to manipulate the construction in an unbound space, a space that is the ongoing result of nature's intensity interlacing itself through us.

Here, following Châtelet among others, post-Kantian thought is not a crude return to metaphysics, or a dogmatic rationalism against the Kantian critical spirit, but various attempts to bring Kant to the unstable moving ground of either a unified ideal activity (Fichte), a polarised but productive nature (Schelling), or the productive logic of the absolute spirit (Hegel). While the first and third have been admitted to the realm of mathematical thinkers, Schelling remains cast out; and yet, I would argue, his adherence to the problem of nature makes his thought all the more relevant for thinking mathematics. Ultimately, Schelling's mathematical contributions amount to an arithmetic and a geometry that not only attempt to incorporate differing quantitative and qualitative magnitudes, but also show that the very structure of the series that is the dynamic stages of nature (*Stufenfolge*) must admit to an addition that cannot be erased in the progression of such a series.

An avenue that demonstrates this influence, one explored by Marie-Luise Heuser, is Schelling's influence on the mathematician Hermann Grassmann and his father J. G. Grassmann. Both Grassmanns began to formalise the *Naturphilosophical* self-organisation of nature in mathematical terms by studying why various units of matter in nature extend in particular ways. Heuser argues that Hermann Grassmann attempted to develop a theory of extension that took dimensionality, and in particular the notion of a non-trivial infinity, into account to describe the non-linearity of the development of matter across time and in space.[68] Similarly, but not identically, to Oken, both Grassmanns attempted to diagram the inner forces of nature as they appear as phenomenal products. The difference lies in the formal separation between dimensionality or direction on one hand and quantity on the other, since, for the Grassmanns, quantity is the necessary but *a posteriori* division of a universal continuum of nature under constant morphogenesis. Far more work needs to be done to further flesh out these historical connections.[69]

Heuser traces this influence not only in the strictly mathematical world, but also to the history of crystallography and in particular the work of C. S. Weiss. Weiss, under the general influence of *Naturphilosophie*, developed a theory of continuous, that is, non-atomised crystalline matter to explain inorganic growth, and made the transition from *Naturphilosophie* to the mathematics of Grassmann possible. In an essay entitled 'A Dynamic View of Crystallization' (1804), he argued that crystalline matter developed dynamically, and that the faces of a crystal were determined along axes offset by non-material polarities.[70] Weiss's emphasis on polarity, in turn, allowed him to describe the faces of crystal formations as snapshots of the movement of polarities, of the forces acting according to their vectorial nature. In this sense Weiss can be seen as following Schelling, whereas Oken differed from him in relation to the generative nature of zero, or the indifference point. In the aforementioned essay Weiss writes:

> All of nature can be thought of as a development of opposing magnitudes (in the pure sense of mathematics) out of zero or null. One must not attribute an absolute existence to any material substance; each is nothing but a magnitude, a pole which is separated from its opposite and which exists at all solely in that separation.[71]

Weiss later developed this theory in a mathematical notion of crystal growth in his essay 'An Improved Method for the Identification of the Various Surfaces of Systems of Crystallization, combined with Observations on the

State of Polarization of the Surfaces of the Lines of Crystalline Structure' (1816–17).[72]

The tension between location and direction speaks not only to Schelling's emphasis on the physics of his time, but also to his unwillingness to abandon either the importance of form in Plato, or the messiness of soul-as-entelechy in Aristotle. Or, against Fichte, mathematics and *Naturphilosophie* are contained in the same world of worlds (or we might simply say nature). Whereas Fichte's intuition is taken as inspiration for L .E. J. Brouwer's intutionist approach to mathematics, it is unclear, given the intuitionists' thrust towards establishing the *existence* of mathematics, why they would steer away from Schelling.[73] Whereas Fichte's brilliantly argued self-generating form of the I is clean of nature, it seems doomed in its isolation.[74] It is not the intensity of the I's activity that divides the continuity of nature into non-continuous realms of inert matter (not-I), but nature, in not reflecting, operates on its own intensity, thereby spreading out the ideas and concepts of mathematics into the continuum. This is why the philosopher must look into the act of construction itself or, in other words, engage in the realm of activity, which makes up the form and trajectory of thought.[75]

Yet, at the same time, the free construction and wild synthesis of mathematics is a remarkable example not only of a means of suspending (without obliterating) reflection but also the non-trivial importance of intuition; that it does not reduce but fully acknowledges the pressure or momentum of the abstract. It is for this reason that philosophy, as *Naturphilosophie*, must be ultimately concerned with forces, and more fundamentally with the *Potenz*. Our enacting of the ideal does not mean that only we are capable of it, but that we are caught in its force and, as a result, the world of measure does not stand apart from nature just as we do not stand apart from nature.

Ultimately, and as Michael Vater has suggested, Schelling's emphasis on the trajectorial nature of mathematics as an additive procedure is what separates him most sharply from Hegel and Hegel's speculative logic.[76] While Vater argues that this shows Hegel's dazzling conceptual breadth as over and above Schelling's dusty formalism, I would argue, and hope to show in the following chapters, that it is in fact Schelling's restraint about philosophy's capacity for determining conceptual content that is the core of his later project of positive philosophy. Put otherwise, Schelling attempts to describe the embodiment and conceptual weight that the structures of nature engender without fixing their effect to particular concepts. The crux of this attempt, as we will explore in the next chapter, is Schelling's development of the *Potenzen*. The *Potenzen* are Schelling's attempt to create the leanest structure of nature possible in order to determine both transcendental and immanent conditions for, and beyond, human cognition.

Notes

1. While a whole different project in itself, there are identifiable traces of Fichte's and Schelling's influence in the work of Brouwer, who fathered intuitionist mathematics in the early twentieth century.

2. See, for instance, Michael Vater, 'Fichte's Reaction to Schelling's Identity Philosophy in 1806', in *After Jena: New Essays on Fichte's Later Philosophy*, ed. D. Breazeale and T. Rockmore (Evanston, IL: Northwestern University Press, 2008).

3. Grant is not alone in this; both Bruce Matthews and Jason Wirth similarly argue that Schelling should not be viewed as a divided figure.

4. Herman Weyl, *The Open World* (Woodbridge: Ox Bow Press, 1932), 61.

5. Schelling, 'Of the I as a Principle of Philosophy', 114–15.

6. Kant, *Critique of the Power of Judgment*, 134–5 (5:251–2).

7. Schelling, *Ideas for a Philosophy of Nature*, 5.

8. Ibid., 45.

9. Ibid., 53.

10. Ibid., 53.

11. Ibid., 161–4.

12. This pivot is also essential for understanding Schelling's mixture of harsh attack and excited praise when it comes to the mechanism and immanence of Spinoza's philosophy. While Spinoza's use of immanence holds the promise of a complex understanding of identity that Schelling begins to entertain in the *Ideas* and develops more rigorously in the *System of Transcendental Idealism*, Schelling is damning of Spinoza's philosophy for being too mechanistic.

13. By naïvely Platonic I mean the view that numbers exist independently of the manifestations of matter in the cosmos.

14. Iain Hamilton Grant, 'Being and Slime', *Collapse: Philosophical Research and Development*, 4 (2008), 308–9.

15. Ibid., 289.

16. Ibid., 290.

17. Ibid., 291.

18. Ibid., 300–1.

19. Lorenz Oken, *Elements of Physiophilosophy*, trans. Alfred Tulk (London: The Ray Society, 1847), 1.

20. Ibid., 4.

21. Grant, 'Being and Slime', 299.

22. Oken, *Elements of Physiophilosophy*, 201.

23. Ibid., 27.

24. Grant, 'Being and Slime', 305.

25. Ibid., 312.

26. Ibid., 315.

27. Schelling, *System of Transcendental Idealism*, 17.

28. Ibid., 13.

29. Kant, *Critique of Pure Reason*, 273 (A141/B180).

30. Michael Vater, 'Introduction', in Schelling, *System of Transcendental Idealism*, xvi.

31. Schelling, *System of Transcendental Idealism*, 136.

32. Ibid., 80.

33. Ibid., 119. It is here along with several moments in the *First Outline* that Schelling appears to be involved in some form of proto-asymptotic thinking in the vein of Peirce, Weyl and others.

34. F. W. J. Schelling, *On University Studies*, trans. E. S. Morgan (Athens, OH: Ohio University Press, 1966), 45.

35. Ibid., 47.

36. Ibid., 47–8.

37. Ibid., 49.

38. Schelling, *First Outline*, 205.

39. Schelling, *System of Transcendental Idealism*, 143.

40. F. W. J. von Schelling, *Presentation of My System of Philosophy*, in J. G. Fichte and F. W. J. von Schelling, *The Philosophical Rupture between Fichte and Schelling: Selected Texts and Correspondence (1800–1802)*, trans. M. Vater and D. Wood (Albany, NY: SUNY Press, 2012), 189.

41. Here it would be prudent to address the relationship between Maimon's injection of rationalism into the critical project via mathematics to Fichte's utilisation of calculus. Like Schelling's actants in the *First Outline*, Maimon's infinitesimals operate on the border between real entities and ideal footholds; hence opposing claims as to whether, via the infinitesimals, Maimon is maintaining a concept of the in itself or a more rigorous notion of the synthetic.

42. As Grant helps to make clear, it is not the method of artificial isolation which is damnable but that such a method of isolation in Fichte makes the practical as such causally immune from nature. See Grant, *Philosophies of Nature*, 82.

43. Schelling, *First Outline*, 202.

44. Markus Gabriel makes a similar argument towards the end of his *Transcendental Ontology* by equating *das Unvordenkliche* (the unprethinkable) with the analytic concept of logical space. See Markus Gabriel, *Transcendental Ontology: Essays in German Idealism* (London: Continuum, 2011). As I will discuss in Chapter 5, Gabriel's account too easily erases nature as a constraint in his articulation of the engine of predication as a factual necessity and not a natural one.

45. Schelling, *First Outline*, 207–9.

46. Ibid., 209.

47. Schelling, *Ideas for a Philosophy of Nature*, 161.

48. Ibid., 163.

49. Schelling, *System of Transcendental Idealism*, 140.

50. Gilles Châtelet, *Figuring Space: Philosophy, Mathematics, and Physics* (London: Springer, 1999), 56.

51. Fernando Zalamea, *Synthetic Philosophy of Contemporary Mathematics*, trans. L. Fraser (Falmouth: Urbanomic, 2012), 374.

52. Schelling, *First Outline*, 207.

53. Ibid., 210.

54. One can relate this shift back to the realm of knowledge in terms of what Robert Batterman has emphasised as the importance of inter-theoretic reduction. Batterman argues that asymptotic thought is important for understanding the way in which reduction functions within a field as opposed to across fields. Or, in other words, asymptotic thinking signals the quantitative/qualitative split as operating differently within immanent abstraction and inter-theoretic abstraction. See Robert Batterman, *The Devil in the Details: Asymptotic Reasoning in Explanation, Reduction, and Emergence* (Oxford: Oxford University Press, 2002).

55. Châtelet, *Figuring Space*, 75–6.

56. See Beach's *Potencies of the God(s)* as discussed in Chapter 1 as well as below in Chapter 4.

57. See Grant, *Philosophies of Nature*, 169.

58. Châtelet, *Figuring Space*, 101.

59. Grant, 'How Nature Comes to be Thought', 25–44.

60. F. W. J. von Schelling, 'Einleitung in die Philosophie der Mythologie', trans. Iain Hamilton Grant (unpublished manuscript), 8–9. An avenue worth exploring, though this is not possible here, would be to investigate Schelling's influence on intuitionist mathematics more generally, and particularly in relation to Leopald Kronecker (who studied with Schelling) and his proto-intuitionism coupled with finitism, which could throw light on Oken's and Schelling's work.

61. F. W. J. von Schelling, *Darstellung Lecture 16*, trans. Iain Hamilton Grant (unpublished manuscript, 2014), 2.

62. Ibid., 3.

63. Schelling, *Darstellung Lecture 19*, 3.

64. Ibid., 8.

65. Ibid., 9.

66. Ibid., 10.

67. In relation to gesture and mathematics I am heavily indebted to numerous conversations with Reza Negarestani.

68. Marie-Luise Heuser-Kessler, 'The Significance of *Naturphilosophie* for Justus and Hermann Grassmann', in H.-J. Petsche et al. (eds), *From Past to Future: Graßmann's Work in Context* (Basel: Springer, 2011), 55–6.

69. Various commentators have suggested that Grassmann's alliance with *Naturphilosophie* may have led to the poor reception of his work at the time. For a summary of these views, see Michael J. Crowe, *A History of Vector Analysis: The Evolution of the Idea of a Vectorial System* (Mineola, NY: Dover Books, 2011).

70. See Andre Authier, *Early Days of X-Ray Crystallography* (Oxford: Oxford University Press, 2013).

71. C. S. Weiss, 'Dynamische Ansicht der Kristallisation', quoted in Kenneth L. Caneva, 'Physics and *Naturphilosophie*: A Reconnaissance', *History of Science*, 35 (1997): 55.

72. See John G. Burke, *Origins of the Science of Crystals* (Berkeley, CA: University of California Press, 1966).

73. For such a treatment of intuition and its historical relation to mathematics, see Roberto Torretti, *Philosophy of Geometry from Riemann to Poincaré* (London: Reidel, 1978).

74. Grant, *Philosophies of Nature*, 90.

75. Ibid., 178.

76. Addressed in Vater's notes to F. W. J. von Schelling, *Bruno, or On the Natural and Divine Principle of Things* (Albany, NY: SUNY Press, 1984).

Chapter 4

The Red Threads of the World: *Potenzen*, Construction and Inexistence

Everything, absolutely everything, even that which by nature is external, must have already become internal to us before we can present it externally or objectively.[1]

First of all, everything that is in Nature, and Nature considered as sum total of *existence*, is not even present for us. To philosophize about nature means to *create* Nature.[2]

This chapter provides a historical outline of Schelling's theory of powers, otherwise known as the *Potenzen*. Schelling's theory of the *Potenzen* emerges from his explorations of dynamics via Kant and Spinoza on the one hand, and from attempting to place human thought properly in the world, following Fichte, according to the constraints of identity and the capacities of construction on the other. Between these theoretical poles, Schelling's *Potenzen*, I argue, function as a structuration of freedom-as-dynamics, thereby criss-crossing the mind–world boundary. For Schelling, an unavoidable tension of this naturalised form of freedom, particularly concerning philosophy, arises between the free construction of philosophical systems in general and the totalising form of philosophy as such. As was suggested in Chapter 1, this tension manifests itself in that the philosopher is never to complete a final system, a final container for all being and knowing, but always provisionally to create systems that attempt to do justice to the open-ended world. This open-endedness disavows any heavy reliance upon either origin or goal, as either ontological states or normative imperatives.

The immediate problem that arises, one that should be evident following the discussions of space and sense in Chapter 2 and of space and motion in relation to construction in Chapter 3, is how to locate such constructive activities and their results, if there are no knowable contours of the world. The immediate temptation, and the reason why I believe Schelling utilises the cosmology of Plato alongside the biology of Aristotle, is to metaphysicalise dogmatically, or to ontologise enthusiastically. Schelling recognises, in philosophy at large, what could be called the metaphysical-ontological demand. This demand is simply the fact that philosophy aims at the All; it attempts to explore the totality of things, as well as each and every thing equally. Regardless of one's stated philosophical aims, goals or methods, Schelling seems to suggest, particularly in the advent of the so-called positive philosophy (arguably beginning after 1809, and surely by 1815), that philosophy will unavoidably explore and generate errantly, hence why mere reflection is a spiritual sickness.[3] Philosophy, according to both the early and late Schelling, should not create for the mere sake of creating, but nor can it ignore the creative impulse of philosophy as such in the form of the metaphysical-ontological demand.[4]

The uncertain spatial bounds of Schelling's conceptualisation of nature (as having no beginning and no end) necessitate his utilisation of the *Potenzen*. The *Potenzen* meet the metaphysical-ontological demand while reasserting nature's autonomy, but simultaneously acknowledging our high, or highly augmented, place in nature. As a result of this complexity, the *Potenzen* are one of the least understood (and often outright ignored) aspects of Schelling's philosophy on the whole. This difficulty is exacerbated by the fact that Schelling is not given much, if any, theoretical autonomy, and is seen as either simply agreeing with Kant, Fichte or Spinoza, or as being a transition point between Fichte and Hegel – one that does not warrant deeper investigation.[5] Yet taking Schelling's view of constructive knowledge via mathematics into account, the degree to which a powers-based ontology sets Schelling apart from his contemporaries becomes clear. The transition from the Fichtean activity of the 'I' or a general notion of intellectual intuition does not overdetermine nature (e.g. by suggesting that nature is *merely* the unconscious side of the I), but further buttresses the strength of Schelling's abstract and formal approach to the quantitative *vis-à-vis* the qualitative. This approach allows Schelling to assess what the structure of nature is in so far as thought is productive with nature, and not of nature in any straightforward sense. Or, put otherwise, Schelling's powers-based ontology allows him to navigate the pitfalls of both mechanism and dynamism in physics via a non-naïve notion of construction – a mode of construction that must epistemologically and ontologically maximally obtain in terms of the diversity of individuation and the stability of nature as a world system over time.[6] Construction by nature does not differ from construction by us in kind, but only in location and degree.

Schelling illustrates this continuity by simply arguing that thought is the field in which we experience the *Potenzen*, or powers, as thought. That is, our relation to thought demonstrates the ungroundedness – or inexistence – of nature at both temporal and spatial 'ends'. If one asked 'Where are you thinking in relation to the start and end of thinking, or of even a single thought?', a feeling of both positive and negative freedom would result – a feeling of seemingly unlimited creativity coupled with an apparently unassailable blockage at locating the thing that thinks in relation to the process of thinking. In other words, origins can never be absolutely recovered. This question demonstrates the apparent unavoidability of the *Potenzen* as an active oscillation between being and becoming.

Overlooking this ungroundedness and the constructive account of Schelling's nature often serves to straw-man his notion of freedom as a *naïve* form of faith,[7] or as demonstrating an impossible immediacy of conceptual acquisition (i.e. of overemphasising the capacity of intellectual intuition, a tendency I hopefully dispelled in Chapter 3). The immediacy of Schelling's articulation of intuition is not one of content (since the very concept is only ever a recapitulation of the real series), but an immediacy of form that Kant utilises in simultaneously connecting the analytic to the synthetic and matter to experience, in the ether proofs of the *Opus Postumum*. As we have seen, this raises numerous questions in terms of whether Kant's final synthesis is dogmatic, Spinozistic, critical or something else altogether. What separates Schelling from Kant in this regard, however, is the ungroundedness of the meontological powers in Schelling's philosophy. On this point, Schelling is also seemingly close to and yet distant from Spinoza. As Schelling makes clear on numerous occasions, he views Spinoza's system as too realist in a mechanistic sense, or as lacking in dynamics, thereby restricting any sense of contingency or freedom.[8]

Schelling's emphasis on dynamics and his powers-based ontology suggest a broadly Aristotelian orientation, whereas ungroundedness as such is distinctly Platonic, in that it functions, like the Platonic idea, as a real universal condition.[9] That is, the Aristotelian view that powers inhere in particular natural kinds or essences is abstracted – via Platonic cosmology and through a general creation or motion – so that power now inheres in the world. For Schelling, essences are always bifurcatory, moving in two directions between their Aristotelian naturalistic basis and their structural or abstract capacities following a Platonic conceptualisation of the world-soul – of that which is taken as the first motion of the world. Since, as we saw above, Schelling states that the philosophical life 'should begin with Plato and end with Aristotle', it is not surprising that the *Potenzen*, as a concept used throughout Schelling's work, would attract both historical valences. Put broadly, Schelling's theory of the potencies allows him to assert the importance of a nature 'outside us', while simultaneously acknowledging our limited ability in understanding it because it is already within us. Or, put otherwise, the *Potenzen* are created to appease both scepticism and the metaphysical-ontological demands, in order to avoid the limitations of a brute mechanical philosophy, and to navigate through a possibly mystifying dynamic atomism by asking 'Why is there neither merely being, nor merely becoming?'

Schelling does not achieve this delicate balance by asserting human finitude in the face of nature, nor by overdetermining nature's capacity for infinitude. Most importantly, nature is that which precedes and produces us, but is, in itself, incomplete or open, in that anything that it could be said to contain actually determines its borders. To flesh this out I will attempt to construct a history of Schelling's development of the *Potenzen*. I will begin by addressing the dynamic forces in his work prior to his formal presentation of potencies *per se*, and then move on to the discussion of the *Potenzen* proper in the *Presentation* and *Further Presentation*.

My more specific goal in producing a historical survey of Schelling's *Potenzen* is to demonstrate how he attempts to construct and maintain a minimal difference between motion and space or, more generally in the terms of the *Potenzen*, between creation and structure. This difference lies in determining the status of the *Potenzen* as an inexistent necessity.[10] While I will return to this in the conclusion, I would for now state briefly that inexistent necessity, which is similar to but not the same as the contingent necessity of necessity, is Schelling's argument for a *consequently* original momentum to creation which, because of its inexistence, is necessarily ungraspable (or unprethinkable) for us, yet is the condition of all forms of creation, noetic and otherwise. This does not mean that nature as such *are* the *Potenzen* as such *are* the unprethinkable (this is unacceptable, since it makes the unprethinkable into an entity), but rather that finding them in thought has potential ontological consequences. Yet just because we discover the *Potenzen* in thought, this does not mean that thought *contains* nature or the *Potenzen*, but that the construction of the *Potenzen* (as always being in thought) is how we have a provisionally minimalistic ontology. Thus, to say that a *Potenz* or power *is* only means that there are general classes of can-be-states (or dispositions, or tendencies) that function across numerous dimensions.

Given the necessary, yet minimal, ontological consequence of thinking, the fact that Schelling is conscripted to both anti- (or post-) metaphysical camps, and high- (or ultra-) metaphysical camps at once is not surprising, given that he attempts to create a lean metaphysics of modality as such or, put otherwise, to construct a theory of how construction occurs with and without human participation. For Schelling, modality is the merely ideal expression of the concept of potency. As he puts it in 'Of the I as a Principle of Philosophy' – modality is not, *pace* Kant, synthetic, but merely sylleptic. For Schelling, the sylleptic names what functions as a category but is not necessarily easily categorisable and thus more like a tendency. However, what is sylleptic is also categorical in that it can be applied to a wide range of entities that share some behaviour. I return to this point in the conclusion of this chapter.[11]

Furthermore, this is why it is difficult to cleanly disentangle Schelling's epistemological claims from his ontological claims. While the next chapter will deal with the former, the following pages attempt to trace the development of Schelling's notion of the potencies throughout his career, treating them as minimally ontological. Approaching Schelling's use of powers or potencies historically, I have two subsequent aims: first, to uphold and do justice to the continuity thesis, that is, that Schelling's work is not fractured into periods conceptually, but only in focus. Secondly, by moving historically through Schelling's use of the *Potenzen*, I hope to demonstrate how their lack of domain-specificity (whether in thought, art, production, natural processes, etc.) exhibits their basic functional use as opposed to them being viewed as metaphysically domineering or ontologically superfluous. Finally, discussion of texts that briefly mention the *Potenzen* has been relegated to notes in the relevant time frame.

Schelling's dynamics as proto-*Potenzen* in the *First Outline,* the *Ideas* and *System of Transcendental Idealism*

> Perhaps the most important contribution of Schelling to the development of field theory was his recognition of what was only implicit in Kant. If matter and material phenomena could be seen only as the results of attractive and repulsive forces, then it seems obvious that all phenomena should be reduced to those forces.[12]

In her text *Schelling and the End of Idealism*, Dale Snow argues that Schelling's earliest discussion of dynamic forces sets the stage for the later development of the potencies. Schelling's adoption of dynamic forces follows a lineage from Kant, which allows him to simultaneously break from Kant, Fichte and Spinoza.[13] To begin, one must distinguish Schelling's *Potenzen* from Spinoza's powers. At the most basic level, Spinoza's doctrine of powers is one ultimately ruled by divine adequation. That is, regardless of Spinoza's pantheism, a power or potency is always measured by how it would be in the mind of God, that is, powers are ultimately under the rule of the One-All; or, put otherwise, potencies for Spinoza function as *measures within* a domain of pure immanence. For Schelling, the potencies are bifurcated between being additive trajectories and exponential qualities (as we saw in the last chapter). They are additive in their geometrical dimension (as going from having one dimension to three is due to adding degrees of freedom in a physical sense), but exponential in that they are always increasing in intensity, as the function of thinking them, or of construction itself, is one of identity-as-intensification. Or, put another way, since conceptual space and actual space are inseparable for Schelling due to the primordial continuity of nature, more of something means more of something in space and/or with more intensity than previously.

The rudimentary source-material for Schelling's generation of the *Potenzen* also separates them from a Spinozist provenance. Schelling's notion of the *Potenzen* combines mathematical and organic notions of power (taken from Eschenmayer and Kielmeyer respectively). Where Schelling seems to downplay the mathematical aspect of the *Potenzen*, and play up its biological aspects in terms of how recapitulation is deployed in his notion of natural history, for example, I argue that the mathematical (and particularly spatial) aspects of the *Potenzen* guarantee their historical dimension, but in a futural, rather than historical, sense.[14]

Given this, how can Edward Beach assert that Schelling's *Potenzen* are similar to, or even the same as, Spinoza's powers? Beach's emphasis on the Spinozistic quality of Schelling's potencies is due to the fact that he reads Schelling as relying heavily on the potencies to give determination conceptual rigour against Hegel's reliance upon the conceptual as being capable of capturing the totality of the world thus determined.[15] That is, Beach suggests that Schelling uses the potencies primarily to contradict Hegel's utilisation of and reliance on logic following Schelling's temporalisation of being; or, in other words, that the potencies are how Schelling *justifies* the inadequacy of logic to grasp being.[16] In terms of their purely negative, or critical, function, Beach's account seems adequate. However, once he begins to discuss the positive explanatory function of the potencies, I believe that his discussion suffers from an over-reliance on viewing them in an anti-Hegelian and, at times, pseudo-Spinozist fashion. Beach, following Snow and others, claims that not only do the *Potenzen* function in a dialectical, albeit modified, form, but that they are ultimately manifestations of a primordial will. While the discussion of will lays bare the need to explain the creativity of the world in time, which can be related to the metaphysical-ontological demand above, the will is overly psychologised, even spiritualised, in Beach's text.[17] Furthermore, this move substantialises the potencies more than Schelling would allow. While the potencies act to transform the possible into the actual, and to subsequently treat the possible as material, they themselves cannot be said to be merely, or even primarily, material in nature in a substantive manner. I will discuss Beach's work at more length below, as he largely focuses on Schelling's work after 1815. His general suggestion regarding Schelling's Spinozism, however, seems to require addressing Schelling's earlier phases, given the general assumption that he was functioning under a largely Spinozist mode from 1797 until 1802.

Schelling's repeated critiques of Spinoza indicate that a substantialist reading of the *Potenzen* does not comply with his general call for substratum independence in both philosophy and science. Furthermore, the temporal unboundedness of the *Potenzen*, which rely neither on limited nor on total being (pure immanence *à la* Spinoza), nor on pure or unruly becoming (*à la* Bergson or Deleuze), break Schelling out of the purely Aristotelian trajectory of philosophy. The notion of inexistence, which has roots in medieval philosophy, better fits the status of the *Potenzen* and of Schelling's conceptualisation of nature in general: that of always coming to be but affected by what it already is. Thus, I argue that taking the *Potenzen* as part of a metaphysical holism, which leads many commentators back to Spinoza's immanence, is the wrong move. As mentioned above, Schelling sees any notion of origin or end as provisional, hence his utilisation of the terms *Prius* and *Posterior*. Therefore, while everything exhibits the All or the cosmos, no claim can be made that this All is a closed whole.

Schelling writes in the *Ideas* that 'form and matter are inseparable [. . .] every organisation is a whole; its unity lies in itself, it does not depend on our choice'; but, at the same time, unity is a concept, and something constructed by us through reflection.[18] This relation of the absolute ideal and the absolute real is a lynchpin of philosophy itself, and of philosophy as a science.[19] Or, as Schelling puts it earlier in the *Ideas*:

> we require to know, not how such a Nature arose outside us, but how even the very idea of such a Nature has got into us; not merely how we have, say, arbitrarily generated it, but how and why it originally and necessarily underlies everything that our race has ever thought about Nature.[20]

The use of 'originally and necessarily' should give some pause, given the opening statements of this chapter; namely, that necessity is always consequent for Schelling, and that origin is always provisional. Nature enables the processes by which we come to have a concept of nature, a concept that leads us to posit an origin only if it functions as an ideal starting point to organise our thoughts about a nature that has long pre-existed us as a race. Yet the being of nature is what makes it impress its limits on us. Since these limits are at least discoverable indirectly by us through the grasping of concepts, particular concepts can be taken to be structurally, that is, maximally, consequential in that their non-conceptual impact appears limitless.

Thus, there appear to be some resistant granules, some traces of structure, which do not disappear in the creative folding and unfolding that are the processes of nature. These entities are not origins but are *more original* than other products so far discovered. This is evident in Schelling's early interest in chemistry, which arguably foregrounds his construction of the *Potenzen*. Chemistry, as an early combinatorial model of dynamic nature, helps justify the use of the original actant in the opening sections of the *First Outline*. Schelling writes: 'The individuality of the original actants, however, strives against this universalisation. The individuality of all actants ought to be maintained in the absolute product together with the most complete combination.'[21] Towards the end of the *First Outline* he writes: 'This idea of pure intensity is expressed by the idea of the actant. It is not the product of this action that is simple, but the actant itself abstracted from the product, and it must be simple in order that the product may be infinitely divisible.'[22]

The specificity of the relation between terms here foreshadows the particular contours of the *Potenzen* to come later. The actants can participate in universality, and in all combinations of nature's products, but something of their *individuality* must remain. This individuality is then later connected to pure intensity, but pure intensity is an idea that is *expressed* by the actants. The simplicity of the actant is not that of a decomposable object or product, but that which allows any given product, any collision of forces that registers as a *Scheinprodukt*, to be viewed and measured quantitatively, because its being depends upon the intensity of the powers that comprise it.

Iain Hamilton Grant takes issue with the articulation of actants as natural monads in his *Philosophies of Nature after Schelling*:

> 'The units of activity' or natural monads effectively recover the Kantian project in the *Physical Monadology*, and do not serve to buttress the identity of forces in nature (the identity of which in any case lies in the construction of matter) but rather to identify units of natural activities with those of transcendental ones.[23]

Here I believe that Grant's anti-Kantianism is overemphasised, albeit slightly. It is less the case, I would argue, that Schelling is transcendentalising action in nature as such, but rather that he is problematising the question of access between the transcendental position and that of *Naturphilosophie*, while taking into account that the transcendental perspective is thoroughly natural. The act of making cuts into nature, of treating the flow of nature in a punctuated fashion, rehearses, *in utero*, the difference between the various potencies *to the extent they can be detected in thought*. Thus, the dynamic atoms, or actants, are expressions of intensity *as a self-contained idea*, that is, as another potency translated into thinking as a kind of interference pattern or distortion, which requires an asymptotic or otherwise highly experimental approach. Another way of putting this is to view the actants as a temporary concretion and localisation of a potency, knowing that, in fact, it is only an instance of a potency. The notion of the *Potenzen* in relation to real patterns, and thus to Plato's ideas, leads us to Schelling's *Ideas for a Philosophy of Nature*.

Ideas for a Philosophy of Nature (1799, 1803)[24]

Schelling's introduction of the potencies ties them immediately to both Leibniz's monadology (therein linking them, albeit slightly, to Schelling's actants of the *First Outline* just discussed) as well as to the proper means of reading the Platonic ideas (*Idee*). Throughout Schelling's *Ideas*, experiments in the physical sciences, particularly regarding magnetism, light and gravity, are attached to discussions of how nature is conceived transcendentally. In this regard, the *Ideas* can be taken as the reverse image of the *First Outline* in which transcendental philosophy is set into nature, where, in the *Ideas*, nature makes transcendental philosophy as such possible. This latter point is further unfolded in the *System of Transcendental Idealism* while the former is worked out in the *Presentations*.

In relation to the Platonic ideas, the potencies function as a means of explaining how a hierarchy of difference emerges from within nature's unity without relying upon holism or pure immanence. The infinite is embodied in the finite, but this finite is added to the unity that is nature. In this sense, nature is best viewed not as *a whole* but as an extensive All (or the whole so far). Thus, nature creates by adding to itself its failure to recreate itself, to reflect fully or to contain itself as a finite entity, thereby expanding outward.[25] Potencies function as a way of particularising types of unities that contribute to this expansion, and Schelling uses them in attempting to explain how nature unfolds itself through particularities, which are always relative infinities, or unities.[26] He writes:

> These unities, each of which signifies a definite degree of embodiment of the infinite into the finite, are represented in three potencies of Nature-philosophy. The first unity, which in embodying the infinite into the finite is itself again this embodiment, presents itself as a whole through the *universal structure of the world*, individually through the series of bodies. The other unity, of the reverse embodiment of the particular into the universal or essence, expresses itself, though always in subordination to the real unity which is predominant in Nature, in *universal mechanism*, where the universal or essence issues as *light*, the particular as *bodies*, in accordance with all dynamical determinations.

Finally, the absolute integration into one, or indifferencing, of both unities, yet still in the real, is expressed by *organism*, which is therefore once more the *in-itself* of the first two unities.[27]

This organism, or living unity, enters ideality as reason reflecting upon itself, as complete but ongoing creation by reason. But this process is not mere reflection, as it is expressed by something outside of it – the unity and indifference of the infinite in the finite and the finite in the infinite. It is important to note that the whole is a *presentation* of a series (pointing back to the expression function of the actants above), while the particulars also can be extrapolated as demonstrating their place in the All. In the language above it is important to note that the potencies are neither things, nor even processes, but second-order tendencies that appear as unities, although they are unities that are always imperfectly captured because of their mediated expression. However, this image is slightly complicated, since throughout the rest of the text the potencies are used in a plural sense as if they are physical powers, that is, chemical or magnetic potencies as opposed to the strictly structural sense that Schelling seems to emphasise earlier. Later on, in the supplemental texts to the *Ideas*, the potencies are further broken down into a three-step system as is common in Schelling's texts. The first dimension, also known as the formative principle, is discussed as the repetition of the same process in the attempt for stability (where matter emerges as the first existent), while the second is the contraction of such irritability represented by electricity, and the third is the emergence of sensibility via light (the expansive force).[28]

It is important to note once again that while the *First Outline* can be read as a transcendental account of the *Naturphilosophie*, that is, a discussion of nature from the view of thought (as the epigraph about thinking nature being a mode of creation suggests), the *Ideas* attempts to view nature in terms of particular physical theories and experiments. What remains the same, however, and what Schelling will formalise most directly in the *Presentation of My System*, is that in both a transcendental and an empirical sense, the *Potenzen* are those tendencies that *seem* identifiable as individuals but, at the same time, are infinite in their particularity. Pursuing the transcendental view in the following years, Schelling develops this particularity as infinite in kind in terms of a self, thereby modifying the Fichtean inspiration of activity, as we saw in Chapter 1.

It is worth returning here to Beach's aforementioned emphasis on will and its relation to the potencies above. Given the notion of self as an activity that is particular, yet seemingly infinite in its expressibility, it would seem that the notion of primordial will is even more likely a means of discussing the potencies. Yet the notion of the self, or of the subject, must be taken in its fully complex Schellingian articulation. This notion, for Schelling, does not refer to a subject in a Kantian sense, or to personality as rooted in a particular soul or person, but to the self as a particular whose expression is also particular, but, importantly, such that this particularity, and what the self is expressing, *are not of it alone.* This will become clear in investigating the *Potenzen* further in the *System of Transcendental Idealism* and how this relates to Schelling's use of the concept of identity.

System of Transcendental Idealism (1800)

In the *System of Transcendental Idealism*, the discussion of the potencies seems to shift, at least in terms of describing them as potencies in nature, as opposed to potencies or powers that are integral to the development of consciousness as such. In the text, Schelling is attempting to relate Fichte's exacerbation of Kantian selfhood to some account of an external, or natural, world. This requires addressing the relation of a subject to an object in a way that preserves that capacity of both. In discussing the Fichtean proposition 'self = self' or 'A = A', Schelling argues that this is not a statement of identity traditionally understood, but one of synthesis.[29] He claims that synthesis and identity are synthetic and identical together, most obviously when spoken about in terms of a self. He states that this is because the notion of self clearly, at least for us, nominates that which is a duality *within* identity, or a subject-object, a thing that is simultaneously a thing and a process, or activity.

Schelling then brings this into relation with the *Potenzen* as follows:

> Natural science proceeds arbitrarily from nature, as the simultaneously *productive and produced*, in order to derive from the concept the particular. The identity in question is an immediate object of knowledge only in immediate self-consciousness; in that the highest power of self-objectification, to which the transcendental philosopher raises himself at the outset – not arbitrarily but through *freedom*; and the fundamental duality in nature is itself ultimately inexplicable only inasmuch as nature is taken to be intelligence.[30]

Thus, the potencies are discovered necessarily in the very structure of thought thinking something, of some content being taken as a thing at all. The immediacy of knowledge here is not one of full understanding, but of a structural necessity, which states that in order for a self (an activity particularised) to interact with another activity, a form of self-objectification is to be accomplished by a power that, while encountered by intelligence, must be other than intelligence, but not too other (i.e. not outside the unity) in order to allow these activities to interact. At the same time, the above quote serves as a meta-philosophical or methodological note on Schelling's own approach to the *Potenzen* in his earliest work.

But the raising of the philosopher's consciousness mentioned above and the importance of the *Potenzen* for synthesis is not merely a bridge of communication, but a means of augmentation. The self-objectification of the philosopher can be taken to be 'higher' in the sense of viewing conceptual space, that is, she can be taken to place the conceptual space beneath her for critical overview, thereby connecting the exponential nature of the *Potenzen* as having a quantitative increase coupled with a direction (and not an arbitrarily 'better' or a more abstract qualitative shift in and of itself).

As Schelling writes:

> I find that the consciousness of an objective world is implied in every moment of my consciousness, and conclude, therefore, that something objective must already enter from the beginning into the synthesis of self-consciousness, and must again issue from the latter in its developed form [. . .] The self, once transposed into time, consists in a steady passage from one presentation to the next; yet it remains, after all, within its power to interrupt this series by reflection.[31]

This interruption, which activity has the power to do, is not an ontological break in the fabric of things, but an ideal series that treats the break *as if* it were an origin, even though origins cannot be found and are always artificial. In treating the necessary or the original as free, as a choice, it is turned into a new series of acts (at least *for us*), but this does not entail a 'blank cheque', or an easily won form of freedom. The imitation must be exact in order to do justice to the real, which forms the basis of the ideal copy – and yet the ideal copy is an addition to the real only insofar as the consequences and investigations of the real, via the ideal, allow for more about the real to be discovered.[32] Again, the exponential nature of the *Potenzen* should be evident – it is a sameness with the addition of a trajectory that may or may not add to that from which the power issues as ground.

The testing of whether or not the ideal methods of the self-as-activity obtain on the world results in the self, once it limits itself via intuition, and appears as a being caught between constant expansion and contraction. The self-as-activity must encounter its own limits in order to expand beyond them, otherwise idealism and the very notion of the ideal would simply make all the world illusory.[33]

Whereas in the *First Outline* Schelling encounters, and begins to sketch, the actants (or pure qualities) as having a distinct dynamic power, in the *System* he engages productive intuition in order to explain how the very notion of potencies has come to be for us. Both terms exhibit the synthetic identity of the real and ideal series: the actants are speculative entities that make thinking about intensities or the world outside of us possible, whereas in the *System*, the pure activity of the self is only possible through the invasion of an outside world into us.

Once again, the tensions and difference between the transcendental and *Naturphilosophical* use of *Potenz* is reflected in the arguments over whether the *Potenzen* are derived more from mathematical (algebraic) sources or organic sources. In the *System*, Schelling defines transcendental philosophy *as such* as the capacity of raising the self to a higher power which, in the history of the genesis of intelligence, means the redrawing of the origin of a decision from blind necessity to free choice. This choice, or general act of intelligence, however, does not mean that human decision ruptures the ontological fabric of the world, *pace* Johnston and Žižek, but that methods that trace the consequences of a particular world at least *appear* as freedom, appear as redirecting the succession of the activities of a self.[34] It is more the case, as Schelling puts it in relating human intelligence to that of animals, that it is in recognising the 'naturalness' of the succession of representations and intelligence's hand in moving those representations along, or of reflection effecting the natural capacities of sense, for instance, that a different direction, or act of free choice, occurs.[35]

Here Schelling appears to be shifting back to the notion of the *Potenzen* discussed above in the *First Outline*. As Schelling argues, the organisation and individuation of nature are simply nature operating on itself, thereby leading to the emergence of things from a dynamic and relative oneness.[36] This self-operation has fascinating consequences for the analysis of nature, and makes a spatial and motive account of natural processes embodied in their particularities an interesting avenue of analysis. But this is not the direction that the *System* pursues. Schelling entrenches the raising of the self-as-activity to the higher power in stricter and stricter human terms in the closing pages of the text.

While this is recuperated in the *Philosophy of Art*, in subsequent years Schelling is more interested in discussing the *Potenzen* in ways less directly applicable, it would appear, to the internal functioning of human consciousness. In the so-called Identity philosophy to which we now turn, Schelling attempts to abstract the notion of the *Potenzen* to their formal and natural limit. This is evident in the next phase of Schelling's use of the potencies applied to physics, art and geometry, particularly with regard to Platonism, most evident in the *Bruno*.

Schelling's *Potenzen* in the 'Universal Deduction', *Presentation, Further Presentations* and *Philosophy of Art*

Whereas our discussion of the potencies in the last section relates to Chapter 2 in terms of connecting the actants, or proto-physical sin-gularites, to the transition problem of moving from the conditions of physics to physics as such, the break with Fichte, which occurs in the letters and in the *Presentations* (*Presentation of My System of Philosophy* and *Further Presentations from the System of Philosophy*), demonstrates a more geometrical or spatially constructive approach. In a broader sense, the second phase of Schelling's utilisation of the *Potenzen* (from 1800 to 1804) appears split between diagrammatic and *Naturphilosophical* means (the *Presentations* and the 'Universal Deduction') as well as more artistic, or generally creative, attempts to express them (*The Philosophy of Art*). The reason for this is already evident in the above discussion, that is, it is Schelling continuing to struggle with identifying creativity in general, and separating expression from nature, or being itself. The diagrammatic becomes a way to discuss abstract expression of quality, *vis-à-vis* quantity, whereas the Platonic style of *Bruno* and the litany of examples in *The Philosophy of Art* attempt to demonstrate a unity through continuous creativity.

'Universal Deduction of the Dynamic Process of the Categories of Physics' (1800)

Following both the style and content of the *Ideas*, Schelling begins his abstraction of natural processes via the diagram in the 'Universal Deduction'. He states that in order to understand nature one must specu-late as to its universal properties, even if investigating these properties is an infinite task. Schelling speaks of these 'primitives' (thereby echoing the language of the *First Outline*) as 'the self-construction of matter repeated at different levels'.[37]

Construction is the overwhelming theme of the 'Universal Deduction', as it follows, generally, the language and method of the *Ideas*, but addresses the nature of the *Potenzen* through a geometrical mode also found in the *First Presentation* and *Further Presentation*. The 'Universal Deduction' also makes references to the *Potenzen* as types of forces in nature, as exhibited in the *First Outline*. These general motions can be detected from the first line of the text – 'The sole task of natural science is to *construct matter*' – to just a few paragraphs later:

Our entire endeavour can therefore be restricted only to seeking out the universal principles of all natural production; but it must also treat their applicability, which runs to infinity in all dimensions, as a non-finite task. – Just as the astronomer knows the general laws governing the motions of the universe, without for that very reason penetrating to the very depths of the heavens.[38]

Here the transcendental goals of the *First Outline* are expressed in the applications of knowledge within their particular field (which, while present in the *First Outline*, is closer in its specificity to the *Ideas*). A few pages later Schelling introduces points and lines in order to explain how various magnitudes of different kinds of forces are in fact on the same continuum.[39] Schelling repeats this theme half-way through the text in direct relation to the *Potenzen*. The *Potenzen* in the act of potentiation turn out to be the key to uniting forces that appear dynamically opposed, yet united, in the intuition of the natural scientist or philosopher.

Schelling writes:

We will arrive at a resolution of this problem through an exact determination of its consequences. The two forces are to be exhibited as opposed in one and the same intuition. When the two are opposed and separate, then just as in the preceding moment, each will produce a surface for itself (§§18–19). But the two must again be posited as identical for intuition. Since the antithesis of forces itself must persist, this is possible only when their productions are exhibited in a common third, and since, as was said, each of these forces produces the surface for itself, the common force (which must be thought not as a mere addition, but rather as arising through an actual penetration or multiplication of products by one another) must be the surface to the second power, or the cube. With this reciprocal potentiation of production on either side, the construction first breaks away from the merely geometrical, the third is added to the first two dimensions, and the genuine mediating link by which the two forces may be posited as simultaneously non-identical and yet as united in intuition, is (not the line or the surface, but rather) space itself, i.e., magnitude extended in three dimensions.[40]

Thus the question remains whether Schelling's discussion of the *Potenzen* shifts from the biological to the mathematical, or whether it was always already something else altogether. The biological impulse appears in the movement that allows the diagrammatic to occur at all, whereas the compact mathematical expression of such motion, to be extended outward in an abstract sense, is the consequence of the diagram. In either case, the *Potenzen* appear as the least noetic account of Schelling's philosophy; they appear as the most real, maximally consequential, or perhaps the only non-sheerly ideal components of nature. This is evident as early as 'Of the I as a Principle of Philosophy', where Schelling claims that the unconditioned, which is comprised of the potencies, is not affected by modality (possibility, necessity, etc.) and therefore *determines* logical categories rather than being *defined* by them.[41] As he writes in a dense note a few pages later:

> The result of these deductions is that only the forms of being, of not-being, and of not-being determined by being can belong to logic, since they precede all synthesis and are the basis of all synthesis, and since they contain the original form according to which alone any synthesis can be performed. It also follows that the schematized forms of possibility, reality, and necessity, made possible only by an antecedent synthesis, belong to logic only because they themselves are determined by those original forms. Thus, for instance, problematical theorems do not belong to logic insofar as they express objective possibility but only inasmuch as they express objective-logical possibility; not insofar as they express a being-posited in the synthesis as such, but only inasmuch as their logical thinkability has been transmitted at all through this synthesis.[42]

Arguably, Schelling's reliance on the *Potenzen* put him in a difficult situation: that of attempting to argue that a determinable structure of nature can be detected, but that it is not logical *per se*. While we will investigate the epistemological difficulties of this claim in the following chapter, for the argument that follows I will attempt to demonstrate how Schelling's *Potenzen* minimally formalise creativity *as such*. It is in facing the difficulty of trying to formally, but non-logically, present or exhibit creativity as such that Schelling will rely more and more heavily on the diagram and the algebraic expression of the *Potenzen*. Schelling's most direct expression of the *Potenzen* can be found in the *Presentation of My System of Philosophy*.

Presentation of My System of Philosophy (1801)

Following from the above section, Schelling's introduction of the *Potenzen* in the *Presentation* is tied to questions of individuation in nature. Schelling writes:

> *Each individual is certainly not absolute, but it is infinite in its kind.* It is not absolutely infinite, since there is something outside it and it is determined in its being by something external. It is infinite in its kind, however, or, since mode of being is determined by the quantitative difference of s.[ubjectivity] and o.[bjectivity], and since this difference is expressed in the potency of one or the other, it is infinite within its *potency*, for it expresses absolute identity for its potency under the same form as the infinite. Therefore the individual is itself infinite within the scope of its potency, even if not absolutely infinite.[43]

How the *Potenzen* grow out of the difficulty of thinking abstract dynamic processes on the one hand, and how to represent factors or actants within such processes on the other, becomes clear following the above paragraph. Schelling identifies the *Potenzen* as localisations of the infinite in terms of kinds, tendencies or qualities. Localised in a particular way, that is, relative to its proper *Potenz*, kind-internal infinity does not appear ontologically or epistemologically strange. Taking the example of the colour blue can be instructive here. That a shade of blue is infinitely blue according to its kind (that is, according to its colour) is quite different from saying that this or that instance of blue is infinitely blue. There is a quantitative measure of blueness, but it cannot be said to be infinite or absolute in a way that would eliminate, for instance, all other colours. One of the connected footnotes to this passage is crucial and is the closest Schelling ever comes to defining what a potency is outright:

> The concept of *power* or *potency* can be most accurately understood in the following way. *What is in existence* is always [and] only indifference, and nothing truly exists *outside it*: but it exists in infinite ways too, and it never exists otherwise than under the form A = A, i.e., as cognition and being.[44]

One way of parsing this would be to argue that things that exist are only ever indifference points between potencies. Any given organism, for instance, is a point of indifference or balance between its capacity to grow, change, heal, eat, reproduce, etc. and the various forces, environments and events that constitute it and threaten it. But of course, and as Schelling says, there are an infinite number of ways in which this can take shape.

Once again, and to return to the above discussion of the *Potenzen* being discovered *in thought*: this discussion means that the meta-stability of phenomena is due to the fact that subjecting and objecting tendencies have reached a point of indifference. This indifference is not an absolute indifference, since if absolute indifference occurred, then all creation would cease, since one would then have only becoming or only being. As I will explore in Chapter 5, the indifference point can be treated as a hinge or point from which new bifurcations can be measured.

In *The Philosophy of Art* Schelling attempts quite a different way of expressing how raising things to a higher level can manifest without assuming that the change is necessarily qualitative.[45]

The Philosophy of Art (1801–04)

In the introduction to his lectures on *The Philosophy of Art*, Schelling introduces the potencies as if for the first time. In discussing the construction of the forms of art, Schelling discusses the potencies, in the highest sense, as the battle between necessity and freedom.[46] Yet throughout *The Philosophy of Art* Schelling describes the potencies as 'ideal determinations', referring to the 1804 *Wurzburg* system as a secondary account.[47] Strikingly, Schelling discusses the potencies as the flight of creation from mere matter. As he writes:

> The essential nature of art clothes itself here, as does the pure essence of nature, completely in matter and body. That matter becomes ideal through the second potence: in nature through light, in art through painting. Finally, in the third potence, the real and ideal potences become one. That which is bound to or informed into the real or into matter becomes sonority or sound; within art it becomes music and song. Here, then, the absolute cognitive act is more or less freed from the fetters of matter; positing that matter as a mere accidental, it becomes objective and recognizable as the act of the informing of eternal subjectivity into objectivity.[48]

At least two points are worth emphasising here. First, given Schelling's emphasis on matter in the 'Universal Deduction', and the construction of matter as a *Platonic problem*, it is worth noting that what Schelling means by matter appears to be rather a question of material construction, and not of existence or being more generally. The second point, which I will discuss further in what follows, is that the above appears to be an almost mirror reflection of the way in which Schelling will talk about matter in the *Freedom Essay*. Once again, this relates to Schelling's concept of the potencies being individuals yet infinite in their kind, that is, the potencies are infinite powers interior to their organic consistency or algebraic self-referentiality, but limited by one another. Again, the trajectorial, vectorial or spatial emphasis explored in Chapter 3 shows why Schelling emphasises that the adding of potencies creates formal differences, or what appears as qualitative changes. In *The Philosophy of Art*, for instance, the potencies correspond to different kinds of art. However, since Schelling refers to potencies as unities (note the plurality here), the notion of ideal determination is not one that supervenes on real creation. This is particularly evident in the following lengthy passage:

> One can extract the individual potence out of the whole and treat it in and for itself, but only insofar as one really presents the absolute within it is this presentation itself philosophy. In every other case, where one treats the individual potence as a particular and presents laws or rules for it as a particular, it can only be a theory of a specific object, such as a theory of nature or a theory of art. One can comprehend this in a more general sense by noting that all antitheses and differences are merely different forms that are nonessential within those differences. Only in their unity are they real, and since the unity of all cannot itself be a particular, they are real only to the extent that each

in itself represents the absolute whole, the universe. By basing laws on the particular as particular, one thereby removes the object from the absolute, and science from philosophy.[49]

Much can be gleaned from this passage. For one, Schelling demonstrates, once again, how the *Potenzen* can be treated as individuals in the form of a useful fiction (again pointing to the actants of the *First Outline*). Furthermore, the general notion of Schelling's theory of knowledge can be taken to be summarised by the following: individuals are articulated as ideal determinations or extensions, which must be treated as representations or mirrors for the entire cosmos. I will address this further in Chapter 5. For now, I wish to focus on the use of extraction with regard to the question of matter and unity. As argued above, I believe that the multiplication of unities, coupled with the fact that an object or an individual can be real or ideal, leads to the conclusion that realness, or the absolute, underlies every ideal determination. But it is not the case that we can finally discover the singular absolute realness, since all notion of singularity is relative to the location of this singularity and the means of its expression. Thus, when Schelling speaks of matter, and of thought escaping matter, there is an arbitrariness in play – namely, that of the choice of expression, which matters far less than what it represents. Realness is determined by how maximally consequential the representation is or how universal it is, and not by what it is made of.

Philosophy and Religion, the Freedom Essay, the 'Stuttgart Seminars'

In his short text that serves as a response to C. A. Eschenmayer, Schelling focuses largely on the concept of the absolute as it relates to reason and faith as capacities capable of determining the absolute and whether it has an outside. Schelling argues that the only way towards knowledge of the absolute is through intuition, in that the process of intuition is continuous with the absolute, whereas both faith and rationality address the absolute in a different register.[50] Schelling struggles to define the absolute as, on the one hand, 'the only actual'[51] and yet, on the other hand, as something from which, and in which, creation occurs without the absolute containing all that is created (this containment would constitute falling back into Spinozist immanence) or decaying via the ancient and medieval doctrine of emanation.[52]

Both the containment and emanation conceptions of the absolute predetermine an origin for the absolute that overly determine what follows from it. Schelling argues, in a line of thinking that will reappear shortly thereafter in the *Freedom Essay*, that one can apply neither finitude nor infinitude to the absolute or the universe because we cannot grasp what it is that predication (cause and effect or antecedent and consequent) is applying to.[53] This feeds directly into the aforementioned darkness of Platonic matter that he explores, particularly which regard to predication, in *On the Relation of the Ideal and the Real in Nature, or, Development of the First Principles of Naturephilosophy from the Principles of Gravity and Light* (1806). But before moving on to this text, Schelling's short text *Philosophy and Religion* must be addressed.

Philosophy and Religion (1804)

Schelling begins this text by noting that it should be read as a continuation of the project that failed to mature within the pages of *Bruno, or On the Natural and the Divine Principle of Things* (1802) to launch a series of new philosophical dialogues. Just as the *Bruno* attempted to demonstrate the movement of the potencies in various works of art and in the formulation of the capacity to produce art as such, *Philosophy and Religion* attempts this by separating philosophy's treatment of the absolute from faith's relation to God.

Philosophy and Religion does not deal with the *Potenzen* in the *Naturphilosophical* fashion or the more formal Identity philosophy mode, but in the letters to Eschenmayer that follow the text Schelling addresses the *Potenzen* in relation to the concept of the absolute as such. He writes to Eschenmayer, 'the *Absolute* is not a potency since it comprehends and dissolves all potencies within itself. This *Absolute* is what you seem to call God.'[54] The dissolution of the potencies mentioned by Schelling does not mean that a great being contains them, but rather means the principle by which the potencies exist to the extent that they do not override other potencies in their determinations. The absolute in question is not a big object or even an infinite process, but the indifference of all the creative powers of the cosmos. For Schelling, the absolute as absolute cannot be equated with God, since this absolute is structurally prior to, or above, all unities or composites. The absolute cannot be the unity of unities, nor merely their indifference, but that space which makes both unities possible as open yet coherent structures.[55]

The question that is raised by such an articulation, however, is how to account for the particular *Potenz* or even the particular *experience* of creation *for us*. This is what Schelling attempts to address in the *Freheitschrift* (or *Freedom Essay*) of 1809.

The *Freedom Essay* (1809)

With regard to the role of the potencies, Schelling's much-vaunted *Freedom Essay* is concerned with the *Potenzen* as they relate to the problem of individuation and the non-totality suggested in *Philosophy and Religion*, which in turn is tied to issues of predication, or the bond and the bonded, in *On the Relation*. Schelling attempts to reconcile the experience of freedom, of the capacity to perform seemingly free acts, with the notion that every consequence, every purportedly free agent, is dependent upon a ground. He attempts this by arguing for a non-modern concept of identity, which stands in direct relation to the *Potenzen* in his *Presentation.*

These themes are all immediately evident in the opening pages of the text. For instance, Schelling argues that the statement 'the body is blue' does not imply an identity between being a body and being blue, but that the notion of 'a' blue body follows.[56] Thus, the statement individuates a thing in that it determines it as having bodiness and blueness, but does not equate the qualities, nor even the level of having them. Thus, for Schelling, 'the body is blue' means 'there is here a thing which has blueness and, in a different way, has bodiness'. Furthermore, the making of the statement itself admits a perspective, as do the 'the' and the 'is', which exhibit the cost of making determinations as such; namely, the making of a determination arrests and removes a thing from its environs. Or, put otherwise, the blueness unfolds from the body, whereas the notions of bodiness and blueness unfold, but in a different sense, from the determinator's determination.

Through a subsequent engagement with the pantheism controversy, Schelling arrives at the problem of freedom within identity. His point is that identities, even in tautological statements or seemingly lifeless unities, are creative in the act of these statements being made.[57] To quote Schelling at length is helpful here, as the following passage encompasses the aforementioned issues:

> In the relation of subject and predicate we have already shown that of ground and consequence, and the law of the ground [*Gesetz des Grundes*] is for that reason just as original as the law of identity. Therefore, the eternal must also be a ground immediately and as it is in itself. That of which the eternal is a ground through its being is in this respect dependent and, from the point of view of immanence, also something contained within the eternal. But dependence does not abolish independence, it does not even abolish freedom. Dependence does not determine its being and says only that the dependent, whatever it also may be, can be a consequence only of that of which it is a dependent; dependence does not say what the dependent is or is not. Every

organic individual exists, as something that has become, only through another, and in this respect is dependent according to its becoming but by no means according to its Being.[58]

Freedom is thus not a container of ontological liberalism, nor is it a specifically human, yet ontological, capacity.[59] Furthermore, Schelling argues that the One (which is not, or non-total) cannot be created from the combination of things deriving from the original into the original; or, put otherwise, the All cannot be made into the One, and yet the All is the closest form to the One.[60] In so many words the All is the One (so far thought). Thus, there is a freedom that in part entails treating sets of Alls *as if they are Ones*, or absolutes. An easy but incorrect path to take here would be to assert, in the vein of Žižek, that Schelling is claiming that human freedom is *ontologically exceptional*, that human freedom is a rupture in the absolute or in the ontological fabric of being; that the non-All or, more accurately in Schelling's account, the non-One, is not due to the status of human subjectivity, but is the status of the world as such.

Schelling argues that human freedom cannot be different *in kind* from the freedom that is nature's dynamics. This is evident in his stating that idealism's task is to demonstrate the difference of human freedom in the absolute.[61] Yet since the potencies demonstrate that there is neither first nor last, not alpha nor omega that can be discovered, but only asserted, then freedom *within* the absolute cannot be viewed as exceptional – it is, after all, only possible as a consequence of what came before, and there is no boundary we know of that freedom could be said to be rupturing.[62]

An overemphasis on freedom, or on any particular potency, can lead to misrepresenting the absolute. Hence Schelling warns his audiences regarding the erasure of nature[63] and he is furthermore critical of those who would assert the priority of the understanding – in his description, 'attempt to make smoke from lighting'.[64] As already mentioned, and as he will further elaborate in *The Ages of the World*, Schelling articulates potencies as individual unities that are infinite in their capacity, yet specific or determinable from one another.

The 'Stuttgart Seminars' (1810)

In the 'Stuttgart Seminars' Schelling has a long digression on powers, focusing on the real and the ideal as subordinate unities, subordinate forms of the absolute.[65] Powers are outlined as periods of the absolute that move in a series, where the ideal must logically follow the real. The first power takes logical precedence but this does not cancel the balance of the powers in the absolute. The real difference that emerges between the two unities, and that is so important for the aforementioned capacity of freedom discussed above, is that of their position or location relative to one another. Real difference between unities, between the real and the ideal as methods, sets value judgements against ones of existence. The relation of real and ideal begins to shift to that of actual and potential as the actual becomes the position from which the real and ideal are treated as either actual or potential.

Positing is the procedure by which the potencies are identified as powers for us.[66] The point of engaging in an analysis of powers means retreating into one of them – for us that is often the power of reason. This retreat is not a reduction, but the only means of forming a position from which to distinguish powers, to formulate priorities and a chain of consequences. These chains are only methodologically useful and cannot simply override the bifurcation of matter and spirit that necessarily takes place in nature,[67] of which humans, as a relatively recent natural development, are at a threshold.[68]

In some ways, Schelling's presentation of the *Potenzen* in the 'Stuttgart Seminars' is rather condensed and matter-of-fact in comparison to the *Bruno*, or even to the diagrammatic version in the *Presentations* and *Further Presentations*. That is, Schelling merely describes how the powers ground themselves in one another as they exponentially augment one another, passing from the form $A = B$ to $A = B^3$ through the asymmetrical dialectic by which nature natures.[69] While it may simply be that the lecture structure forced Schelling to present the *Potenzen* in such a form, it is there that he appears potentially to be falling simply into a return to dogmatic metaphysics.

The Ages of the World, History of Modern Philosophy, Philosophy of Mythology, The Grounding of Positive Philosophy, Presentation of Pure Rational Philosophy

In the 1813 version of *The Ages of the World*, Schelling engages with material quite similar to that of the opening pages of the *Freedom Essay*, namely, identity and predication. Although the text sets out to address temporality more specifically, Schelling quickly moves from the past, as a necessary concept for philosophy to recognise its own history, to notions of the unconditioned and contradiction in order to demonstrate how the past can be known in a way that does not merely identify it as that which was the present.[70] In essence, Schelling argues that that which is and that which has existence are the same, and refers to them – or rather, to it – using the *Naturphilosophical* term of the unconditioned.[71] Repeating language and phrasing from *Philosophy and Religion*, Schelling attempts to articulate that-which-is and that-something-is with unity and eternality respectively. This relates to Schelling's view of contradiction influenced by Plato, as contradiction is not absolute but merely a difference that has not yet been properly articulated. Following this, unity cannot exist but is required to have existence (as indifference), while eternality only occurs through demonstration of creation, not through the stasis of being. Eternality is the unity of mere being (*blos seyn*) in its active and actual (and not merely potential state). Or, in other words, the continuum that allows things to be is the base of being or of whatness, whereas the emergence of particularities has to do with the continued attempt at unity or continuity – at constantly being produced. For Schelling, unity can only be unity by producing particularities.

Thus, time and contradiction are bound together because the mobility of the unconditioned, or the eternal, appears as time, since the eternal cannot be being and existence simultaneously.[72] By the same logic, unity must appear as heterogeneous continuity in order to appear at all.

The key term for Schelling, with regard to these conditions, is that of expression. An expression cannot express contradiction as such, but only equally express two active powers in a statement.[73] This leads Schelling back to the formula of identity expressed in the *Freedom Essay*. He writes: 'The true sense of each judgment – for example, that "A = B" – can only be the following: THAT *which is* = A IS THAT *which is* = B, or, THAT which is A and THAT *which is* B are as one.'[74]

Schelling goes on to say that the 'is' is the ground of being, which is the unity of unities in that all expressions are expressions of this ground.[75] Thus, anything resembling a contradiction must in fact be merely a tangled or lost connection, and not an absolute breakage, given that the expressed is only expressible because of an underlying unity.[76] As already mentioned, the difficult aspect of predication is the problem of articulating difference in kind, or the qualitative distinction between things (things being limitations or conditions of the unconditioned) and their relative infinity. Again, pointing back to the *Freedom Essay*, Schelling addresses this problem with regard to will or personality. He writes:

> The unconditioned can express itself as what-is and as being, and it can refrain from expressing itself as both; in other words, it can be both, or it can let both alone. Free will is just this ability to be something along with the ability to not be it. But further, the Highest can be what-is, and it can be being.[77]

Freedom, or will, is thus the same as the unconditioned, except that freedom, which is connected here to the highest potency (which, elsewhere, Schelling defines as the onto-epistemological location of human beings), is a maximally extensive view of conditions, an indifference not only between conditions or choices, but also between what is and what is being. These two tendencies are unified in a third moment, which Schelling expresses in the exponential language of the potencies.[78]

Once again, potencies become the structures that attempt to explain how qualitative difference, which is infinite in kind (will, or personality for example), can exist as equally powerful when all power as such can only ever be measured as quantity. That is, since like can only be known by like, and because there could be no motive contradiction unless there was an underlying unity or continuity, the difference between potencies must be one that is not absolute contradiction, but relative. Yet at the same time, this relativity appears differently, and is viewed differently depending on the conditions it takes up, that is, on where a potency is located in the All. This leads Schelling, in the 1813 *Ages of the World*, to shift the emphasis from contradiction to one of grounding (*Verhältnis des Grundes*), in which there is neither a total sublation, nor contradiction, but a cooperation that issues a trajectory, whether spatial or temporal.[79] As Schelling puts it, a judgement that expresses a ground and a consequent does not determine a different degree of existence or contradiction, but a relation of dependence and independence (again repeating the opening pages of the *Freedom Essay*). The difference between the antecedent and consequent, or the subject and the predicate, is one that can be defined in terms of potencies: 'The preceding will would act as the ground of its successor, and hence as the first potency. Now it could certainly fail to be active in the potency of the other will, but this does not stop it all the while as active in *its* potency as the other is in the *other's* potency.'[80] In addition to the potencies restricting one another and determining succession depending on their grounding relation or ratio to one another, this co-determination is reoriented by a particular act or decision of will or motion.[81]

> Because the negating will is posited as preceding, it is also posited as the ground of existence [*Existenz*], as *being*, as the (A = B) of what is higher. Moreover, the affirming will (which is grounded by the negating will) would act as A^2. Finally, the third – their living unity would be to them A^3 is in the expressible.[82]

At the end of the text Schelling settles back into a discussion of eternality and appears to abandon the discussion of how the will, or a particular aspect of willing, constructs or expresses itself as a particular existence or as a particular *Potenz*, or how construction relates to the potencies as coming out of the eternal and exteriorising it. The 1813 version of *The Ages of the World* appears unable to address the problem of how the eternal relates to the reorientation of the world, or how a particular world relates to the particular agent doing the constructing. Before addressing how Schelling attempts to solve this problem, it is worth addressing the 1815 version of the *Ages*.

The Ages of the World (1815)

In the 1815 draft of *The Ages of the World* Schelling introduces the potencies in relation to the question of unity and how it relates to the law of predication. The potencies are introduced following Schelling's statement that knowledge requires 'movement',[83] as the exploration of knowledge is the unfurling of a judgement into a conclusion.[84] This unfurling cannot be mere change but must be a form of creation that does not fully erase its immediate grounding and potential direction; hence all potencies have a degree of selfhood or, perhaps better put, an auto-catalytic nature.[85] Later Schelling defines this selfhood in terms of having being,[86] of being potencies amid the All and not merely immanently internal to the One. In relation to the 1813 version, the 1815 version of the *Ages* highlights the tension between the eternal, the individual, and how powers fit in between. It is clear that there are potencies (plural) and that they are infinite in kind. While individuals are generally inhibitions of underlying forces, the potencies are defined as externalisations (or expressions) of the eternal.

Schelling writes:

> The true meaning of this unity that has been asserted in the beginning is therefore this: 'one and the same = x' is as much the unity as it is the antithesis. Or both of the opposed potencies, the eternally negating potency and the eternally affirming potency, and the unity of both make up the one, inseparable, primordial being.[87]

And then:

> And here, first after the consummate unfurling of that initial concept, can we glimpse the first nature in its full vitality. We see it, in an equally originary way, decomposed, as it were, into three powers. Each of these powers can be for itself. Hence, the unity is a unity for itself and each of the opposite powers is a whole and complete being.[88]

Beyond noting the *Naturphilosophical* language of the above (powers and their relation to decomposition), the completeness of each *Potenz* is a particular statement, since the *Potenzen* determine one another's limits, and their wholeness is limited externally. However, given the central

themes connected with the potencies, particularly that of the All replacing the One, and first and last – or low and high – replacing origin and
teleology, there is nothing external to the external, to the totality of the
potencies. This totality cannot be at rest or merely being, since, to quote
Schelling again:

> This [being at rest] is impossible in that initial equivalence since both poten-
> cies, so to speak, want to be in a single point because both make the same
> claim to be that which has being. But if the negating / principle (A = B)
> only knows itself as a potency of the being and thereby makes space for the
> other principle opposed to it (the A^2), then the opposed principle can become
> helpful to it and become its liberator from contradiction since the opposed
> principle is, in accordance with its nature, unlocking and liberating.[89]

The phrase 'making space' is the important emphasis here, as the will or
particular directionality made possible by one potency in relation to another
is not merely determined by the grounding relation, but also by one of relative spatiality. Just as the potencies can be related to the succession of times,
they should be articulated as an orientation of spaces – although, I argue,
this is only implicit in Schelling's work.

As Schelling goes on to write:

> Now, we maintain the possibility that what does not now have being could
> endeavor to emerge from out of the state of potentiality and elevate itself again
> to what has being. From this comes an intensified concept of what does not
> have being which we are often enough forced to acknowledge in nature and
> life. This clearly persuades us that there would be something mediate between
> what is and nothing, namely, what is not and also should not be, but which
> still endeavors to be. It is not because it only endeavors to be. And it is not
> nothing because in a certain way it must be in order to covet.[90]

Furthermore, Schelling goes on to state that the *Potenzen* determine the
succession of time, given the fact that powers cannot exist all at full force
at the same time, or, for that matter, in the same place.

Schelling makes the important distinction of noting that as individuals,
the *Potenzen* are different in that they *have being* in every time.[91] Or as he
puts it again:

> When one potency is compared with another potency, the proceeding potency
> appears lower than the preceding potency, because the preceding potency nec-
> essarily appears as a higher potency in its time than the proceeding potency
> does in its time. But when one time is compared with another time and one
> epoch is compared with another epoch, the proceeding one appears decisively
> higher. Hence, such seeming regressions are necessary in the history of life.[92]

There is, I argue, an epistemological consequence here in that the *Potenzen* can be read from above, in terms of the various potencies limiting one another, or they can be viewed in a temporal sequence, in terms of higher and lower. In addition, it could be argued that it is the concept of essence that suspends this temporal difference. The essence of something suggests being and existence but also spreads these possibilities into the past and future simultaneously. But I will address this in greater detail in Chapter 5.[93]

The History of Modern Philosophy (1833–34)

In his lectures in Munich, Schelling returns to the history of philosophy, starting with Descartes and working up to his present. In the section on *Naturphilosophie*, he once again goes over the *Potenzen* and their relation to individuation and temporality in particular. In passing over Descartes, Spinoza, Leibniz and Wolff, Schelling indicates tensions between how they utilise being and how, and in what ways, being can be active in their relative systems. In particular, he focuses on how delicate the problem of the origin of being – of what he transforms into the firstness or *Prius* of being – is. Schelling adds the caveat that this firstness is a determination, but not merely a fact, that is, the first being is determined as first but can be thus determined because of the innumerable consequences that firstness would mean. In such a move Schelling attempts to simultaneously critique and absorb the dogmatic gesture of necessity. Quoting Schelling:

> we ourselves spoke first of all of what Is and determined it as the *Prius*, as the original state (*Urstand*), i.e. as the possibility of being. Quite right; but we also immediately added that it could not be sustained in this priority, therefore, even though the Prius, never *as* the *Prius*; the transition was inevitable, *what* Is should not be, thus to think it as not-being (*nicht seyend*).[94]

In this way Schelling attempts to separate the necessity of necessity (as inexistence) from a necessarily existing being. A necessarily existing being would, for Schelling, eliminate the dynamism within any system. Yet at the same time, Schelling's thinking maintains a concept of necessity, in that necessary stages determine subsequent ones (whether viewed as the historicisation of nature or the structure of predication), but there is no means of determining the original necessity, only that a chain of necessitation occurs and that material existence is a primary, not originary, step. Schelling approaches this the other way around with regard to Spinoza. Instead of focusing on the *Prius contra* the originary, he notes that Spinoza's immanent monism requires an absolute outer boundary in order to make coherent the correspondences between modes. Schelling argues that Spinoza's notion of being swallows possibility inside it[95] and that the great flaw of Spinoza's system is that it lacks an independent notion of infinite.[96]

Schelling finds Spinoza's account unsatisfactory as he believes that Spinoza cannot account for creation within the closed being of God as anything but combinatorial, yet somehow infinite. Thus there is not infinite capacity in Spinoza but only contained capacity, which is measured relative to God. Again, against commentators such as Edward Beach who would place Schelling's *Potenzen* close to Spinoza's powers, the difference between the two lies in the fact that for Schelling the *Potenzen* have behaviours, or possess an infinity relative to themselves – this infinity cannot be contained, but only limited by the activity of other potencies.

Returning to the language regarding the dynamics of nature, Schelling argues that nature must have the structure of a being that would be pure becoming if it did not have a desire to be something to itself, to come to rest as finitude.[97] This contradictory notion of becoming is one of intensification, since the infinitude of creation or becoming raises itself to a higher level by attempting and failing to become an object to itself.[98] The uninhibited power of creation appears as nothing until it inhibits itself, until it attempts to become a being. Here Schelling is repeating, though perhaps less poetically, ideas from his earliest texts. The passages cited sound similar to those of *The Ages of the World* in particular. The rotary motion of creation, which even God cannot escape, is cast in the *History* as an originary motion which turns in on itself, thereby creating finite things. This creation is a necessity, but not an pre-existent necessity, and therefore the emergence of contingency comes with existence, with finitude. The threefold structure of the *Potenzen* then demonstrates how finitude emerges as a consequence of infinity, and how that consequent infinity becomes a particular infinity by locating itself in the world as a kind, as a potency.[99] The finite being, working as a pure subject, can likewise treat itself as infinite (in the A^2) after it has submitted itself to finitude. The pre-history of the *Potenzen* is thus folded into their status as an essence, thus having no 'proper' origin, which allows for further augmentation or intensification.[100]

Schelling then quickly shifts to the language of the dynamic processes from the *First Outline* and the *Ideas* in discussing the dynamic treatment of the potencies as categories of physical emergences within the threefold structure. The first stage, A^1, is connected to matter, A^2 to light, and A^3 to the organic – this latter level operates on both as real and ideal material, that is, material that could be classified as either in the mind or outside it.[101] Schelling thus indicates, by way of a cursory review of his earlier texts, how the potencies mark the stages of augmentation which, in a linear view of nature, led up to the emergence of humans. A difficulty emerges, however. These stages of potentiation lead to the capacity of thought and to the possibility of pure knowledge since, in the past, potencies eventually become essences, or mere forms, in order to make room for further augmentation. But how would such a sublation be conceivable once the process of conceiving emerges? Schelling states that the human, burdened with the apparent infinitude of thought, finds herself in the position of the *Prius* of nature as unconditioned becoming. Thought appears to itself as completely unconditioned, yet it has come after a long chain of determinations in nature. Because of this, thought copies the determinations in nature as ideal, but in order for thought to intensify and progress, it treats the stages of this ideal copy as objects or tools, whereby action can be justified.[102]

Historical-Critical Introduction to the Philosophy of Mythology (1842)

Schelling's lectures on mythology expand his concerns regarding the personality of God expressed in *The Ages of the World* as well as his discussion of the *Potenzen* as personalities or subjectivities.[103] Like *The Philosophy of Art* or *Bruno*, Schelling attaches the *Potenzen* to a particular discourse which, in the case of this text, is of course mythology. As is the general function of the *Potenzen*, Schelling argues that mythology, taken in a very general sense, cannot be merely subjective but, on the contrary, must be an instance of powers manifesting themselves through consciousness. He writes:

> In this explanation there is also a return to the primordial Being [*Urseyn*] of man: mythology is no less the consequence of a nonarbitrary process, to which man falls prey because he stirs himself from his original position. But as you yourself see, according to this explanation mythology would be only something false [XI 207] and also something merely subjective, namely, what exists in such representations, to which nothing real outside them would correspond, for divinized natural objects are no longer actual ones. But especially to be accentuated, however, would be the contingency that the drawing-on things brings into the explanation, while alone the manner in which we have reached the concept of the process brings with it that nothing is required for this process except consciousness, nothing outside the principles it itself posits and constitutes. It is not at all the things with which man deals in the mytho-logical process by which consciousness is moved, but rather it is the powers arising in the interior of consciousness itself. The theogonic process, through

which mythology emerges, is a subjective one insofar as it takes place in consciousness and shows itself through the generating of representations: but the
causes and thus also the objects of these representations are the actually and in
themselves theogonic powers, just those powers through which consciousness
is originally the God-positing consciousness. The content of the process are
not merely imagined potencies but rather the potencies themselves – which
create consciousness and which create nature (because consciousness is only
the end of nature) and for this reason are also actual powers. The mythological
process does not have to do with natural objects, but rather with the pure
creating potencies whose original product is consciousness itself.[104]

While much can be said about Schelling's articulation of God and of the
theogonic (the origin of the Gods) in general, I will restrict myself to how
Schelling's articulation of the potencies emerges within the discussion of
mythology. Immediately, one can note that the general thrust of Schelling's
argument regarding the potencies here concerns their environing in the
consciousness of humans.

Powers arise in consciousness, but are not merely due to consciousness,
since nothing can be self-grounding. Because of this outsideness, this exteriority, the mythological content is not only determined by consciousness,
but myth, as a creative act, is a narrativisation of powers in which thought
encounters its own creativity. As Beach emphasises, Schelling's discussion
of the *Potenzen* is connected to his distinction of whatness (*Was*) and thatness (*Dass*), or Being and Existence again mirroring the above distinction of
unity (indifference) and eternality (demonstration).[105] This distinction, particularly in relation to the *Potenzen*, will become more central in Schelling's
lectures on the split between the negative and positive philosophies. The
potencies thread themselves through any particular domain of representation, but this does not mean that such a domain is only ever an example of
those powers. The expressive nature of any domain of representation/action
aligns its own local notion of modalities with and against the larger exterior
of potency or pure-possibility – possibility as such. This tension between
possibilities interior to their kind and possibility-as-such is why Schelling
finds it necessary to divide philosophy into positive and negative kinds.

Negative philosophy, which Schelling will associate most directly with
Kant, is negative because it forecloses the possibility of creativity and,
according to Schelling, makes a dogmatism out of an *a priori* logic. Or,
to return to the language above, Kant attempts to define whatness in
a way that predetermines all possible forms of thatness without taking
into account how thatness forces us to redefine whatness. Mythology is
one attempt at narrativising such genesis in its most primordial state by
attempting to outline how certain *a priori* structures came to be from what
was before – from what Schelling designates as the *Prius*.

The Grounding of Positive Philosophy (1842–43)

Schelling's lectures on positive philosophy, myth and revelation in Berlin in place of the recently deceased Hegel maintain the overtly historical trajectory of the lectures on modern philosophy, albeit with different emphasis. In particular, he focuses on how the potencies function in reason following Kant's rearticulation of reason in the critical enterprise. Quoting Schelling at length:

> According to Kant, reason is nothing other than the faculty of knowledge as such, so that what is posited within us becomes, from the standpoint of philosophy, an object for us – so that reason itself considered entirely objective is the infinite potential of cognition (for reason remains this even apart from its subjective position, apart from its being in [63] any one subject). Potency is the Latin *potentia* – power – and is opposed to the actus. In the conventional use of language, one says, 'The plant in its seed is the plant in its mere potency, in *pure potentia*, whereas the real mature or developed plant is the plant in actu.' Here, potency is considered merely as a *potentia passiva*, as a passive possibility; the seed is not necessarily the potential of the plant; there must be other external factors – fertile soil, rain, sunshine, and so on, added to it so that this potency becomes actus. As the faculty of knowledge, reason also appears as a *potentia passiva*, insofar as it is a faculty that is capable of development and, in this respect, is admittedly also dependent on external factors. Here, however, reason is not the faculty of knowledge subjectively considered, rather that standpoint has already been assumed from which reason itself is its object. Considered as an object, where the limitations of the subject are removed through abstraction, it can be nothing other than the infinite potency of cognition.[106]

Once again Schelling's scepticism regarding a necessary being, or any existent that contains all its own potential, is apparent. He will formulate this sentiment more directly in one of his *Darstellung* lectures, a point that has been highlighted by Iain Grant: '[n]o primal germ, scattered into chaos by ourselves as if fallen from the creator's hand, is required. Everything is primal germ or nothing is.'[107]

In stating that 'only the infinite potential of being can correspond to the potency of being', Schelling distances himself from the Scholastic notion of *Ens omnimod interminatum*. In essence, he wishes to argue that pure possibility and pure contingency do not exist, and neither does being as such always-already, but only a tension between potentiality and actuality.[108] Schelling attacks Hegel, and in particular his use of logic, as failing to recognise that predication – the activity of the potency recognised in the move from antecedent to consequent – is not the same as that move *actually* occurring. To equate the motion of the concept with the thing is, for Schelling, to erase the effect of experience, as it would be merely superfluous to the real-conceptual motion occurring. Or, in other words, to confuse embodied motion with conceptual motion is to confuse *that* something is with *what* something is, to confuse being with a being.[109]

While I will address the use of experience in Chapter 6, and remain with the notion of the *Potenzen* for now, Schelling states that reason chases the *Potenzen*, since reason, like nature, strives to be their original content, to be infinite potentiality – and yet to be this, it must continually empty itself of specific content. Thus, it continually chases potencies and finds content that is not itself, therefore having a negative concept of being as its motor.[110]

Schelling attempts to address this by returning to the language of will that he utilised in the *Freedom Essay* as well as *The Ages of the World*. Following a discussion of the relation between individuation and the *Potenzen*, he shifts to the language of movement. He here focuses on the experience of reason as movement, in that reasoning, as a kind of motion, only encounters possibility and not being as being. This is because sublated being, being treated like essence (that is the perspectival position of the self), is what allows the particular individual example of will, or reason in motion, to occur at all.[111]

After a detour through Kant, Schelling returns to the motion of reason via the *Potenzen*, arguing that being is the content of thought only as potency, since potency is a leap towards a being. If this leap is objectified or verified – that is, becomes relevant for experience – thought must move beyond itself again in order for thought to remain thought.[112] Later on, Schelling states that this moving within the *Potenz*, as the science of reason, is a negative philosophy, one that sets aside the philosophical ramifications of experience. Experience, for Schelling, is one category of empiricism that treats reason alongside that which is, taking existence as infinite in itself, and not merely as infinite possibility as it is conceived in reason. Schelling states that:

> The pure or infinite potency (the beginning of the negative philosophy) is the content identical with thought, which, because it does not go toward thought (since it is identical to it), only proceeds out from thought. In contrast, that which simply is the content that is not identical with thought; indeed, it is excluded from the very start and, for this very reason, it can and must be first conveyed to thought since it is originally external to thought.[113]

It is Schelling's focus on Aristotle's work, which appears in the *Erlangen Lectures* (1821) and which intensifies for the rest of his life, that is crucial for the positive philosophy – a philosophy that, instead of exploring the *Potenzen* in their development following an inhabiting of being, constructs an ultimate goal, or free choice based on the fact of existing things working as potential; yet, importantly, not a potential that can be sublated and is possible in theory, but a notion of potentiality that follows from the reality of its actualisation. While Chapter 5 will address the epistemological ramifications of such a split between the negative and positive view of the *Potenzen*, I wish to close by articulating how Schelling's *Potenzenlehre* can be taken in the context of the last period of his life via a return to Plato, Aristotle and Kant.

Presentation of Pure Rational Philosophy (1847–52)

The negative/positive split in Schelling's work is complicated by the *Presentation of Pure Rational Philosophy*, in which he attempts to refashion what Kantian criticality means – or what it means to thoroughly apply the power of reason to itself, alongside a discussion of the philosophy of mythology. Schelling's last period of thinking tends to combine Aristotelian naturalism with Platonic cosmology in order to get at the core of philosophy as a science of reason. To this end, Schelling engages often, and at length, with Kant's critical system. In the 13th *Darstellung* lecture, he discusses the *Potenzen* as representing that which is ineliminable in thought *contra* Kant. Schelling argues that Kant's determination of tenses (past, present and future) cannot be a mere logical form, representing rather that which thought obtains upon, only incompletely.[114] It should be evident that Schelling's language is returning to that of his earliest writings on potentiality, as exemplified by 'Of the I as a Principle of Philosophy', where he makes the claim that Kantian modality incompletely grasps the possibility outside of it. This return to his earlier thinking is repeated again, only a few passages below that referenced above, where Schelling invokes the relation between Aristotelian dynamism and Plato's concern about motion in the *Timaeus*. He emphasises that the pure actuality of a being cannot be captured by a concept.[115] Here Schelling references the line from the *Timaeus* that fascinated him as a young man:

> What is that which is Existent always [28a] and has no Becoming? And what is that which is Becoming always and never is Existent? Now the one of these is apprehensible by thought with the aid of reasoning, since it is ever uniformly existent; whereas the other is an object of opinion with the aid of unreasoning sensation, since it becomes and perishes and is never really existent.[116]

Schelling continues this line of thinking in the subsequent *Darstellung* lectures. In the 16th lecture he writes:

For in what has being, i.e. in reason, not only the material but also the law of movement is predetermined. The principles that, in the Idea – in what it is that is being – are merely possible or are potencies, were in pure thought the hypotheses or presuppositions of what the actual in itself is, but each of them is however immediately the hypothesis of what is consequent upon it, –A is the hypothesis of +A, both together the hypothesis of + –A: all ultimately of what is the pure principle, the purely actual, in which there is no longer any possibility. This connection amongst the potencies entails that the converse of the usual order holds, that, namely, the antecedent has its actuality in the consequent in respect of which it is accordingly mere [376] potency.[117]

Once again, Schelling emphasises the difference between possibility and pure possibility, or potentiality (*Potenz*). The endless productive determinations of the potencies consist in the following: if they are treated as pure potentiality, they can upset the normal causal order of things in that the consequent of a hypothesis contends that the hypothesis, as an activity, *already existed prior* to its hypothesising, though it would seem that the instance of the potency caused the hypothesis. It is this expressive function of the potencies, mentioned above via the actants, that can be misread as human-caused. In the 17th lecture, Schelling continues to discuss the *Potenzen* in terms of the problem of causes. Due to the complexity of the text I quote Schelling at length:

The three causes are the first, the pure possibilities, from which the concrete possibilities lying between beginning and end are derived. And they too act in relation to each other as beginning, middle and end. The beginning, first at the gate of Being, is what immediately can be, and by nature, is pure can-being. Following it is the pure being [*Seyende*] from nature, to which the strength (potency) for actualisation must first be given. The end is what is itself originally powerful, self-possessing. Due to this natural order we have also spoken of a first, a second and a third potency, and without thinking of an analogy with mathematical thought, we have designated them accordingly. Given what can be in general = A, the immediately able to be must be designated as A^1, but as such it first appears at the end, in the process (for with the relations of the causes a process is also promised) it appears immediately as 'unselved', i.e. as subjectless Being and would thus be designated as the B, which is first to be brought back into A; the pure being, first posited by B in *potentiam*, is elevated to the subject, and thus A^2, and the last, which as object is subject and vice-versa, will be designated A^3. I demand of these designations only that they serve clarity and brevity; nor, for the same reasons, would I reject to designating what stands higher than all potency, that is what is and is the cause of Being and itself pure actuality, as earlier, A^0, although we are not thinking here of the arithmetical $A^0 = 1$.[118]

Immediately one can see Schelling returning again to the critique of Kantian modality, as well as re-emphasising the open-endedness of any determined system. Modality, temporalised as beginning, middle and end, functions between the unprethinkable beginning of end that lies in the pure possibilities as potencies. The appearance of immediacy, or givenness, must be fed back into the notion of pure can-being to treat the given as if it is the consequence of pure being. The givenness as immediate A becomes B, and then is fed back into A and thus is registered as A^2. Thus the action of B, as a determination, is merely ideal and a hypothesis, unless its consequences can be viewed as being that of A and thus be re-designated as A^2 (as always-already a part of A but more of it, A to a higher power). It is then in the subsequent work of determining those aspects of the higher power that are not merely based on our determination as subjects, that it can be treated as adequate ground for future testing (and thus can be treated as A^3).

Here one can begin to see how Schelling is struggling, but not without purpose, to create an open system of being, and subsequently, of philosophising, which accepts the consequences of contingency as well as those of necessity *without relying upon or metaphysically reifying either*. In the quote above, Schelling carefully toes the line between ideality, or human thinking in particular, creating the world, and humans being merely participatory in the *Potenz* that is thought, thought being merely a consequence of nature's self-augmentation. Since we 'have' the capacity to think, we participate in this augmentative process and affect it.[119] But the important third motion (the A^3) indicates that this movement is itself only fully potentiated in its capacity to be a ground for another.

The consequences that this structure has for human knowing and for the practice of philosophy will be the focus of Chapter 5. To close this chapter, however, I would like to look at how Schelling's notion of potency relates to the notion of world, and, in turn, to modality (as related to possible worlds).

Potencies and modalities: potency and world

In conclusion, the ontology of powers, with its modal determinations (necessity, contingency, possibility, actuality), can only be regarded as a reducibly metaphysical problem if the physical dimensions of its actuality are ignored [. . .] powers necessarily involve modal concepts. Against Hegel's denial that the categories of Modality determine anything objective, objectality is nothing other than a set of potentials for actualisation, as Plato insisted. Powers make contingency into an ontology, a metaphysics and a physics.[120]

[A]ccording to modality – pure being [*Sein*]. Specifically this determination separates the original concepts [*Urbegriffe*] of being [*Sein*], not-being [*Nicht-Sein*], and existence [*Dasein*] from the derivative concepts of possibility, actuality, and necessity.[121]

> The concept of not having being, but especially the not being that occurs everywhere in so many forms, has always led the beholder astray and, like a real Proteus, manifoldly brought them into confusion. For just as it is manifest to hardly anyone that actual power lies more in delimitation than expansion and that to withdraw oneself has more to do with might than to give oneself, so is it natural that where they encounter that which through itself does not have being, they rather regard it as 'nothing' and, when it is asserted that it 'is' precisely as that which does not have being, they rather explain this away as the greatest contradiction.[122]

Given this admittedly cursory examination of Schelling's development of the potencies, one may ask: why does Schelling use them, and why does he feel as though he needs them? Fundamentally, I wish to argue that Schelling's use of the *Potenzen* is about the insufficiency of the usual notion of modality, that is, that it does not obtain as such. More than the Leibnizian question of 'Why is there something instead of nothing?' it would seem that the *Potenzen* try to answer the awkward question of 'How does our thought thing?' or, less awkwardly: if there are no absolute divisions between thought and nature, how do we account for creation and motion when everything is potentially naturalised? At the same time, and taking into account Schelling's proto-pragmatic emphasis on positive philosophy, the question of 'How does our thought thing?' might be coupled with the question 'How does experience think?'

As the epigraphs above show, Schelling was concerned with how to separate knowledge, or reason, from representation. To conclude the investigation of the potencies, the present question asks after Schelling's need for the potencies in relation to creation and reason's categories (specifically modality). Or, to point to the discussion above in relation to the negative–positive split, the potencies are what allows for Schelling's method of construction to function, which does not reduce them to merely subjective constructions.

Returning to the introduction above, I argued that Schelling's *Potenzen* make up for the insufficiency of modality as mere categories, as well as marking the importance of necessary inexistence. That is, in both the negative and the positive philosophies, there are constraints of generation which themselves become sublated in the process of generation, whether merely ideal or merely real. The relation between the real and the ideal is skewed by Schelling's utilisation of the *Potenzen*, hence the questions above. Instead of the general question of 'How do mental acts or representations obtain?', Schelling assumes that they do and asks how it is that thought creates things. In dealing with everyday existence, Schelling does not ask after the relation between theory and practice, but rather posits the question 'How does experience think?', assuming that being within existence and existing as a particular thing – 'this will' – is an admixture of theory and practice, which is the price of human freedom. The further danger of the closeness of Schelling's epistemology and his ontology is to risk a complete conflation of deontic modality and alethic modality. Deontic modality has to do with morals and choices (should and can), whereas alethic modality has to do with truth claims (contingency, necessity, and so on). Since the following chapter focuses on Schelling's epistemology and, in particular, on how it relates to intuition, I wish to end here by discussing the philosophical import of his *Potenzlehre* for alethic modality.

Importantly, Schelling's *Potenzen* point to a notion of creation or novelty existing before the world, at least before any thinkable one. Yet in opposition to philosophies of the event (such as in Deleuze and Badiou), Schelling is far more sceptical about the means and capacity of human beings to harness this evental status, or even think it. *Potenzen* are can-beings but they are, to some extent, particular, or can only be detected in the tracing out of their consequences. Schelling appears to be straddling two sides of a split in the history of philosophy, namely that between Spinoza and Leibniz. While Kant attempted to suture this split, the German Idealist tradition spread it open by questioning Kant's grounds in building the critical system.

This split can be read in numerous ways, but perhaps most clearly through tracing the status of human freedom. As was hopefully apparent in the first chapter – we will also return to this in the conclusion – Kant forced the question of whether human freedom is exempted from or submitted to the causal structure of the world. This can be summed up quite simply in the question: 'While our free acts always seem free for us, are they free in themselves?' While Žižek has famously argued that Hegel ontologises Kant's indecision to decide between noumenal and phenomenal freedom, I do not see his account as taking Hegel's scepticism seriously. While the German Idealists on the whole attempted to seek grounds for Kant's critical conclusions, these grounds are not clearly ontological, but take up differing processes as a middle ground between sheer being and sheer becoming, or between scepticism and dogmatism.

As has hopefully been outlined above, this is evident in the case of Schelling's *Potenzen*. The potencies are tendencies that are more or less stable depending on how many consequences issue from them; they are the forces behind real patterns in the cosmos and are apparent in physical processes and noetic endeavours alike. So, in this sense, it appears that Schelling must therefore abnegate any difference between deontic modality (morals and choices of should and can) and alethic modality (ontology and questions of truth via necessity and contingency). This, however, overlooks the centrality of position, or location, in Schelling's thought. Location or determination puts limits on the constructivism implied in Schelling's *Potenzenlehre*, while remaining attentive to the ontological status of the potencies not as things, but as universal tendencies or qualities.

Schelling's potencies point to his Platonism and, in particular, the 'realness' of ideas – which he maintains from his earliest work (such as *On the World Soul*) to the late *Darstellung* lectures. Yet at the same time, Schelling emphasises that physical and perceptual limitations (such as those that arise with different species' sense capacities) affect where and when we detect such ideas. To separate these conditions according to real and ideal assumes a 'view-from-nowhere', but, at the same time, Schelling is not endorsing a full-blown constructivist or perspectival system, where there are no matters of fact or universals. Things are facts or universals in so far as the *Potenzen* are can-beings. Universals are in-process but should be viewed as absolute until they are overturned or viewed as simply another process among many, whereas the *Potenzen* are speculated to have being, but can only be seen, or encountered, in the process of tracing them. Again, while I will investigate the epistemological consequences of this in the following chapter, for now I am interested in the ontological stakes of these claims. This talk of can-beings immediately brings us to talk of possible worlds and modality, given that a common view construes something possible as existing in some possible world. These themes are generally discussed primarily in semantic terms, following Saul Kripke and David Lewis, whereas Alexius Meinong, the primary originator of possible worlds, is dismissed as being too literal, or ontological, in his discussion of them – he states that beings usually construed as non-existent (i.e., fictional beings) exist, since for him being is to be understood in a proper sense as beyond being (as actual) and becoming (as creation).[123] This relation is complicated directly in Schelling's theory. As Bruce Matthews writes in the translator's introduction to *The Grounding of Positive Philosophy*:

> Thinking is movement, but it is not self-propelled; rather, thought is carried along incessantly from predicate to predicate by the power of what Schelling calls the infinite potency of cognition. Like Kant's unconditioned absolute, the *actus* of this potency is transcendent to the series of its members, but transcendent only in the sense that it is absolutely other than thought: as the pure actuality of reality [*Wirklichkeit*], that which simply exists excludes potency, and thus the possibility indicative of thought.[124]

Numerous thinkers and commentators on Schelling have, following Wolfram Hogrebe, read his philosophy of the *Potenzen* as primarily a theory of predication. Iain Grant, in his essay 'Remains of the World', complicates this view, albeit slightly. While Markus Gabriel and others have focused on predication as a particularly human capacity, rooted in judgement as defined by Kant, this leaves out not only the ontological constraints on logic and judgement, but also overlooks inexistence as well as existence as having actual consequences on predication and on its logical-ontological function. As Grant writes: 'Powers cannot originally inhere in some essence or existent, but must, as powers, exceed that existence, and since what exceeds existence is inexistence, inexistence must be a power paradoxically ineliminable from nature.'[125]

Schelling's theory of the *Potenzen* attempts to generate the most creative world in which creation is not bounded by pre-set limits, nor overly determined by thought. Modality is then a formal re-presentation of the *Potenzen* or powers. Furthermore, whereas Kant famously argued that existence is not a real predicate, Schelling argues against this, not for ontological reasons, as was commonly the case, but due to the fact that realness for him can only be provisionally asserted in its consequences. As Beach outlines, Schelling thinks through Kant's idea that existence is not a real predicate by questioning what the jump from being to existence is.[126] Or, while actualities are being in the mode of existence, it is not a straightforward matter to determine what the being of an actuality is, different from its mode of existing. Following Matthews above, the volition of reason is as powerful as it is because it is of the potencies. As Schelling emphasises in the 1815 *Ages*, the potencies limit one another's existence or inexistence, in a reciprocal fashion.[127]

As Gabriel has highlighted, the relation of mind and world is explicitly addressed (particularly with regard to creation, contingency and necessity) in David Lewis's theory of possible worlds. Lewis's theory, as Gabriel outlines, has at its core the position that the semantic variability of language suggested by modal statements necessitates taking seriously the idea that possible worlds are as real as our world. Put crudely, words like 'can' or 'maybe', referring to events, suggest that one should treat worlds in which those events take place as being as real as our own.

While Lewis's theory is (in)famous for inviting the 'incredulous stare' of other philosophers, since the positing of so many worlds spits in the face of Occam's razor, it can be argued that his position is one of pragmatics, and not an ontology at all. Either way, Schelling's *Potenzen*, in a similar sense, demonstrate the necessity for positing a lean ontology, if for no other reason than to stave off dogmatic or overly reckless or enthusiastic speculation (such as asserting that all logical statements have ontological consequences or that all ontological predicates are completely translatable into currently existing logic).

Following Schelling's reading of Plato put forward in the introduction, there is only one world and not separate realms for ideas and for things. This seems an uncontroversial proposition. Yet because of the way Schelling views Platonic ideas as being real, his singular world could invite incredulous stares of its own. The distinction between real and ideal is one of method, and not one that can be constitutively separated either in terms of separate realms (such as the natural versus the normative) or in terms of material (physicalist reduction and rampant idealism on the other end).

Schelling distinguishes the real and the ideal in terms of actual and potential. These latter terms do not map on to the former directly, but instill a concept of motion and a derivative form of judgement. Being actual and being potential are modes, which are more than formal modality (necessity, contingency, etc.), but whereas Lewis suggests that modal statements imply possible worlds, for Schelling the plasticity and creativity of the singular world manifests, however imperfectly, in modal categories. Because of the actual and potential relation, whether something is real or ideal is more a question of what something does than what it is. Subsequent analysis of a thing's consequences determines its actuality and potentiality. Given the potential ubiquity of creation, the tracing of consequences in turn requires means of determining one's location in the world and, therefore, one's own creative or constructive capacities.

How one determines one's own location epistemologically and pragmatically will be the emphasis of the following two chapters.

Notes

1. F. W. J. von Schelling, *The Ages of the World*, trans. Jason Wirth (Albany, NY: SUNY Press, 2000), xxxvii. Translation modified.
2. Schelling, *First Outline*, 14.
3. Schelling, *Ideas for a Philosophy of Nature*, 11.
4. See Schelling, 'On the Nature of Philosophy as a Science'.
5. In the editor's introduction to *The Reception of Kant's Critical Philosophy*, for instance, Sedgwick notes that Schelling is basically consistent with Kant, but provides no textual evidence. Sally Sedgwick, 'Introduction', in *The Reception of Kant's Critical Philosophy: Fichte, Schelling, Hegel*, ed. Sally Sedgwick (Cambridge: Cambridge University Press, 2007), 1–18.
6. Karl Jaspers, in *Schelling. Größe und Verhängnis* (Munich, 1955), refers to the *Potenz* as indicating a 'construction field'. Quoted in Iain Hamilton Grant, 'The Remains of the World: Grounds and Powers in Schelling's Later Naturphilosophie', *Schelling Studien*, 1 (2014): 3–24. Beach affirms this but in terms of Schelling's notion of will (*Potencies of the God(s)*, 115).
7. Sedgwick, 'Introduction', 13.
8. See Schelling, 'Stuttgart Seminars', 214, as well as Schelling, *On the History of Modern Philosophy*, 65–6.

9. Frederick Beiser suggests this in 'Dark Days: Anglophone Scholarship since the 1960s', in *German Idealism: Contemporary Perspectives*, ed. Espen Hammer (New York: Routledge, 2007), 81–3.
10. I choose the term inexistent with some trepidation as it has roots in Anselm's ontological proof of God's existence as well as Brentano's theory of inexistent intentionality, neither of which I wish to directly address. However, both of these usages lend some coherence to Schelling's *Potenzen* as inexistent. In terms of Anselm, Schelling can be seen as trying to argue that existence does add something to being (*contra* Kant) and, in relation to Brentano, inexistence functions as an intentionality in terms of the momentum of creation in Schelling's concept of nature.
11. Schelling, 'Of the I as a Principle of Philosophy', 224. This relates to the discussion in Chapter 1 regarding the discussion of Kant's application of purposiveness to nature.
12. L. Pearce Williams, *The Origins of Field Theory* (New York: Random House, 1966), 46.
13. Dale Snow, *Schelling and the End of Idealism* (Albany, NY: SUNY Press, 1996), 155–6.
14. Grant, *Philosophies of Nature*, 122.
15. Beach, *Potencies of the God(s)*, 117–27.
16. Ibid., 111.
17. Ibid., 114–15.
18. Schelling, *Ideas for a Philosophy of Nature*, 31–2.
19. Ibid., 44.
20. Ibid., 41.
21. Schelling, *First Outline*, 28.
22. Ibid., 208.
23. Grant, *Philosophies of Nature*, 151.
24. The fact that the *Ideas* was written in 1799 and revisited in 1803 creates difficulties for my chronological attempt here, especially given the fact that the explicit mention of the *Potenzen* occurs in the 1803 Supplements and not the original text. I leave the discussion of the *Ideas* here, however, since Schelling relates the *Potenzen* to the natural sciences, and it is thus in the same spirit as the *First Outline*.
25. Schelling, *Ideas for a Philosophy of Nature*, 49.
26. Ibid., 49.
27. Ibid., 51.
28. Ibid., 137–8.
29. Schelling, *System of Transcendental Idealism*, 30.
30. Ibid., 30.
31. Ibid., 48–9.
32. Ibid., 49.
33. Ibid., 76.
34. Ibid., 118.
35. Ibid., 124.
36. Ibid. 126.
37. Schelling, 'Universal Deduction', 1.
38. Ibid., 1.
39. Ibid., 3–4.
40. Ibid., 18–19.
41. Schelling, 'Of the I as a Principle of Philosophy', 114–15.
42. Ibid., 118.
43. Schelling, *Presentation*, 156.
44. Ibid., 252.

45. Here I am skipping over Schelling's *Bruno* (1802). It must be immediately noted that, given that the form of the *Bruno* is that of a Platonic dialogue, it is difficult to count it in the progression of Schelling's thought in the same fashion. For one, Schelling does not speak in his own voice but in the titular character of Bruno (named after Giordano Bruno). This fact itself, however, points to the importance of the potencies in an interesting sense. The Platonic style of the *Bruno* allows Schelling to place the *Potenz* in a cosmological context, something that would remain important for the rest of his career. That is, instead of oscillating between discussing the *Potenz* in *Naturphilosophical* or transcendental terms (although the limits of the latter are strained in the *Presentation*), Schelling makes the *Potenz* as abstract as possible within the *Bruno*. As will become more clear in Schelling's later works and is first detectable in 'Of the I as a Principle of Philosophy', the *Potenz* are a means of explaining the modality of existence as more than merely cognisable modality.

46. F. W. J. von Schelling, *The Philosophy of Art*, trans. Douglass Stott and David Simpson (Minneapolis, MN: University of Minnesota Press, 2008), 247.

47. Ibid., 281.

48. Ibid., 200.

49. Ibid., 282.

50. F. W. J. von Schelling, *Philosophy and Religion*, trans. Klaus Ottman (Putnam, CT: Spring Publications, 2010), 18.

51. Ibid., 26.

52. Ibid., 24.

53. Ibid., 36.

54. Ibid., 60.

55. Ibid., 60.

56. Schelling, *Philosophical Investigations*, 13.

57. Ibid., 17.

58. Ibid., 17.

59. Ibid., 28

60. Ibid., 13.

61. Ibid., 49–50.

62. Ibid., 28.

63. Ibid., 26.

64. Ibid., 29.

65. Schelling, 'Stuttgart Seminars', 203.

66. Ibid., 203.

67. Ibid., 216.

68. Ibid., 217. See also F. W. J. von Schelling, *Clara, or On Nature's Connection to the Spirit World*, trans. Fiona Steinkamp (Albany, NY: SUNY Press, 2002), 79–80. The particularity of human existence in relation to the potencies is taken up in *Clara* (1811). This strange pseudo-novelistic text places the potencies as both characters (foregrounding the connection of potency to personality present in the *Ages*) and as marking the transition from the natural world to the spiritual world. This transition is not absolute, as the worlds are of one world or one unity and are different only in the position (or character) from which they are articulated. Furthermore, the process of transition or transcendence (the movement of development) individuates or turns inward in the form of a conflict. *Clara* can be read in conjunction with Schelling's scattered remarks on philosophical anthropology, found in his writings on mythology in particular. At the same time, the concepts and characterisation (thought of in a more literal narratological sense) preview the emphasis on the potencies being modes of expression in Schelling's work to follow.

69. Schelling, 'Stuttgart Seminars', 216–18.
70. F. W. J. von Schelling, *The Abyss of Freedom/Ages of the World*, trans. Judith Norman (Ann Arbor, MI: University of Michigan Press, 1997), 123–5.
71. Ibid., 126.
72. Ibid., 126.
73. Ibid., 128.
74. Ibid., 129.
75. Ibid., 130.
76. Ibid., 131.
77. Ibid., 131–2.
78. Ibid., 170–3.
79. Ibid., 172–3.
80. Ibid., 173.
81. Ibid., 177.
82. Ibid., 177.
83. Schelling, *The Ages of the World*, 4.
84. Ibid., 8.
85. Ibid., 9.
86. Ibid., 24.
87. Ibid., 10.
88. Ibid., 11.
89. Ibid., 11.
90. Ibid., 48.
91. Ibid., 82.
92. Ibid., 84.
93. Chronologically speaking I am skipping over Schelling's *Erlangen* lectures (due to their brief referencing of the potencies) as well as Schelling's *Darstellung* lectures, as I will focus on them in Chapter 6.
94. Schelling, *On the History of Modern Philosophy*, 53.
95. Ibid., 65.
96. Ibid., 71.
97. Ibid., 117.
98. Ibid., 114–15.
99. Ibid., 116.
100. Ibid., 117–18.
101. Ibid., 122.
102. Ibid., 125–6.
103. Beach makes this argument as well in *Potencies of the God(s)*, 136–40.
104. F. W. J. von Schelling, *Historical-Critical Introduction to the Philosophy of Mythology*, trans. Mason Richey and Markus Zisselsberger (Albany, NY: SUNY Press, 2007), 145.
105. Beach, *Potencies of the God(s)*, 147.
106. Schelling, *The Grounding of Positive Philosophy*, 132.
107. Quoted in Grant, 'Remains of the World', 5.
108. Schelling, *The Grounding of Positive Philosophy*, 133.
109. Ibid., 134.
110. Ibid., 137.
111. Ibid., 138.
112. Ibid., 160.

113. Ibid., 209.
114. F. W. J. von Schelling, *Darstellung Lecture 13*, trans. Iain Hamilton Grant (unpublished manuscript, 2013), 8. Translated excerpt from Schelling, *Sämmtliche Werke*, Vol. XI, 294–320.
115. Schelling, *Darstellung Lecture 13*, 10.
116. Plato, 'Timaeus', in *Plato: Complete Works*, ed. John Cooper (Indianapolis, IN: Hackett Publishing, 1997), 1234.
117. Schelling, *Darstellung Lecture 13*, 2.
118. F. W. J. von Schelling, *Darstellung Lecture 17*, trans. Iain Hamilton Grant (unpublished manuscript, 2013), 4. Translated excerpt from Schelling, *Sämmtliche Werke*, Vol. XI, 386–408.
119. Here I skip over the 19th *Darstellung* lecture in which Schelling does discuss, though not extensively, the *Potenzen*. I discussed the relevant passages above in Chapter 1.
120. Grant, 'Prospects for Post-Copernican Dogmatism', 450–1.
121. Schelling, 'Of the I as a Principle of Philosophy', 71.
122. Schelling, *The Ages of the World*, 14.
123. Alexius Meinong, 'The Theory of Objects', in *Realism and the Background of Phenomenology*, ed. Roderick M. Chisholm (Glencoe, IL: Free Press, 1960; repr. Atascadero, CA: Ridgeview, 1981), 76–117.
124. Schelling, *The Grounding of Positive Philosophy*, 49–50.
125. Grant, 'Remains of the World', 8.
126. Beach, *Potencies of the God(s)*, 142.
127. Schelling, *The Ages of the World*, 22.

Chapter 5

Lamps, Rainbows, Unicorns and Horizons: Spatialising Knowledge in *Naturphilosophical* Epistemology

> Since I seek to ground my knowledge only *in itself*, I inquire no further as to the ultimate ground of this primary knowledge (self-consciousness), which, if it exists, must necessarily lie *outside* knowledge. Self-consciousness is the lamp of the whole system of knowledge, but it casts its light ahead only, not behind [. . .] *Whether it is absolutely* autonomous can be left undecided, until such time as the science itself has determined whether anything whatever can be thought, which is not to be derived from this knowledge itself.[1]

In this chapter, I address the apparently problematic status of epistemology in Schelling's work. Given the (at times) overblown emphasis on Schelling's anti-Kantianism, there would seem to be little hope of articulating anything like a theory of knowledge in his thought. For the sake of brevity, and to touch on the thrust of this project, I will emphasise knowledge's spatial and navigational function in Schelling's texts. For Schelling, the navigational is that which locates, and constructively constrains, the capacity of the subject to synthesise. This is best understood, I will argue, via a spatialised reading of his notion of intellectual intuition. While this form of intuition initially resembles that of Fichte, Schelling soon transforms the term, using it in tandem with construction, in order to maintain both the sensory immediacy and abstract form of intuition as the initial means through which a knowing subject, immersed in the activities of nature, comes to recognise its own capacities and begins to form claims about the world.

Epistemology in Schelling can be taken to revolve around the problem of location and synthesis on two axes. The first, vertical axis is the purportedly asymmetrically causal, or generative, axis of nature represented by

Schelling as the *Stufenfolge* (or graduated stages of nature). The second axis is the horizontal representation of nature in terms of fields, or domains, of knowledge. Or, put otherwise, Schelling's epistemology must deal with the vertical axis of the transcendental method that manifests as the *Stufenfolge*, as well as the horizontal axis that manifests itself as fields or the scientific classification of the progression of the potencies (*Potenzen*) via a form of Peircean abduction. Abduction, which will be addressed in detail in the following chapter, is Peirce's name for a non-deductive inference, a hypothesis, or more generally the logic of creation. This is, to point back to Chapter 1, merely an extension of Schelling's attempt to radicalise the materiality of Spinoza and the ideality of Leibniz, in order to do justice to the creative capacity of both nature and the idea.

If either of these axes could be perceived purely abstractly, the horizontal axis would view all domains, or fields of knowledge, as co-determining one another in a massive web or network. Viewing the vertical axis purely abstractly (as the *Stufenfolge*), one would see an evolutionary series, a line of higher and higher potentiation. These two views are complicated by the fact that, for Schelling, being an embodied spectator or observer does not allow for these views to be abstracted from one's embodied position. Furthermore, and as the above epigraph suggests, Schelling advocates a form of constructivism, but one that is augmentative, in which powers express themselves at ever higher levels and are never found completely within things constructed via these powers. The question becomes: 'What remains of the epistemological enterprise given a world of potencies on the one hand, and co-determination of facts, or objects, on the other?'

As was illustrated in the previous chapter, the potencies project the unity of subjectivity and objectivity as subject-object, the two sides of which are methodologically separated for the sake of thinking their counterparts, while they can never, on pain of contradiction, be separated ontologically. Schelling claims that due to this function of the potencies, an irresolvable dualism wedges itself in the very attempt to think philosophy, and thus one ends up with negative and positive philosophies, or philosophies that think in terms of the 'what there is' (the negative) and the 'that there is' (the positive). Hence Schelling makes consistent references to a third thing (*tertium quid* in the early work), which eventually shifts to the indifference point in the Identity philosophy. Gilles Châtelet, who will be engaged once more here, demonstrates the importance of indifference points for examining the relation between intuition and construction, between scientific theories, and between philosophy and science.

Extensively laying out the positive, the negative and the indifferent would be an altogether different project and one too massive for the present concerns. These concerns can be oriented and narrowed following the spatio-temporalisation of intuition mentioned above: that of the horizontality of fields and the verticality of the *Stufenfolge*. This in turn will lead us into the proto-pragmatism of the next and final chapter in that, as Schelling argues in *The Grounding of Positive Philosophy*, positive philosophy is a 'higher empiricism' because it utilises the world of sense as a material for an epistemological gesture that expands the power of reason. Or, in other words, positive philosophy uses experience's relative sensorial stability as a ground for reason rather than concerning itself with the deeper structures of reason (as Kant does in the *Critiques*). The threat remains that such a positive philosophy can be misconstrued as a romantic or naïve phenomenological enterprise, but I believe that this is clearly not the case, especially when the Berlin lectures are viewed in light of their rearticulation in the *Darstellung* lectures which immediately followed them.[2]

To address these issues, and to set the stage for Schelling's late proto-pragmatism (the positive philosophy), the present chapter will deal with his attempt to articulate a theory of knowledge that is co-constructive within the natural (as derivation), that isolates and extracts kinds of knowledge as fields (or determinations), and that relies upon an account of intuition or sense that is neither naïve nor purely factical. That is, one must construct a notion of determination that neither relies on the apparent self-evident appearance of things in sense, nor is addressed merely as facts in a human-centred system of meaning. The alternative to these two paths is ultimately best represented as a form of navigation following the work of Gilles Châtelet.

Epistemology and the *Stufenfolge* (derivation)

The *Stufenfolge*, as a divided series of graduated stages, involves a logic of ground that functions to impart the transcendental as an *a priori* logical structure to the genesis of both nature and consciousness over time. Yet, in addition, the *Stufenfolge* can be read as the non-reductionist or expansively naturalist demand in Schelling's thought, as it asserts an asymmetrical generation that affects humans as deeply as all the rest of nature.

Derivation, as a natural occurrence, arises from the fact that nature, to be as productive as it can be, must self-inhibit in order to create at all (otherwise there would be either pure creation, or pure stasis). As Schelling argues in the *First Outline*, the dynamic graduated series in nature (*Stufenfolge*) is what must be deduced in order to argue that these inhibitions maintain some level of permanence as things, as individuals in nature.[3] It is with the advent of the *Stufenfolge* that Schelling may be 'trying his luck' with regard to the kinds of claims he can make about nature without falling back into pre-critical dogmatic metaphysics. In other words, does the *Stufenfolge* fall into the same trap as Leibniz's monads or Spinoza's singular substance? It is these kinds of worries about the relation between causes and reasons (or nature and norms) that lead many contemporary analytic thinkers who invoke German Idealism to abandon the former for the clarity of the latter. Following in the footsteps of thinkers such as Wilfrid Sellars and John McDowell, it is presumed by Robert Brandom and Robert Pippin that the space of reasons, the place of normative commitments and operative reasons, must be strictly divorced from the realm of causes or the realm of nature. The root of this separation lies in Kant's treatment of teleology in relation to human freedom and the nature this freedom purportedly escapes.

This normative cut-off is utilised by current strands in analytic philosophy that have taken up German Idealism in order to complicate, if not to combat directly, the possibility of a ground of naturalism. This is done largely by an appeal to categories of normativity, due to the fact that the normative dimension of human behaviour seems operationally (if not necessarily causally) divorced from scientific explanation or some other epistemological articulation of the natural world. To put it otherwise: if we assume, as is the case in Schelling, a one-world physics as suggested in the Introduction, we are faced with a question: what is the best way to account for the seemingly non-natural tools of human existence (morals, values, laws, etc.) without conceding a form of pure relativism, scientistic nihilism, or as David Bell has aptly demonstrated, a strange patchwork world where local ideal claims are somehow made to supervene on a natural, or physical world?[4] As I will argue in relation to reductionism below and Mark Wilson's work in the following chapter, this patchwork approach may be fundamentally unavoidable. We are left then with the difficult task of ascertaining Schelling's position between bald naturalism and anti-naturalist idealism. Whether this means that Schelling is a liberal naturalist or some other kind altogether will also be addressed below.[5]

As has been the case throughout this book, scepticism is the operational pivot between naturalism and idealism, or between nature and freedom. But unlike Kant's scepticism, that of Schelling does not attempt to ground itself in the reality of our experience in order to determine its conditions (those being the definition of the form of transcendental argumentation according to Kant) but, as we have seen in Schelling broadly, the naturalisation of the transcendental means that the *apparent necessary conditions of our being-as-experience must defer to the seemingly necessary conditions for Nature to be as productive as it is.* This statement is the general form of what Schelling takes from Fichte, and transfers from the structure of the *Ich* to the structure of nature. That is, the productivity of nature is a postulate that seems unavoidable if one is to make any further claims about any-thing, let alone nature or the entity that is postulating. The subsequent difficulty lies in how we get from such a weak meontology (as I believe that to be what Schelling advocates) to knowledge claims that are neither ontologically liberal (all things have being) nor anti-ontological (ontology as only a verbal dispute).

As was touched on in Chapter 2, the exploration of the epistemological navigator requires re-entering the fray between the normative examina-tion of German Idealism (with its deflationary account of the school's connections to nature and naturalism) and Schelling's one-world physics as something between a hard (or reductive) and soft (or liberal) natural-ism. The problem with these articulations of naturalism is that the former hard naturalism transforms epistemological certainty into a metaphysical frame (we might say ignoring the difference between structure and form or between what we find and what we know), whereas the latter over-relies on an anti-reductionism that reinstates its epistemological premises against investigation. Essentially, the former approach discusses the normative as absolutely separate from the natural and then transcendentalises a non-parochial (but not quite universal) practice as a norm, whereas the latter crude or bald naturalist approach immantises a field of knowledge into an exacerbated ontology. This brings us again to the methodological split of Schelling's epistemology, which, I would argue, ignores the false choice between soft or liberal and hard or bald or reductionist naturalism, as well as avoiding a crude notion of reductionism. The same methodological move is also seen in one of Peirce's greatest heirs, and the figure who stands before the split between the natural and normative, namely Wilfrid Sellars. But before getting to Sellars and Peirce, several other territories need to be crossed and examined.

The apparent alternative to a normative approach (which argues that reasons are fundamentally distinct from causes) and bald naturalism (which argues that there are only causes and entities) is one of an exchange between epistemological and ontological minimalism or weakness. That is, a normative approach is epistemologically strong but ontologically weak in that it asserts the importance of knowledge claims over and above onto-logical claims, perhaps dismissing ontology altogether. Bald naturalism may be equally strong about epistemological claims, but may claim that the knowledge claims of science displace those of philosophy, if the arbiter of choice serves to protect human freedom and action from the judgements of neuroscience, for example. Another possibility is to argue that ontology supplants all other claims, but to then establish a minimal ontology, such as that 'things exist'. A fourth option, and one I believe Schelling takes up, is to claim that there is a speculative meontology that is necessitated by being in a world that limits our capacity to know it, but seems simultaneously to engender thinking agents to create with and beyond what we know of it. The problem becomes how to locate and properly delimit the capacity to know against (and with) other capacities.

Despite broad claims about the systematicity of German Idealism, I would argue that the problem of locating reason emphasises the non-totalising character of this approach of systematicity. Whether it is Fichte's internal light of determination, Schelling's unprethinkable as engine of predication, or Hegel's constant reinstatement of the measure of necessity (or what Žižek has referred to as the contingency of necessity), it becomes apparent that German Idealism, even though it was attempting to be far-reaching, was not attempting to construct a view from nowhere. In fact, it is German Idealism's very emphasis on capacities such as construction, derivation, determination and the like which stresses the work that is always required in order to make any kind of claim to universality or the Absolute, or to nature, from a somewhat limited locale.

In fact, it is Kant's inability to properly ground how transcendental schema come to be known and function that can be read as the impetus for the German Idealists to set about their project.[6] For Schelling, productive intuition, which follows from the immediate world of sense, sets the powers of the imagination off in constructing and creating outwards. But once the subject, or more generally any constructive force, recognises its limitations, it turns inwards and accesses itself, albeit diagonally. Even these earlier stages of conscious development, restricted to the human, demonstrate for Schelling the difficulties in asserting a schematic universality as Kant does. Yet Schelling does not discount that something like universality is possible, given the fact that the universality is expressed from a local point that may very well dislocate the place from which that thought occurs. Schelling's conceptual bind here is this: how can we invoke a concept that is far-reaching (consequently or potentially universal) given the locality-constraint he has put on conceptual production? In part, this is possible because Schelling cautiously utilises concepts as demonstrations or exhibitions, and never as things-in-themselves or meta-stable categories. The *Stufenfolge* adapts the genetic version of the transcendental from Fichte, which, as Daniel Breazeale lucidly outlines, sought to demonstrate how the kind of subjectivity or consciousness that Kant presupposed could be demonstrated by accounting genetically for the series of acts by which it comes to recognise itself as such.[7] Schelling, as we will outline more fully below, specifically in reference to intuition, sees this as a middle step (as intellectual intuition) which cannot, for him, be the sole, or at least main, ground from which construction/derivation occurs. For Schelling, to maintain the continuity between sensory experience, the production of the imagination, the recognition of the self as a producer and the subsequent production, one must set the very process of derivation or self-construction as graduated, as partially outside the subject's control. While for Fichte, anything set outside the sheer production-by-consciousness would be merely factical, for Schelling the assumption that the creative activity is proved by demonstrating *our ability to act* overly localises the underlying dynamics of action as such.[8] At the same time, Schelling does not wish merely to ignore the impressive constructive capacity of the mind, hence the transcendental is naturalised via its being opened at both ends, in that our schematisation of it is a selection of a potentiated evolutionary process which the thinker only views from a place, though a temporally 'late' one 'inside' of it.

For instance, Schelling's *Stufenfolge* model presumes, for better or for worse, that the human organism sits atop the graduated stages – that the human is the *highest* production of the cosmos thus far. 'Highest' here does not, of course, mean perfect (as Schelling is consistently critical of perfection as well as any notion of completeness), but the most potentiated. The strangeness of the *Stufenfolge* model is that while we are viewing the series of developments from a high point, this gives us the responsibility of being so potentiated as to see how potentiated we are.[9]

As Schelling writes in his lecture 'The Exhibition of the Process of Nature' (1843):

> We must of course assume that the Earth is the point of emergence for humanity – why, we do not know, it refers to relations we cannot survey, but humanity is therefore not specifically a product of the Earth – it is a product of the entire process – not the Earth alone, the entire cosmos contributes to humanity, and if of the Earth, as, continuing from the earlier standpoint, he is, then humanity is not exclusively created for the Earth, but [390] for all the stars, since humanity is created as the final goal of the cosmos. If humanity appears to be a local essence, this is not what it originally is, but has become localized.[10]

Also relevant is the following sentiment from the Introduction to the *First Outline*:

> But if Nature is absolute productivity, then the ground of this limitation cannot lie outside of it. Nature is originally only productivity; there can, therefore, be nothing determined in this productivity (all determination is negation) and so products can never be reached by it. – If products are to be reached, the productivity must pass from being undetermined to being determined, that is, it must, as pure productivity, be canceled. If the ground of determination of productivity lay outside of Nature, Nature would not originally be absolute productivity. Determination, that is, negation, must certainly come into Nature; but this negation viewed from a higher standpoint must again be positivity.[11]

While I will address determination below, derivation, as graduation, must be a natural process and not something merely added to nature from the outside. The struggle here is expressed as follows: how can Schelling claim that structures and forms are real, but discoverable by humans, and also that there are some concepts that refer to things we cannot discover or have not yet discovered? How can any claim to knowledge be more than only an artificial claim, how does any statement of fact in Schelling obtain on reality if everything is nature, yet we are limited or localised aspects of it? This is also complicated by the fact that Schelling no doubt realigned, in various ways, the relation between *Naturphilosophie* and transcendental philosophy during the almost fifty years separating the above quotes. While the human, as organism, hardly appears in the *First Outline* or the *Ideas*, as human beings are discussed in terms of their thought processes in idealistic language, this division between organism and idea-wielding entity seems slowly to disappear over time.[12]

While these questions are more directly addressed through determination (and the horizontal model of knowledge), the concept of the *Stufenfolge*, of the discovery of non-trivial derivation as a natural occurrence, addresses the temporal dimension, or temporal pressure, that *is* creation. That there is generation proposes the hypothesis that generation can be understood, or can be mapped as a consequence of that generation. The status of the human as the highest comes from the fact that, as far as we know, our understanding of generation allows for an augmentation of that generation in a way that is often used to support the fundamental difference of thought from nature, that is, the realm or space of reasons over and above the space of causes or nature.[13]

The *Stufenfolge* is, above all, the problem of entities, or points of inhibition from within creation which seems, by definition, as if it should be unceasing. The standpoint of the highest issues a perspective downward into the chain of causes (as well as upwards in terms of speculation). The perspective of the human, being as high as it is, allows for the creation of a concept such as the *Stufenfolge* whereby we can attempt to place ourselves within the chain of ongoing causes, within the dynamic stages of nature. Thus anything functionally akin to a space of reasons in Schelling (from the vertical view of the *Stufenfolge*) would be consequent upon a natural process even when that space of reasons is absolutised. In this sense, the *Stufenfolge* is a radical form of epistemological perspectivism or constructivism, but one that admits not only the foundational limit-factors of nature in the process of constructing knowledge systems, but also the ongoing ones. Thus, the transcendental, as a *provisional* subordination of the real to the ideal, can be viewed as a vertical orientation in that it attempts to trace the evolutionary or augmenting repetition of forms over time from above what is traced.[14] Whereas Fichte's geneticism could also be claimed to be vertical, broadly evolutionary, the difference is that, for Fichte, the external or the not-I functions as a boundary, and thus human subjectivity is always at the bleeding edge of construction. For Schelling, on the other hand, our capacity to think is a late development, but it also demands that we properly localise its emergence naturalistically *even in a transcendental context, because thinking is derived from nature.* Thus activity is more than simply an ideal propellant for Schelling – it is also the not-sheerly think-able medium by which, and on which, humans act.

Epistemology and the field problem (determination)

Unprethinkable being is the fundamental presupposition of all determination.[15]

Unprethinkable being is Schelling's name for the facticity of reason. This facticity for him is resultant of the fact that a mere dimension of distinc-tion without anything distinct still has no relationship to a differentiation in judgments and is therefore indeed a necessary proposition.[16]

The fundamental question of fields of knowledge, as I see it, is that of how Schelling's system can account for meta-functions, such as systems of knowledge, if he claims no special capacity of the human to know the depth of things, and if (on the side of nature, we might say for conceptual clarity) being and thinking are within a heterogeneous monism (nature as subject-object). That is, whereas the emergence of things or facts is credited to the self-inhibition of an abstract identity (put most directly: in order for anything to be something, it must inhibit itself into things), the question remains: how is it that we have privileged access to domains such as biology, chemistry, physics and so on?

To bring the question specifically to the domain of epistemology: how is it that the domains which we have constructed (such as the physical sciences) seem more than ontological, but less than metaphysical?[17] Or, put another way, does Schelling ontologise knowledge claims, epistemolo-gise ontology, or pursue a different path altogether? The unprethinkable (*Unvordenkliche*) is referenced above, since instead of pointing to a brute metaphysical or ontological claim about the impossibility of complete knowledge, or to the simple fact that there is always more knowledge to be produced, the unprethinkable is the status of the continuum as an ongoing synthetic activity, an activity that is as real as it is ideal.

As has hopefully become evident in the previous three chapters, Schelling's semi-abductive method follows from the fact that one cannot merely remove oneself from one's own sensual domain. This does not mean, however, as Schelling takes from Kant, that the domain of sense is necessarily physical or real – and nor is it simply factual (*contra* Fichte), as I will address below. Schelling argues that nature produces real structures or universals but that these are discovered only through the constant tracing of their consequences. This problematic situation, I would argue, centres on forgetting that the field problem is one of assumed authority, that is, that the question of fields belongs to science and philosophical investigations into nature – concerns which, unfortunately, are no longer the purview of continental philosophy but, increasingly, that of analytic philosophy. The former, more often than not, simply stands behind a blind rejection of the validity of the hard sciences, while the latter stands behind blind acceptance (both the rejection and acceptance are often of seriously outdated forms of science). While this is not always the case, and various fields such as science and technology studies or philosophy of cosmology in analytic fields are generally more open to finer questions of method, experiment and the conceptual history proper to science, the analytic–continental split has done serious damage to cross-disciplinary communication. While this may seem a trivial concern, or one that forces the thinker into either accepting or rejecting the total authority of the physical sciences, I believe that the avoidance of this question has become accepted as a central characteristic of post-war thought.[18] This avoidance is part and parcel of the avoidance of the investigation of nature as a philosophical problem. As Schelling noted:

> The entire new European philosophy since its beginning (with Descartes) has the common defect that nature is not available for it and that it lacks a living ground. Spinoza's realism is thereby as abstract as the idealism of Leibniz. Idealism is the soul of philosophy; realism is the body; only both together can constitute a living whole.[19]

Before pursuing the ontology–epistemology relation in a general sense to move towards Schelling, a historical excursus is useful here. An added complexity arises in discussing Schelling's use of fields, as his work, in a broad sense, functions as a base for field theory in modern physics. This is a contested claim, but one that, for the sake of this project, finds additional support in that field theory, abstracted into the field problem, appears central to Schelling's thought. Or, put otherwise, the status and treatment of physical fields (such as electric or electromagnetic fields) cannot be separated from the question of what the borders of epistemological fields are in Schelling's work. This is not merely to claim a generic irreducibility of historical context, but to demonstrate that whether in the case of physical fields, or that of fields of knowledge, the diagrammatic and explanatory function of field is necessary, given Schelling's removal of objects or any substratum as final explanation of both how we act and how we know.[20]

As L. Pearce Williams argues convincingly in his book *The Origins of Field Theory*, the history of certain physical theories (such as electromagnetism) appears odd if the influence of German Idealism, and particularly Schelling, is not taken into account.[21] Williams demonstrates that in contrast to the Newtonians and atomistic chemists of his time (such as Lavoiser), Schelling influences a field theory that fundamentally embraces the synthetic construction of scientific concepts – a belief that discovery must be supplanted with the creation of concepts that must be extended until they break. Williams writes: 'The fertility of these mental concepts will be determined by the manner in which these mental conceptions lead to further discourses and causal chains.'[22]

The connection between physical field theory, or what is more often than not called classic field theory, and fields of knowledge is not too difficult to make. Field theory came into existence as a means of describing how forces act in a space not dependent upon matter but acting upon matter or in matter's place. Classical field theory generally discussed gravity and electromagnetism – forces that were important for Schelling from his early works in *Naturphilosophie* until his later lectures on *Pure Rational Philosophy*. In several places Iain Hamilton Grant has indicated the importance that field theory has for Schelling, and Schelling for field theory.[23] But what Grant does not emphasise is the diagrammatic function that the field theories instil in German Idealism and vice versa. That is, the scientific success of field theories is not just explanatory across domains, but the diagrammatic thrust of fields also allows for a non-trivial constructive approach by loosening the break between the space of reason and the space of nature via an intuitive placing of the observer, as Châtelet puts it.

To link back to the previous two chapters, the importance of field theory and fields of knowledge for Schelling demonstrates once more the importance of continuity and the asymmetrical production of nature before thought, that is, that the idealism of the I follows from the idealism of nature. The emergence of field theory particularly in the work of Humphry Davy (who was influenced by Coleridge's Schellingianism and adopted *Naturphilosophical* terminology),[24] as well as in the work of Michael Faraday and James Clerk Maxwell, shows how diagrammatic non-material forces were imperative for understanding the productivity and general functioning of nature at scales both small and immense as the eighteenth century shifted into the nineteenth. Furthermore, because of the synthetic nature of these domains, the diagrammatic and the geometric become the methods best suited to present them as part of nature. Whereas, for Châtelet, the diagram is any mark on a material surface, the geometric presupposes a system of relation into which the diagram may, or may not be, added. This transition is evident in the first diagrams of field physics. These diagrams mapped lines of force, bent lines of magnetic poles and, later for Oersted, the cosmos itself, which was a plenum of forces, a net of surging lines of powers generating all things. Field theory was an area of study that allowed further discovery coupled with diagrammatic rigour, which productively formalised the forces of nature but did not restrain them. As Schelling's synthetic philosophy emphasises, and again as Williams indicates, any philosopher who relies upon a physical substratum is no philosopher at all.[25]

As Châtelet remarks, German Idealism writ large can be taken as that which attempted to trace the generation of structure *as such* from apparently 'free' speculation or intuition. The leaps made possible through intuitive means in the same stride freed certain forms of mathematical and scientific creativity, but this is not a freedom from rigour but a freedom from certain common-sense or sensorially hardened constraints – we might say constraints of the practical, which, again as we will see below, Markus Gabriel emphasises (perhaps indirectly).[26] Thus, it is imperative to determine what exactly replaces the physical substratum in the wake of fields. If not facticity, or matter, then what? Châtelet suggests an abstract answer – that any mark retroactively identifies its *potential medium*, whereas the assumption of a medium quickly becomes epistemologically restrictive. Châtelet highlights how intuition functions to lace together thought and nature in a way that is neither purely real (where the real determines the ideal only) nor purely ideal (where thoughts produce entities). As we will discuss in the following chapter, Schelling too does not support a merely ideal separation of the real from the ideal, that is, a normative cut-off endorsed by thinkers such as Robert Brandom and John McDowell. And as Châtelet will highlight, any act, as evidenced by the diagram, immediately threatens to contaminate the normative, given the fact that it is creative yet stable. For Schelling the substratum is a gesture: it is posited, and its consequences are either found, or not, in the act of tracing its potential consequences. This act of tracing is essentially one of abductive demonstration built on speculative motion. It is this tension that Châtelet emphasises in the use of the gesture. The gesture and the figure are two means of demonstrating the intuitive field or open space of motion while, at the same time, demonstrating the material effect of such a motion as caught in the 'memory' of the gesture or as a diagram.

In terms of substratum and intuition, Schelling, like those who pursued field physics after him, creates an electromagnetic space, or a space that is boundless except for those dimensions created by motions that appear to occur 'within' that space. This speculative 'within-ness' is defined only as being neither at the beginning nor the ending edge of the space in a spatiotemporal sense, that is, at the alpha or the omega of creation (pointing back to the use of the *Stufenfolge* above). Before addressing the relation between fields (whether scientific or philosophical) in the following section, it is worth examining the diagrammatic ways in which Maxwell and Faraday attempted to draw the motions of an intuitive substratum.

As Williams highlights, Maxwell dealt the final blow to the physical substratum by mathematising the work of Faraday[27] and discussed the interaction of various forces and fields analogically as vortices or gear wheels.[28] As has been indicated earlier, the genesis of field theories can be traced from Schelling's influence on Davy via Coleridge. Faraday, as Davy's laboratory assistant, picked up the language and it, in turn, influenced Maxwell. Châtelet traces this progression through the ways in which the electromagnetic space as such is visualised. Drawing on Schelling's 'Universal Deduction of the Dynamic Process', Châtelet discusses how a free space is produced in the barest notion of system following Schelling's combination of intuition and the potencies (the virtual or intensive force of construction).[29]

For Châtelet, Faraday and Maxwell use diagrammatic figures such as gear wheels and vortices in order to organise a wilful or 'deliberate ambiguity'.[30] To attempt to situate these figures as real or ideal would be insufficient and the emphasis on figures and diagrams indicates the complex interplay of fields and asymmetrical generation between the two methods. Châtelet goes on to argue that Faraday and Maxwell utilise metaphorical wheels, gears and screws to demonstrate collections of motions, but that these figures are to be expanded and unwound as the consequences of experiments emerge: 'Lines of force are neither "real" nor "artificial"; they do not mathematise forces; they do not pin geometrical onto physical, rather they substitute an ideal, but elastic and tough, network, which allows virtuality to reclaim its rights.'[31] In addition: 'The lines of force weave a "field", a system of reverberation and resonance between the space and the geometer or physics: one might speak of a preparation of space for experimentation, analogous to that of the moved awakened to mobility.'[32]

He goes on to write:

> Faraday takes an inspired position: the diagrams of interlaced axis and loop possess a peculiar autonomy and an allusive power that must be respected and not treated like an exercise in which a mathematical 'form' is applied to physical 'phenomena'. Faraday's experiments are not enslaved to 'predictions', but instead strive to establish a new overhanging point in physics by defining a ritual of gestures which is always carefully accompanied by diagrams. Their aim is to produce a protocol for approach that is sufficiently bold and sufficiently articulated to release all the possible reverberations of the interlace.[33]

Schelling's inspiration for the field theoreticians, as well as his later reflections on their experiments, exhibits the difficulties arising from there being an inability to rely upon origin, upon substratum, or upon ideal factors of the idea in constituting any one thing or force.[34] If forces merely are, then what appear as things are intersections of forces, thereby being the result of different co-determinations. It is not sufficient to state that forces are and that everything else is a result of them as a concluding remark.[35] It is the advent of the positive philosophy in Schelling's later work that attempts to do justice to the consequence of determinations as more than merely a net of forces, that is, to ask what it means for us as creatures capable of a peculiar kind of force (ideation) that forces just seem to be.

Esposito reads this ambiguity as a rather hard opposition between experimentation and speculation,[36] but this would seem to read abduction out of Schelling's method of determination. Even speculation would require some embodied resources placed in a particular location. That is, as creatures who produce thoughts, humans are still situated in particular locations and are subject to certain forces over others. In other words, while the doctrine of forces largely addresses the realm of negative philosophy (what things are), the gestural aspect of field physics lends itself to the positive philosophy, in that it addresses what it is that things are specifically. Thus, ideal constructions (or constraints) contribute to a situated form of knowledge not because ideas create things in the same way that forces do, but because ideas are contributory to pre-existing forces.

How this process contributes directly to the practice of philosophy will be examined in the final section of this chapter as well as the concluding chapter, but for now it is important to examine the consequences of how determination is focused in a particular activity, particularly, that of the sciences. Fields of inquiry, whether scientific or otherwise theoretical, are not self-standing but are meta-stable fields of co-determinations which, at least for us, are constituted by the results of experiments. These experiments follow from, and are at times regulated by, entities that lie between our creation of them and their discovery 'in' nature. As Esposito writes: 'Nature itself cannot be an object to anything that is a part of it, so that we must reject any explanation that does not also contain a way of explaining the possibility of such knowledge without the Archimedean assumption.'[37]

However, as Châtelet emphasises, this does not mean that all of our determinations, or observations, are always-already thwarted in terms of their epistemological efficacy, but that a determination is like the potential grasping of a puzzle piece without knowing the final picture. As he writes in 'Interlacing the Singularity, the Diagram, and the Metaphor' (1999):

We are at the antipodes of the 'abstraction' which always results from the violent deduction of a part, and thus of a mutilation, whereas while the 'lever' does not subtract anything and acts like certain fragments of a *puzzle* which, from the outset, emerge and impose or dictate the solution: to be absolutely concrete is to persevere to some extent in *a kind of tangential approach of thought which grasps its own movement.*[38]

Schelling's epistemology, and the field physics with which it is entwined, attempts to minimise (without obliterating) the constraints not only of conceptual creation but creation as such. This entails, as was demonstrated in the previous chapter, that inexistence is a part of nature: a reservoir of creation that is not contained within nature but, in the form of the potencies, runs through it without determinable end or beginning (in space or in time).

Schelling's impact on field theory is not merely of historical note but imperative to understand the relation between philosophy and the sciences broadly. The conceptual work of philosophy on science and science on philosophy is important as long as it avoids being either conciliatory or atavistic with regard to science, as is often the case in analytic circles, or hostile and reductive towards science, as is often the case in continental thought.[39] In the following section I will address this in more detail with an eye to relations between fields, and between fields and the observer.

Rationalising rainbows: between sense and observation

In phenomena, we commonly, indeed, distinguish that which essentially belongs to the intuition of them, and is valid for the sensuous faculty of every human being, from that which belongs to the same intuition accidentally, as valid not for the. sensuous faculty in general, but for a particular state or organization of this or that sense. Accordingly, we are accustomed to say that the former is a cognition which represents the object itself, whilst the latter presents only a particular appearance or phenomenon thereof. This distinction, however, is only empirical. If we stop here (as is usual), and do not regard the empirical intuition as itself a mere phenomenon (as we ought to do), in which nothing that can appertain to a thing in itself is to be found, our transcendental distinction is lost, and we believe that we cognize objects as things in themselves, although in the whole range of the sensuous world, investigate the nature of its objects as profoundly as we may, we have to do with nothing but phenomena. Thus, we call the rainbow a mere appearance of phenomenon in a sunny shower, and the rain, the reality or thing in itself; and this is right enough, if we understand the latter conception in a merely physical sense, that is, as that which in universal experience, and under whatever conditions of sensuous perception, is known in intuition to be so and so determined, and not otherwise. But if we consider this empirical datum generally, and inquire, without reference to its accordance with all our senses, whether there can be discovered in it aught which represents an object as a thing in itself (the raindrops of course are not such, for they are, as phenomena, empirical objects), the question of the relation of the representation to the object is transcendental; and not only are the raindrops mere phenomena, but even their circular form, nay, the space itself through which they fall, is nothing in itself, but both are mere modifications or fundamental dispositions of our sensuous intuition, whilst the transcendental object remains for us utterly unknown.[40]

The aim here is to demonstrate through a detailed discussion of a concrete example (the rainbow) how fruitful it is to study the asymptotic domain between theories. We will see that there are phenomena – various observable features of the rainbow, in particular – that require for their description aspects of both the ray theory and the wave theory. To my mind, from a philosophical point of view, this is an extremely important fact. It means that the reductive programs championed by philosophers actually miss out on a lot of interesting physics [. . .] We ought to give up on the notion of reduction in any sense and consider what of philosophical (and physical) interest can be learned by studying the asymptotic limits between theories.[41]

Rainbows glorify neither the subject nor any region of the universe. As the generic light of the universal continuum traverses regional horizons – each a droplet or a crystallized particle open to light – it enters them. Upon entering a regional horizon, the light refracts, bringing into the equation the internal conditions of the region. Once the light reaches the end of the horizon (the back of the droplet), it reflects back. As the light departs the regional droplet, it changes direction once again, indicating a departure from the regional conditions (the composition of the droplet) into the open, and accordingly, the continuation of this synthetic illumination for other regions.[42]

Taking the asymmetric generation of nature as the model of the *Stufenfolge* above, in tandem with the field problem of substantialising the observer, I move on to the necessity of de-romanticisng the notion of the observer in order to combat knee-jerk reactions (in both directions) in terms of the validity of knowledge claims as either being totally free of, or completely corrupted by, observation bias – whether that bias is coded in terms of naturalistic or normative limitations. I will then, in more specific terms of the sciences, attempt to show, through Robert Batterman's expert analysis of scientific and philosophical reduction, that these moves ignore Schelling's approach, which asserts the reality, yet epistemological graspability, of fields of science (or systems of knowledge), which at different levels approach one another more 'roughly' or more 'smoothly', depending upon the apparatuses utilised.[43]

I want to argue that many of the contemporary hard sciences present an appealing model of the invariance of, and relation between, the fields of knowledge in a way that reflects the use of the potencies in the *First Outline*. Furthermore, and following from Schelling's logic of determination, I will focus upon a somewhat odd example, but one that is quite frequent in discussions of emergence and knowledge claims: that of the rainbow.

Following the quotations above, and given Schelling's complex epistemological stance, how is one to grasp the weight of knowledge claims that can be made about, and based upon, an ephemeral entity such as a rainbow? Beyond this, and as the above epigraphs suggest, rainbows are tricky phenomena because they bring into question the tension between sense, knowledge and existence in that they can be adequately, but not completely, described by different physical theories. As Batterman and others have pointed out, the ray theory of light explains certain aspects of the rainbow, whereas the wave theory of light is preferable in other instances. In essence, rainbows demonstrate universality at the level of particularity, as universality means, for Batterman, that 'systems of very different microscopic constitution exhibit identical behavior under certain circumstances'.[44] For this reason he argues that rainbows point to the need to restrain, but not eliminate, the very concept of emergent entities because emergence operates in a 'no-man's land' of theoretical description. Emergent entities are thus not inexplicable, but only partially explicable according to different, and bordering, knowledge domains.

These no-man's lands, or zones of transition, are not merely ideal but indicate a system's internal structure. Constructing a theory to bridge bordering knowledge domains details, but only obliquely, the relevant correlations between them; the passage from one field to another that makes the locally detected motion important.[45] Thus, the macroscopic or emergent results of a phenomenon's transition are phenomenologically relevant, as is the context of embodiment or, more generally put, locality.[46] Or, in other words: if an object such as a rainbow can be constructed from the materials of two different theories (the ray and wave theories of light), then is the insufficiency of these theories alone a result of some noumenal status of the rainbow, or of the limits of the structure of how theories themselves are constructed from particular perspectives?

In addition, rainbows index the relation between sense and being, in terms of what can be gleaned from something that appears to be a mere illusion. The above quote from Kant suggests that ephemeral phenomena, in particular, point to the fact that all particular entities are carved out of sensuous material (here pointing back to Chapter 2 and the physics of sense), but this raises the question, as Maimon pointed out, of how one then distinguishes analytic propositions from synthetic ones.

Schelling argues that synthesis occurs in any act and that analytic stability is only ever a meta-stability, when another form of synthesis is treated as ground or, more unstably, as reason. This treatment of a particular form of synthesis as ground is what ties Schelling to Peirce and to pragmatism more generally: the asymptotic approach to natural phenomena. Schelling's intuition and speculative temporality-as-derivation are coupled with his horizontal field-based concerns for space and systematicity. In both cases, reasons are the results of grounds being treated *as if they were absolute* in order to test how a particular entity (which, after all, is only an inhibition of natural processes) is connected to nature. This is evident not only in Schelling's emphasis on productive intuition (to be discussed in the following section) but also in terms of the emphasis on location in Schelling's thought. For Schelling, the problem of location, or individuation, is one of simultaneous epistemological and ontological bordering. Reduction and asymptotic investigation both highlight the difficulty in navigating multiple fields of knowledge, where asymmetrical generation over time does not explain but, in fact, inhibits discussion of the resulting field's interaction.

To return to Batterman, the zone between theories demonstrates the problems with the easy critique and utilisation of reduction (both scientifically and philosophically). Reduction is tempting because quite different entities and forces in different explanatory realms (such as an organism on the one hand and the reaction to stress of a metal beam on the other) may exhibit similar (or what Batterman calls universal) tendencies. For instance, we could say at relative micro and macro levels that both can be discussed in terms of being masses of physical material responding similarly to stress. This places one, at least abstractly, in a similar space as Schelling's axis of horizontal and vertical knowledge, or between the difference that thought makes in relation to the difference that time makes (understood from our particular perspective). In other words, one is placed between apparently qualitative and apparently quantitative distinctions; to put things in the language of inter-theoretic relations, between derivation and connection. Schelling engages the inter-theoretic space by extending the possible grounds of phenomena or apparent products (*Scheinprodukt*).

One difficulty here in connecting Batterman's discussion of inter-theoretic relations to Schelling's thought is how to properly relate theory and method. The terms are, of course, mutually reinforcing in that, by using constructive or productive intuition, Schelling is able to take the freedom of the transcendental method and restrict it with the demonstratively unavoidable theory, in his case, that nature is prior to thinking. Nature functioning as *Prius* in turn allows, or in fact necessitates, that thinking functions dynamically, that is, constructively and intuitively. Both theories and methods are tests, or experiments, but the former are speculative grounds that justify the locality of the latter.

As already noted, Schelling's method is one of constructive extension, of extending an experiment to its breaking point (to determine whether something is merely ideal or real according to its consequences and not its substances). This is why, in the *Erlangen* lectures, philosophy is that practice where one must face the infinite. In terms of rationality, this points to a certain asymmetry that we have already encountered: 'the lamp of knowledge that only points forward'. In one sense, Schelling appears to endorse the power of Kant's critical project, of what the science of reason can do and its necessity for the progression of philosophy. Yet at the same time, Schelling does not believe that the critical project can be constructive based on the slim premises it sets out from, or else its method begins to function as a theory to the extent that it does not justify its claim to universality. This is why Schelling classifies Kant's work as negative philosophy. At times this classification has been obscured by readings of Schelling that either emphasise his anti-Kantianism (Iain Hamilton Grant) or claim he is resolutely Kantian (Arran Garre).[47] In essence, Schelling attempts to de-couple Kant's transcendental method, which he sees as a novel development in philosophy, *from philosophy as such.* Partially the issue is that, for Schelling, experience is accessible to reason since determination is about 'whatness' and not 'thatness', or what something is (existence) versus that something is (being). Whatness connects to the augmentative model where the qualitative is only experienced, is only conceptually registered, *post-factum.* This is the most basic division of the negative from the positive philosophies.

Furthermore, Schelling wishes to argue not only that reason cannot fix its experiential content and still remain reason but, with regard to the positive philosophy, that the relation between reason and experience is one in which reason must take experience as essence. The complexity here is that while Schelling acknowledges the myth of the given, that is, he admits that what is sensed is already conceptually laden (since one cannot be sure how real and how ideal a determination is), he also points out that while thought can, and must, set out to see the extent of an object or concept's consequences, experience, as issuing from both conceptually coded sense and that which necessarily is (i.e. existence with us already immersed in it) must be treated as a constructive condition *for the content of reason.* In this regard, Schelling (pre-emptively) follows Wilfrid Sellars in his scepticism regarding the given, but admits that experience must be treated as given not ontologically but as locative, as locally given in a way that is not *immediately* conceptually readable. Or, put in a simplified sense, Schelling rejects givenness as pure or non-conceptual, but accepts the givenness of experience as proximate and local. This is not to denounce reason as such, but to acknowledge the continuing pressure to push reason alongside experience. It is to try and ascertain the mediation between mind and world (ideal and real), to answer the question of the third thing (*tertium quid*) as the consequence *as consequence* (as a non-trivial result of the investigation of mind into world) and as a trajectory (as the appearance of quality in quantity).[48] It is both reason and experience that recognise the potency as trajectory, as having occurred in, and out of, both experience and reason. Thus reason is that which determines the inexistent *as a 'what'* since this occurs in experience, and as sensed, for reason.

In this relation of negative and positive philosophy, naturalism falls somewhere in between in terms of being strictly methodological or strictly ontological. The distinction between ontological and methodological naturalism is made methodologically (and would later be determined by one to be merely ideal) if one follows a Kantian method. As creatures capable of reason, human entities investigate their own investment in the world. From the perspective of a self-conscious entity, a method is a filtering device in order to make motion and navigation (as the systematisation of motion) into determination and speculation.

This determination is more than ideal if it expresses a real potency in an actuality. There appears to be no way of knowing ahead of time (without experience) how many potencies there are or how they function, which is why, as indicated in the previous chapter, they index inexistence. The relation between knowing and being can be articulated in terms of determination and derivation, in terms of horizontal fields establishing one another's boundaries and a vertical evolution, or derivation in terms of evolution. The vertical/horizontal distinction is immediately a rough one, one surpassed and complicated in topological and geometrical mathematics.[49] The spatial articulation of Schelling's epistemology, being one of extensity, of the real–ideal relation becoming one of vertical (evolutionary) and horizontal (recapitulative) exploration, allows for an embodied or enacted form of sceptical knowledge. That is, given that experience is treated as an essence in the positive philosophy, scepticism cannot undo the constraint of experience but questions its applicability outside of its local context (extended outwards).

The question of knowledge then becomes whether to focus on the *Stufenfolge* (the transcendental but naturalised) or fields (methodological cuts into nature that may be more real than their ideal construction). Since there is no ultimate ground nor ultimate end, the vertical model must determine the scope of the derivation taken for a particular investigation, that is, the question becomes how far back (or how speculative) should one go in cutting out a slice of the progression of a particular motion in nature?

Fields, on the other hand, are determinations of kinds of knowing (intuition, reason, speculation) as well as subfields of science (geology, chemistry, physics, etc.). These determinations disrupt or amplify derivations as cause and effect as being purely or absolutely real. If fields are a part of nature, the endless question becomes whether or not the fields of the sciences, to take one example, necessarily correspond to real patterns in nature, that is, does the field known as chemistry point to a set of potencies that is not absorbed or superseded over time? Or, in other words, at what point does the success of a particular field of inquiry imply the existence of a field of being (of a potency), as opposed to that being merely ideal or merely a methodological distinction? Whereas the transcendental pays attention to the motion away from the speculative excess or *ek-statsis* of an augmentation and its potential consequences, fields presume that each augmentation, each creation of a new field, may necessitate a new domain of knowledge, a new method in order to even perceive, let alone measure, the consequences of this potentially new field.

To return to the theme of extensity mentioned above, observing the relation between mind and world (between knowing and being) in terms of extensity, in terms of fields, reveals that creation does not add to an existing world *ex nihilo* but expands the boundary of the known world outwards. In paying attention to fields, Schelling is hypersensitive to the material context of what might be considered otherwise merely ideal creation.

Two immediate concerns and temptations emerge – does the vertical–horizontal reading map directly on to the negative–positive distinction and, furthermore, does it map on to a temporal versus spatial split (reading the vertical *Stufenfolge* as temporal and the horizontal fields as spatial)? These binaries would immediately seem not to match, as the negative and the positive philosophies engage in both spatial and temporal characteristics – the negative potentially being associated with Schelling's own *Naturphilosophie* wherein temporal and spatial characteristics are explored, and the positive philosophy referred to as historical by Schelling. By focusing on a spatial and navigational reading of Schelling's thought generally, and specifically in reference to the positive and negative split, I hope to clarify the relation between mind and world or, in Schelling's terms more specifically, reason and experience.

Rationalising unicorns: facts and intuition

Following the previous section, if Schelling sees intuition as coupled with determination, then a possible means of distinguishing fields from one another arises. This view of determination, as well as the passage between determinations, can be attempted from a different view of the transcendental – that of the irreducible particularity of certain objects or facts. Or, put another way, certain conditions of perception become central facts to any adequate explanation of experience. Numerous commentators on Schelling have remarked on his fascination with the emergence of particular objects following the Leibnizian question of 'Why is there something rather than nothing?'

Given the previous sections regarding Schelling's constructivism and the admixture of the real and the ideal, it would be tempting to suggest that ideation is the same kind of creation as that which happens before, or without, human intervention. This would place Schelling against various forms of naturalism and closer to various forms of ontological liberalism. One of the more common examples or figures of ontological liberalism is that of the unicorn – that is, what does it mean to say that they do or do not exist? In the *Further Presentations* Schelling utilises a similar example, that of the gold mountain. Just as the rainbow is a test case for physical theories of emergence as they obtain or fail to obtain on different explanations, the unicorn is a test case for the relation between facthood and existence.

Markus Gabriel, in his book *Transcendental Ontology*, addresses this relation by bringing reason and experience closer together under the rubric of sense and specifically in terms of what he calls fields of sense. In his later work, and in numerous lectures, Gabriel emphasises that fictional objects such as unicorns exist, but that meta-conceptual objects, such as 'the world', do not. He makes this argument by extrapolating from a particular view of Schellingian determination.

While Schelling's 'knowledge is a lamp that only points forward' sounds fairly idealist, it can be tempered by the statement that nature always remains a book closed in darkness. This darkness is seen productively most notably in Schelling's concept of *Das Unvordenkliche*. Gabriel, against any naturalistic reading of Schelling, has associated the unprethinkable with the very notion of logical space, by claiming that it is the unprethinkable that gives itself as the source of ongoing thought as such. Gabriel thus reads the relation between reason and existence in Schelling in terms of the relation between facthood and sense. The upshot of examining the reason/existence (or thought/world) relation in terms of facts and sense is that it implicitly and explicitly shows the links between the concerns of analytic thought and those of German Idealism or post-Kantian thought more generally. Gabriel argues that everyday use of language points to certain cognitive biases that he sees as central to an outmoded and metaphysical view of the world, namely, in the very concept of world itself. Gabriel argues that the notion of totality, whether described as world or universe, is one that is simply the result of long-standing fears of uncertainty, that behind much of our everyday thinking is the assumption that there is a maximally big object that contains everything.

Rather than making a direct appeal to Cantorian set theory in terms of asserting the impossibility of a set of all sets, following Alain Badiou or Quentin Meillassoux via Cantor, Gabriel argues along similar lines that a thoroughgoing physicalist approach to the universe, or to the world, cannot account for the existence of facts. Facts have an accretative function since for every fact there is the fact of that fact *ad infinitum*. This errancy of logic, Gabriel argues, makes it impossible for there to be a maximally 'big thing' or, viewed in terms of factiality, there cannot be a list of all lists because the most recent list would itself have to be included on a new list.[50]

While not always direct in his references, Gabriel's argument that the world does not exist but that unicorns do is based on the fact that the latter have identifiable contexts that verify certain qualities and aspects of unicorns, whereas the world, having no context but its own, cannot exist. Gabriel argues that instead of totalities we should utilise what he calls fields of sense or *Sinnesfelder*. Thus, for Gabriel, sense is simply the organising (non-factual) power of facts. Hence there can be no world, but there can be fictional entities (as long as they occupy their proper field).

While Gabriel gives a convincing account of the history and current use of German Idealism as that which is best suited to bridge the gap between analytic and continental thought, I find his articulation of fields of sense somewhat unclear other than as a vague form of ontological liberalism in which context itself is ontologised. As Gabriel writes: 'Being is nothing other than a side effect of the transfinite, nontotalizable plurality of fields of sense.'[51] For Gabriel, existence is determined not by real objecthood but by anything appearing in a field of sense, as a mode of presentation most generally.

Relating back to our first section, however, one can see that Gabriel is promoting a weak ontology that, as has come to be expected, poses no epistemological apparatus as to the appeal, for instance, to facthood. Gabriel states that there are facts following a logic of factiality, that is, the self-grounding postulate that facts are stable, that the fact that there are facts is more than a fact. Whereas Meillassoux admits the groundlessness of the regime of facthood as such, Gabriel does not. Gabriel takes it as a given that facts are, that they are as ontologically certain as things we can physically manipulate. He argues that facticity is rooted in sense and that sense need not belong only to subjects. Gabriel takes Frege's full-blooded notion of sense and reduces it to the barest notion possible.

Given Schelling's heterogeneous monism as defined by Paul Franks, as well as Iain Hamilton Grant's reading of idealism as asserting not the triumph of ideas over 'the real world' but exploring the reality of the idea, this seems to fit. Gabriel refers to his own thought as an objective idealism that allows for internal realism (in the sense that the reality or coherence of facthood holds for the sake of reference), yet, at the same time, he argues that facts as facts with the most cosmological meaning – that is, having the widest concept of facthood (such as that a star in a galaxy far away has exploded) – require knowing very little about the object's constitution. In contrast, he states that a subjective mental state requires more specific knowledge about mental states in order to ground its particular context.

Gabriel appears to be following largely in Heidegger's footsteps, given his emphasis on both world and fact and that ontology for him is tied to meaning in a given domain. In Heidegger's text on *The Essence of Human Freedom*, he emphasises the importance of distinguishing fact and factuality.[52] However, unlike Gabriel and like Châtelet, Heidegger does emphasise the naturalistically perspectival aspect of Schelling's *Naturphilosophie* via his incorporation of Kant's notion of world-view into the sciences,[53] stressing furthermore that Kant's discussion of perspectives is taken up but altered by the German Idealists, in that they focus on constructing systematic perspectives alongside being as opposed to finding those structures as *a priori* epistemological.[54]

Against the scientific-synthetic approach, Gabriel argues that ontology, in his sense of it, relies upon and also indexes a transcendental logic. The motor of this logic, as we touched upon in the first chapter, is Schelling's notion of the unprethinkable – that concept that determines that there is always more to be predicated, that there is always another antecedent to be discovered and a consequent to be found or produced. The brilliance behind Schelling's unprethinkable is that it deploys the function of a meta-rule (as Gabriel names the field of sense of all fields, that is, the maximally biggest thing) but is constitutively underdetermined. Thus, it functions as a necessary logical structure but one that is defined so as to make sense as the basic structure of a non-closed world, or an open set of the sensible.

My disagreement with Gabriel's reading is that while anti-Kantian readings of Schelling would usually overemphasise derivation (the naturalist thrust of Schelling's work), Gabriel overemphasises the constructed nature of determination, of determination being only ideal (yet this is called a realism). This is why Gabriel can claim that unicorns exist while the world does not. In essence, he overemphasises determination by putting too much stock in the ungroundedness of things produced being ungrounded because of the lack of all derivation, a lack stabilised, in his view, by fields of sense (his name for the distribution or web of determination).

Given Gabriel's focus however, it is odd that he, like many other contemporary readers of Schelling, sets aside the question of intuition even when he focuses on knowledge and methodologies of knowledge acquisition. In many works on Schelling, intuition is erased or, more egregiously perhaps, equated with Schelling's method as such (as Eckhart Förster attempts in *The Twenty-Five Years of Philosophy*). Gabriel's text is practically devoid of any discussion of Schelling's intellectual intuition whatsoever, which, given his emphasis on how sense and facthood interact to make claims, appears particularly strange. While neglecting one Schellingian concept among many is no crime, it is particularly interesting that Gabriel's text, which focuses primarily on knowledge claims, could make such an omission. It will be helpful to outline a typical view of Schelling's notion of intuition as put forward by Förster.

For Förster, in his *Naturphilosophie* Schelling errs by mistakenly applying a Fichtean form of intellectual intuition to nature. From this Förster argues that Schelling's observations of nature merely function to prove the power of intellectual intuition. Furthermore, Förster argues that Schelling's notion of intuition, as well as that of identity, are dead or inert, in that he claims that Schelling is attempting to add activity to nature via Fichteanism. And yet Förster claims that the observational key of productive intuition, that the intuiting and the intuited are the same, cannot be the case for nature.[55] But he gives no justification for why this is so, as if it is self-evident – but how is this possible?

Förster detours through the question of inhibition and Kant's theory of matter as an influence on Schelling's *Naturphilosophie* before returning to the issue of intuition as a method. He repeats that Schelling's notion of intuition is taken from Fichte and crudely inserted into the *Naturphilosophie*, and that Eschenmayer had raised a similar objection to this transplantation.[56] Yet even though Förster analyses Schelling's response to Eschenmayer, he still claims that Schelling's method 'is wholly insufficient' because the method of cognition must be the same for nature and the I.[57]

Förster writes:

> [Schelling] is fundamentally mistaken when he infers that the method of cognition must be the same for both nature and the I, namely intellectual intuition, for he has clearly failed to learn the lesson of what I referred to above as Fichte's central insight: that 'I am' and 'it is' express two wholly distinct modes of being.[58]

In so doing, Förster is reading Schelling like a Fichtean in assuming that the kind of activity at ground must be a form of cognition, whereas, for Schelling, cognition is a form of this activity, a form that intellectual intuition, along with other kinds of thinking, enacts but as thought. Thought is a form of a more primordial activity and, at the same time, it is the privileged form of human access to that primordial activity. Intuition, as opposed to reflection, speculation or other forms of cognition, is spatially immediate and not non-conceptually immediate, since, for Schelling, reason is always accompanied by experience; there is no mystical connection, but only different articulations of conceptual space. To ignore the spatial aspect of intuition is also to assume a crude notion of synthesis or construction in relation to idealism. So, whereas Förster follows a traditional assumption that intuition is a 'merely romantic' category, thinkers such as Heidegger in his text on Schelling rightly dismiss this naïve assumption. Heidegger notes that Schelling's intuition, as an attempt at systematic or absolute knowing, is merely a knowledge that recognises the original, if obscure, unity between knower and the known.[59]

The evidence pointing to intuition's complexity is clear enough in Schelling's own texts. In the *Ideas* Schelling puts forward the hypothesis that unity only exists for thought, or for the thinking being,[60] but that intuition suggests absolute simultaneity of nature and mind.[61] This might suggest that unity is only intellectual, but the intellectual capacities cannot be separated from nature. As Schelling also makes clear in 'On the True Concept', this does not mean that mind merely generates entities or forces, but that mind and nature realise one another. This is further explained in the *System of Transcendental Idealism* where intuition is a limitation, whereas the self is a localisation of the real and the ideal as limiting one another.[62] As has been addressed already, separated things are ideal determinations, but the ideality of these determinations cannot be known to be merely in the mind since the mind is a part of the world, and hence, the quality of the thing is as real though its location and potential consequences may be limited. Intuition's simultaneity is more structural than temporal; intuition is merely a local instance at the site of an attempt at individuation for the sake of navigation, for navigating between determinations. Intuition, to point back to Batterman, is inter-theoretic.

As Bruce Matthews puts it, Schelling's progressive method, as a combination of a transcendental method and an abductive method, attempts to grasp the unconditioned in terms of combining the sensual and the intellectual in treating both as ground or essence to construct outwards, or, again as Matthews puts it, construction is the human imagining of natural powers.[63] Formally, the question is simply how to incorporate, yet maintain methodologically, the distinction between the particular thinking subject and the nature in which it is embedded, and that it thinks, from its particular location. While I cannot in the space allotted fully elaborate each of these views, what I wish to pursue is the interesting fact that they generally approach the avenues they do only by rejecting the obvious place to go in order to combat Hegel's theory of representation: Schelling's use of intellectual intuition.

Schelling's notion of intuition, I believe, has been largely misunderstood, taken as fundamentally misguided and succumbing to Kant's critique of it in the *Critique of Pure Reason*. However, given Schelling's reading of Kant, I believe that the former's notion of intuition cannot be read as completely compatible with that of the latter's critique.

One of Schelling's later statements on intuition is made in relation to Hegel and is one of the strongest portrayals of the capacity. In *On the History of Modern Philosophy* Schelling lays out how he came to his own formulation of intellectual intuition. He notes that the concept moved from Kant's typically cautious definition to Fichte's elaboration. For Fichte, according to Schelling, intellectual intuition was the fact of the I's immediacy. Schelling argues that, against his former master, he wished to assert the immediacy of the content of the subject-object over and above the immediacy of content in the Fichtean 'I am'.[64] Schelling writes in summary:

> This first basis, this true *prima materia* of all thought, cannot, therefore, be what is really thought, not be what is thought in the sense that the single formation is. When thought is concerned with the determination of this matter, it does not think about this substrate (*Unterlage*) itself, but rather only of the determination of the concept which it puts into it – (sculptor—clay) – it is, therefore, what is not really thought in thinking. A thinking which does not think (*ein nicht denkendes Denken*) will, though, not be far from an intuiting thinking, and, as such, a thinking which has an intellectual intuition as its ground, goes through the whole of this philosophy, as it does through geometry, in which the external intuition of the figure which is drawn on the blackboard or where-ever is always only the bearer of an inner and spiritual intuition. This, then, is said in relation to a philosophy without intuition.[65]

While for Hegel, according to Schelling, it would seem that intuition is completely allergic to anything approaching rational, or even systematic, thought (and therefore is what Kant critiques), Schelling also faults Kant for limiting thought's outer limits. So while one could abandon intuition as a flawed but early attempt on Schelling's part to break through such limitations, for the late Schelling intuition is the fact and embodiment of thought and nature's coexistence. Intuition, as a means of conceptual and constructive navigation, is not mere idealistic fancy, but the vagueness of being in a nature that we can manipulate but not fully understand. In its final rendition, Schelling opposes intuition to Hegel's emphasis on logic, particularly on logic being that which is, and that which ends, once nature starts.[66] Intuition, then, is an important category, as it toes the line between merely accepting a common-sense view of the world and admitting that philosophy's role is to reduce or decompose common sense into simpler, and also potentially deeper, reservoirs. One such instance of this is how Schelling argues that teleology, although a naturalised one, is no less inscrutable than the mechanic causality that Kant favoured.[67] Or, as Joshua Mendelsohn has pointed out, while Kant abjures teleology because it threatens normativity, Schelling sees teleology as an objective part of the world.[68]

To return to the epistemological axes with which we started, intuition can be said to be the necessary passage between the horizontal fields (immanent condition) and the vertical evolutionary *Stufenfolge* (transcendental condition). Or, even the most speculative imagined thought necessarily crosses from one axis to the other in terms of relating capacities to consequences (whether potential or actual). Furthermore, intuition, from the located position of the thinker steeped in experience, is the means by which one can determine the difference between the positive and negative philosophies, between those forms of thinking that work alongside experience and those that abstract away from it.

In the *Grounding* Schelling argues that the positive philosophy is the application of the transcendental within an immanent context.[69] Where the *Naturphilosophie* attempted to naturalise the transcendental, to explore the transcendental as an augmenting motion of natural processes later articulated into fields, in the positive philosophy the transcendental, or act of transcendence, is simply an augmentation relative to a location.

Thus, in taking Kant's critique to heart, Schelling makes the transcendent *of this world*, thereby getting around Kant's prohibition of it as being above, or out of, experience. Experience exceeds the immediate reach of reason, not because it is absolutely separate from it, but rather because of the manner by which reason functions in relation to experience. Experience transcends reason simply because reason cannot 'catch up' to experience as movement in the world. Whereas the transcendental method attempts to reconstruct derivation either by naturalising it or localising it, intuition functions via immediacy, not in the manner which Kant prohibits, but via the processes of knowing that follow from continuous relations between our position as knowing being limited, and being unknowingly connected to, that which we are attempting to understand. Or, put otherwise, whereas the transcendental method attempts to trace the paths of derivation, intuition measures the local co-determinations of subject-objects in an immediate context.

To put this in navigational terms, the transcendental method tracks derivation, moving from the general to the specific in that it reduces a chain of derivations to fuel an instance of action. Intuition, on the other hand, starts from the immediate, or local, and expands it outwards. Once again it is worth returning to the work of Gilles Châtelet as he puts an emphasis on intuition and *Naturphilosophie* in relation to the gestural. As intuition can be said to spatially map the difference between determination as a web and derivation as a chain, Châtelet's diagrammatic approach to intuition and *Naturphilosophie* views potentiation (or the naturalised transcendental) as an unfolding and depotentiation (or the reductive notion of immanence) as a folding.

Gestural scars: Gilles Châtelet and intuitive anchoring

In his remarkable book *Figuring Space* Gilles Châtelet writes:

> Any detailed inspection of a landscape or of a domain of knowledge presupposes a survey, and the horizon is what endows caution with some style. If this survey were reduced merely to prescribing a 'horizontal' reading and a 'vertical' reading, it would lead only to a fixed stratification. The survey induces an axis of distribution of the mobilities that reactivate knowledge: the strata become a field, whose exploration implies a norm of virtual grasp of the statements. This norm never offers itself up placidly for analysis and always evades anyone who would seek it 'on the near or far side' of the horizon that controls it. Its withdrawal is always painful and is paid for by a 'metaphorical' dislocation of the field or by its reduction to significant networks subordinated to a code. The implicit pressure of the horizon is like the scar of a gesture . . .[70]

In *Figuring Space* Châtelet takes up Schelling's focus on the point of indifference as itself the producer of two symmetries[71] – an argument that Schelling uses to situate himself between Spinoza and Leibniz in his *Investigations*. Schelling's intellectual intuition is what makes possible, and in turn is made possible by (though on a different scale), the description of the universe as polarities that can only be adequately described in the diagrammatic register. Where Schelling's concept of the *Potenz* is often dismissed (such as by Beach and Vaughn) as Spinozistic power and nothing more, Châtelet recognises that it speaks to an original tension of fields in Schelling that exponentially produce, and spin out of control, producing more and more stages of being (*Stufenfolge*). Or, put another way, the arithmetic of qualities gives rise to a different order of quantity. This is why, just as identity and subsequently powers must be plural, powers add qualities in such a way that not only are magnitudes multiplied, but the metric of reading such multiplication, as addition of quality, is the production of the ideality of nature.[72]

In examining Châtelet's reading of Schelling, I hope to provide a transition from intuition as a localising function between facts and sense, to intuition as providing a springboard for action in the form of a proto-pragmatism, or positive philosophy, to be addressed in the following chapter.

What are these symmetries exactly? The problem is that fields, viewed one at a time, obscure the fields beneath them, whereas viewing nature as derivation minimises the fields' relation to each other and de-spatialises the *Potenz* (making them appear as nothing but generation over time). Châtelet's emphasis on both gesture and horizon can be used to 'tilt' the *Stufenfolge* (bisected all along the way with fields) over, to deform it slightly into a horizon. As the above quote emphasises, the style of the gesture, the particular form of motion *in the individual*, is what allows for the *Naturphilosophen* in the field to address the horizon through a navigational assertion as that which is ontological and epistemological in equal measure.

The symmetries produced or made possible by the observer as the blank X in the field in relation to the horizon are ones of depotentiation and potentiation. In the case of depotentiation, the synthesis of the *Stufenfolge* and the repetition of fields become the horizon from which the thinker reduces one aspect to a singular ground to then re-expand or construct a new horizon from that one point or ground *as if this were the origin of the world as such*. Potentiation, on the other hand, treats the hybrid of derivation and determination as the foreground, thereby fashioning a speculative vanishing point *as if this point were the goal of nature*.

Following Châtelet, norms function as a reactive gesture to figure out this oscillation between viewing the horizon as such and viewing it as a vertical progression, or as a horizontal (yet flattened) plane. The indifference point, taken as an observation post, functions as a hinge, which is not merely a hinge between material elements, but also *produces* an orientation.[73] Furthermore, Châtelet notices in Schelling's *Naturphilosophie* an emphasis on the productive or constructive function of intuition that not only furthers epistemological endeavours, but also expands nature as we know it.

Châtelet writes: 'We are touching here on the tender spot of the philosophy of nature: that of the intuition of the degrees of articulation, those where Being overhangs, where quantitative difference and "canonical" choices of paramatrege vanish.'[74] Intuition allows the philosopher-scientist to occupy a space by which one can occupy a motion that is not merely of the self. Intuition creates maximal ambiguity, not as a kind of debilitating fog, but in that it frees the observer for creating between things. In this regard, intuition functions as potentiation, as it creates space as space free of all constraints, where construction occurs only according to thought, but this thought is itself of the same kind as the natural forces that produce it.[75]

Relating back to Chapter 3, the exponent as a potentiation of a number is the power, whereas the number is the indifference point, the particular individuation thus either potentiated or depotentiated.[76]

This leap of intuition, a leap that Schelling addresses in the *Erlangen* lectures, sets him apart from either simply following exhaustive deduction or abstraction from common features. Châtelet's understanding of Schelling's notion of intuition comes largely from the *Bruno*. The *Bruno*, as an expansion of the Identity philosophy, attempts to articulate the relation between the potencies as the kinds of thinking of which humans are capable.[77] Furthermore, and to return to our methodological axes, the point of indifference is where the observer locates her or himself and intuits from. This pivot complicates the two methods which, again following Grant, are not reducible to one another.[78] Schelling is neither endorsing deduction or induction but transcendental naturalism and material abduction.

Châtelet masterfully demonstrates how Schelling, following Kant's discussion of negative magnitudes, allows for thought to escape mad and endless deduction,[79] for separation of fields and transcendental generation to set up stakes – to trace consequences not merely real or merely ideal.[80] Thought does not merely produce things, nor is thought produced by things alone, but, again, tracing Schelling's Fichtean roots points to an activity in which thought and nature are of a singular kind.

Châtelet goes to great pains to attempt to demonstrate how the stake, how the particular inhabiting of an indifference point, is not merely arbitrary – that is, it is not a division of two methodological processes within the ideal only, but it has stakes *for nature*. Châtelet attempts to do this by discussing the shift from zero as merely a point (whether merely ideal or material/real as in Lorenz Oken's thought) to where the zero becomes a loop of forces. Châtelet discusses the zero as the heart of the kinematic scale where it is not merely the tipping point of a physical scale, but the point from which negative and positive forces encircle each other, and move away from one another in relation to the zero. Intuition functions as the identification of difference and indifference, as the point from where two different dimensions (such as length or width mentioned above in relation to electromagnetism) emerge.[81]

Following the famous electrical experiments of Volta, Châtelet describes how Schelling's zero becomes a loop. He writes: 'A new around has been grasped diagrammatically in nature and thought and we do indeed rediscover the creative ambiguity of the indifference centre: disrupt a unity to reach the next plateau of Being.'[82] The indifference point, the sprout of intuition,[83] shows how articulation strikes out in the progress of becoming in the stream of becoming. Intuition functions as a form of individuation that is simultaneously a point of observation.[84]

Intuition, as Châtelet understands it, and as Schelling reads it in relation to Kant, is a form of thinking that functions as a non-purposive form of knowledge, or at least, as Förster puts it, a form of knowledge that does not require the assumption of purposiveness.[85] Thus Schelling's position appears quite close and quite far from Kant's, following the navigational mode outlined in Chapter 2. The motive or motile zero also distinguishes Schelling from Oken. Whereas Oken's zero was substantively additive, Schelling's zero is a trace or gesture composed of motion and is thus augmentatively additive. Thus Oken's number is always about the repetition of a substance however general, whereas, for Schelling, material is always secondary to the act of construction, which is itself immaterial and is always a self-augmentation without substance.

Intuition is the introduction of a disturbance that is simultaneously a vantage point and a hinge. The inscribing of this disturbance is never an arresting of becoming, nor the mark of being, but a gesture or inscription of the being of becoming and the becoming of being in tandem. In the case of the zero, the mathematical mark is a knot, or tying of the stream of becoming; it is a gesture or instance of being that, nevertheless, stays in motion. Potentiation and depotentiation occur as either the untying of this knot, or testing its extensity through the application of experiment, which can be represented in the form of the exponent. The gesture or intuition is the transit between these stages that leaves a trace of its action while attempting to emphasise not the means of its path, but the potential impacts of how it has already moved. This is the strange kind of navigation present in Schelling's theory of knowledge: that of a self-inhibiting exploration that speculates about the spaces it may find.

As I will aim to show in the next and final chapter, Schelling's navigational mode differs from Kant's not only with regard to the emphasis on intuition, but also in terms of Schelling's commitment to naturalism, but a form of naturalism different from the more common forms adopted by contemporary philosophy.

Notes

1. Schelling, *System of Transcendental Idealism*, 18.
2. One could tenuously argue that while negative philosophy works ascendentally and positive philosophy descendentally, as Schelling puts it, *Naturphilosophie* is negative philosophy properly made dynamic, whereas transcendental philosophy is positive philosophy properly restrained. See Schelling, *The Grounding of Positive Philosophy*, 196.
3. Schelling, *First Outline*, 53–4.

4. David Bell, 'Transcendental Arguments and Non-Naturalistic Anti-Realism', in *Transcendental Arguments: Problems and Prospects*, ed. Robert Stern (Oxford: Oxford University Press, 2000), 198.

5. The term liberal naturalism is used by several thinkers who accept the claims of scientific naturalism but believe that such a form cannot account for the primacy of rational decision making. While Markus Gabriel has argued that the transcendentalism of German Idealism opposes it to liberal naturalism (which Gabriel aligns with figures such as McDowell), Michael Blamuer has argued that Schelling in fact embodies perfectly the liberal naturalism of figures such as Thomas Nagel.

6. Most famously, this issue is connected to Schelling's letter to Hegel in which he states that Kant has provided the results for thought but that the premises are still missing. This idea is also central to Eckhart Förster's *The Twenty-Five Years of Philosophy: A Systematic Reconstruction*, trans. Brady Bowman (Cambridge, MA: Harvard University Press, 2012).

7. Daniel Breazeale, 'Kantian Questions/Fichtean Answers', in *The Transcendental Turn*, ed. Sebastian Gardner (Oxford: Oxford University Press, 2015), 83–4.

8. Fichte, *The Science of Knowing*, 37.

9. To wax poetic, we could view Schelling's *Stufenfolge* as simultaneously the wreckage heap of Walter Benjamin's angel of history, and the medieval Great Chain of Being.

10. F. W. J. von Schelling, 'Exhibition of the Process of Nature', trans. Iain Hamilton Grant (unpublished manuscript, 2013).

11. Schelling, *First Outline*, 204.

12. I must thank Tilottama Rajan for pointing out the strange non-role of the human in the *First Outline*.

13. I am aligning determination with a horizontal model of knowledge in that it requires a depotentiation of the human's place, as in the vertical view, thereby flattening all kinds of beings on one horizon.

14. Schelling, *First Outline*, 226.

15. Frederick A. Mortensen, 'The Fate of Finitude: Schelling and the Question of the World', PhD thesis, University of Copenhagen, 2012, 108.

16. Gabriel, *Transcendental Ontology*, 134.

17. I would define ontology as being about what exists (and thus being a discourse about objects or things), whereas metaphysics is about the overall structure of reality or of the cosmos.

18. While this is a broad claim, I see very few exceptions in the continental tradition. Besides Whitehead, Merleau-Ponty and scattered adventures into ethology in rather rare moments in hermeneutics and phenomenology, I do not see nature as a productive constraint existing for philosophy.

19. Schelling, *Philosophical Investigations*, 26.

20. As is hopefully evident from Chapter 3, my use of diagram follows Châtelet. For Châtelet, the diagram is the solidification of the gesture which, in turn, is the first act of intuition.

21. Williams, *Origins of Field Theory*, viii.

22. Ibid., 36.

23. Iain Hamilton Grant discusses this aspect of Schelling's work, most notably in 'Does Nature Stay What It Is?', in *The Speculative Turn: Continental Materialism and Realism*, ed. L. Bryant, G. Harman and N. Srnicek (Melbourne: Re:Press, 2010), 66–83, and 'Movements of the World'.

24. Williams, *Origins of Field Theory*, 69.

25. Ibid., 114.
26. Gabriel, *Transcendental Ontology*, 73.
27. Williams, *Origins of Field Theory*, 121–2.
28. Ibid., 129–31.
29. Similarly, Joseph Esposito argues that Schelling's *Naturphilosophie* should be viewed as a precursor to general systems theory. See Joseph Esposito, *Schelling's Idealism and Philosophy of Nature* (Lewisburg, PA: Bucknell University Press, 1977), 10.
30. Châtelet, *Figuring Space*, 162.
31. Ibid., 166.
32. Ibid., 163.
33. Ibid., 164.
34. See F. W. J. von Schelling, 'On Faraday's Most Recent Discovery: Lecture to an Open Sitting of the [*Bayerische*] *Akademie* [*des Wissenschaften*] on May 28, 1832', trans. Iain Hamilton Grant (unpublished manuscript, 2014).
35. This problem is what Schelling viewed as 'the riddle of the world' according to Esposito, *Schelling's Idealism*, 42–3.
36. Ibid., 137.
37. Ibid., 98.
38. Gilles Châtelet, 'Interlacing the Singularity, the Diagram, and the Metaphor', ed. Charles Alunni, in *Virtual Mathematics: The Logic of Difference*, ed. Simon Duffy (Bolton: Clinamen Press, 2006), 43.
39. Esposito argues that Schelling's relation to Kant centres on the conceptual boundaries between philosophy and science, namely that the critical enterprise makes a proper relation between them impossible. Esposito, *Schelling's Idealism*, 55.
40. Kant, *The Critique of Pure Reason*, 84.
41. Batterman, *Devil in the Details*, 77.
42. Reza Negarestani, 'Rainbows and Rationalism' (unpublished manuscript, 2013), 6.
43. This is also expertly explained in pseudo-pragmatist terms by the contemporary philosopher Mark Wilson in his monumental work *Wandering Significance: An Essay on Conceptual Behavior* (Oxford: Clarendon Press, 2006).
44. Batterman, *Devil in the Details*, 37.
45. Ibid., 38–40.
46. Ibid., 43.
47. Bruce Matthews deserves mention for providing one of the more extensive analyses of Kant's relation to Schelling in *Schelling's Organic Form of Philosophy*.
48. Schelling, *The Grounding of Positive Philosophy*, xxxx.
49. As was demonstrated in Chapter 3, Schelling's interest in geometry and the emerging algebra of his time both inspires and limits his ability to spatialise his concepts.
50. Whereas for Fichte, facticity referred to the unquestionability of the status of a fact, for Meillassoux facticity refers to the impossibility of determining an ultimate ground for anything.
51. Gabriel, *Transcendental Ontology*, viii.
52. Martin Heidegger, *Schelling's Treatise on the Essence Human Freedom* (Athens, OH: Ohio University Press, 1985), 15.
53. Ibid., 18.
54. Ibid., 37–8.
55. Förster, *The Twenty-Five Years of Philosophy*, 238–9.
56. Ibid., 247.
57. Ibid., 249.

58. Ibid., 249.
59. Heidegger, *Schelling's Treatise*, 47–8.
60. Schelling, *Ideas for a Philosophy of Nature*, 31.
61. Ibid., 36.
62. Schelling, *System of Transcendental Idealism*, 40.
63. Matthews, *Schelling's Organic Form*, 149, 197.
64. Schelling, *On the History of Modern Philosophy*, 150.
65. Ibid., 152–3.
66. Ibid., 153–4.
67. Esposito, *Schelling's Idealism*, 76.
68. Joshua Mendelsohn, 'Teleology and the Scientific Image in Schelling's Philosophy of Nature' (unpublished manuscript), 8.
69. Schelling, *The Grounding of Positive Philosophy*, 205–6.
70. Châtelet, *Figuring Space*, 54.
71. Ibid., 75–6.
72. See Grant, *Philosophies of Nature*, 169.
73. Châtelet, *Figuring Space*, 75.
74. Ibid., 76.
75. Ibid., 77.
76. Ibid., 89.
77. Schelling, *Bruno*, 100 n. 30.
78. Iain Hamilton Grant, 'The Eternal and Necessary Bond between Philosophy and Physics: A Repetition of the Difference between the Fichtean and Schellingian Forms of Philosophy', *Angelaki: Journal of the Theoretical Humanities*, 10.1 (2005): 53.
79. This is how Brady Bowman describes Schelling's method as opposed to Hegel's sober dialectics in *Hegel and the Metaphysics of Absolute Negativity* (Cambridge: Cambridge University Press, 2013), 227.
80. Châtelet, *Figuring Space*, 81.
81. Ibid., 90, 94.
82. Ibid., 154.
83. Ibid., 85.
84. Ibid., 94.
85. Ibid., 144.

Chapter 6

Speculative Pragmatism: Navigating the *Richtungen* of Nature and Thought

In this concluding chapter I demonstrate how Schelling's emphasis on motion and space, coupled with his particular mode of philosophical speculation, leads to a form of proto-pragmatism. I work out this pragmatism via Schelling's 1821 *Erlangen* lecture ('On the Nature of Philosophy as a Science') by moving through the connections between the great American pragmatist C. S. Peirce and Schelling. I then compare Schelling's proto-pragmatism with the analytic thinkers who have taken German Idealism, in conjunction with the pragmatic legacy of Peirce as well as Sellars, as implying a philosophy that emphasises normativity at the cost of nature, namely McDowell and Brandom (referred to as left Sellarsians or Pittsburgh Hegelians). I close by appealing to the contemporary pragmatist Mark Wilson, who synthesises and operates between the scientific considerations of Peirce and the communicative and practical pragmatism of the Pittsburgh Hegelians. Wilson, through a focus on classical concepts in the physical sciences, demonstrates the limitations of a normative approach to human thought. Specifically with regard to thought, Wilson attempts to argue for a navigational approach to cognition that steers clear of both the normativity of the Pittsburgh Hegelians (or left Sellarsians) as well as the more hard-nosed neuroscientific articulations of consciousness in the work of Daniel Dennett and Patricia and Paul Churchland (categorised as right Sellarsians); the former emphasise reason as *sui generis*, whereas the latter investigate the impact of the natural sciences arguably at the cost of normativity. Peirce, Sellars and, as I will argue, Schelling, all in their own ways, attempt to construct a philosophy where the division between the capacity to articulate particularly human concerns and the capacity to adequately describe and situate our place in the natural world does not make those two capacities incompatible endeavours.

Abducting intuition: Schelling and Peirce

> The heart of the dispute lies in this. The modern philosophers – one and all, unless Schelling be an exception – recognize but one mode of being, the being of an individual thing or fact, the being which consists in the object's crowding out a place for itself in the universe, so to speak, and reacting by brute force of fact, against all other things. I call that existence.[1]

> I carefully recorded my opposition to all philosophies which deny the reality of the Absolute, and asserted that 'the one intelligible theory of the universe is that of objective idealism, that matter is effete mind'. This is as much as to say that I am a Schellingian, of some stripe; so that, on the whole, I do not think Dr. Carus has made a very happy hit in likening me to Hume, to whose whole method and style of philosophizing I have always been perhaps too intensely averse. Yet, notwithstanding my present disclaimer, I have little doubt apriorians will continue to describe me as belonging to the sceptical school.[2]

> My views were probably influenced by Schelling – by all stages of Schelling, but especially *the Philosophie der Natur*. I consider Schelling as enormous, and one thing I admire about him is his freedom from the trammels of system, and his holding himself uncommitted to any previous utterance. In that, he is like a scientific man. If you were to call my philosophy Schellingism transformed in the light of modern physics, I should not take it hard.[3]

In Chapter 5, I demonstrated the epistemological space that Schelling attempts to construct and then navigate in order to re-establish the relation between the real and the ideal, as well as between the activities of determination and derivation. This entailed avoiding the Charybdis, on the one hand, of a factial and logic-based account of our production of knowledge, buttressed by the apparent self-sufficiency of sense (Gabriel) and, on the other hand, the Scylla of a physicalist, or hard-nosed naturalist position, where causal or teleological models of nature can explain all worldly capacities both human and non-human. Schelling attempts this navigation by accepting a naturalist position – but one that admits non-physical or process-based ontological (or perhaps more accurately meontological) powers into nature. Thus, Schelling attempts to avoid an ontologically liberal approach that grants equal being to all things, as well as an appeal to facthood as such in order to avoid negating an appropriate dose of epistemological scepticism. Furthermore, he dodges an over-reliance on becoming or meontology that reduces everything to mere emergence without worrying about positionality or methodology. In other words, Schelling does not allow becoming to replace epistemology as a negative constraint (position, or from where one thinks) or as a positive constraint (knowledge claims are strong because one has established a method).

The complex midway position that Schelling constructs, one that puts him in close proximity to C. S. Peirce, can be summarised in the following manner: there is a self-inhibiting creative structure where the realness of things is determined by the reach of their consequences, that is, realness is simultaneously its synthesis and the testing of its extensity by another agent. Realness is thus less about the matter or substratum upon which a thing or fact rests, but more about the measurable activity of a meta-stable individuation (a *Scheinprodukt*). Ideas are a peculiar part of nature that index inexistence, whereas objects tend towards, and index, existence. That is, the discourse of ideas is explicit about their tentative relation to any real-world things, whereas the discourse of objects is often backed up by another field of reference, whether physical or fictional.

In emphasising Schelling's proto-pragmatism here, I wish to argue that intellectual intuition, as it functions for Schelling, is an abstract form of Peircean abduction, or that Peircean abduction is Schellingian intuition put into disciplined practice. Both concepts represent their respective creator's attempts to find a third way between two extremes: realism-as-mechanism and idealism-as-overly speculative in Schelling's case, and crude empiricism and crude nominalism in Peirce's case.

A passage from Schelling's *System of a Philosophy as a Whole* (1804) captures the predicament nicely:

> Merely reflective humanity has no idea of an objective reason, of an Idea that as
> *such* is utterly real and objective; all reason is something subjective to them, as
> equally is everything ideal, and the idea itself has for them only the meaning of
> a subjectivity, so that they therefore know only two worlds, the one consisting
> of stone and rubble, the other of intuitions and the thinking thereupon.[4]

Schelling's notion of intellectual intuition has been criticised for falsely suggesting the possibility of immediate knowledge (this was Kant's central objection to the very notion of intellectual intuition). But, as I have attempted to show, the immediacy at stake does not suggest an immediacy in terms of intimate knowledge, but rather a faster, more crude form of knowledge in comparison to the slowness of reason in the wake of an immediate natural response of mentation-as-intuition. That is, intellectual intuition is Schelling's way of pointing out the slowness and locality of reason in relation to the kind of information indirectly gathered due to the continuity of reason and nature. Or, in other words, intellectual intuition is the name for the process by which we are capable of localising thought, that is, simply saying 'this thing is here' with the navigational self or observer-as-X being one of those determinations.

As a result, the capacity to determine whatness (or being) is inexorably tied to a thing's whereness, its location. Or, to say what something is requires asking where it is, since the ontological arises from location, insofar as the productivity of the thing is determined by, and determines in turn, its location in terms of origin and emergence. The whereness of intuition is, pointing back to the previous chapter, the question of transit between the negative philosophy of whatness and the positive philosophy of thatness.

If every individual thing is a production of the interaction of powers, as Schelling seems consistently to argue, then the questions of which powers produce a certain thing, and in what proportion they function, index the importance of location. A thing as a location in a nexus of powers is a failed containment or, as Schelling puts it in the *First Outline*, every thing recognised as a product of nature is a failure.[5] Powers produce things that are not strictly reducible to powers, nor are powers reducible to the products they produce; things can be viewed as trajectories of a stalled becoming, or as a mobile capture of powers or potencies. A thing is a mobile capture of those powers, a knot of particular potencies in nature, which is a consequence of them. As Schelling puts it, all definition is containment.[6]

Thus, the immediacy of intellectual intuition is an auto-coincidence of thinking and being, or of the transcendental method and the naturalistic method gaining shared traction on the world. Intuition is immediate because it is ideally determined to be spatio-temporally contained, or intuition functions as the extensity test of an object's roots and consequents. Thus determination-as-such suspends space-time to augment it, or, put otherwise, the isolation of a thing isolates that which is produced and continues to produce it as ground.

To say, as crude caricatures of idealism would have it, that determination is ideal because of its suspension of the not-merely ideal (the mixture of subject-object) is to erase the augmentative capacity of thought in the merely ideal as well as with regard to the non-thought that thought carries with it (the inexistent potentialities it bears). Or, as Schelling puts it in 'On the Nature of Philosophy as Science' (1821), while all ability is a form of knowledge, not all knowledge is necessarily ability.[7] Here we can investigate the reallocation of the ideal, given its determinative capacity being not merely ideal *per se*, but only in the inadequacy of its consequents to be materialised.

That thought purportedly floats above the world at the cost of the earth (as Kant's crude reading of Plato would have it) misses the thought composition of the very notion of the world. The purported motionlessness of the world is itself ideal, but a more real or existent ideal, whose apparent self-evidential status seems to grant it automatic materiality. Yet if nothing is what it is on its own (if nothing is self-standing), then claiming that the world is only material depotentiates the world without augmenting it. In other words, without feeding the notion of the world back into itself properly, such a claim determines the world by re-mobilising the immobilised, that is, by stretching or extending the isolated (or determined) thing *as if* it was the world. Or, as Schelling puts it, thought is a stretching as opposed to knowledge, which is a mirroring.[8]

Once one forgets the space-time suspension of a determination – the fact that determination depends on derivation – then all sense of materiality is lost as anything consequent – it becomes merely that which it is *for us*. But if the world was self-standing or self-determining, how exactly would it be contained? Schelling's notion of the world is consequent and thus any determination is an extainment (*Ausschließung*), an unfolding, but not of a predetermined One or wholeness, but of a self-augmenting non-One that adds its self to the entirety of its existence while being itself possibly inexistent (though no less real).[9]

Thus determination is both stronger and weaker than containment. Determination implies an exploratory model of knowledge, whereas reason attempts to locate the drawing of conclusions, or the self-aware activity of thought, outside of the problem of space-time. Schelling explicitly explores the tension between the exploratory and the navigational, or between systems of reason and the *asystaton* of coexistence.[10] In order to recognise this 'inner tension', the human 'must have already searched in every possible direction', or, as Schelling argues, systems come after not only an internal disarray in thought from individual practitioners, but their imperfect collectivisation.[11] Or, put otherwise, reason is the drawing of conclusions within an already stabilised space, whereas pure navigation, as wandering, would simply be exploring chaos. Systems are the vessels by which knowledge claims can explore the world without replacing the system of the world with the system of reason.

It is in this combination of meontological musings on the notion of individuation in relation to space via local experiences, and time in terms of the slowness of reflection, that Schelling's thought begins to appear in the form of a proto-pragmatism. The term 'pragmatic' should not here be taken as commonsensical in a naïve sense, but as a practical way of handling local existence given the complexities of space-time, the slowness of reflection, or whatever lurks behind the everyday use of concepts and the everyday consequences of actions. This brings us to Peirce and Peircean abduction.

Peirce's notion of abduction is generally situated between deduction and induction (while being 'closer' to the latter), and can be defined crudely as an educated guess, or the form of thought that produces hypotheses, or what functions as the logic of discovery. Despite its wide usage, one may be surprised to find that there is no single text of Peirce's that focuses on the concept specifically; its definitional traces have to be tracked across his infamously wide and rambling *oeuvre*.

K. T. Fann explicates how abduction is a synthetic form of amplifying inference. While induction is also amplifying and synthetic, deduction is explicative and analytic.[12] Peirce asserts that while deduction is secure, its security is at the cost of its creativity, and thus abduction inhabits the opposite end of the inferential spectrum.[13] Here the general character of Peirce's abduction should not seem alien to Schelling's thought. The creative and synthetic nature of abduction, of a risky form of creation, should appear similar to Schelling's notion of intellectual intuition. My hope is that the spatial qualification of Schelling's intuition given immediately above and in Chapter 5 should ease the strain between these contextually disparate concepts. Numerous authors have commented on Schelling's relationship to Peirce. Most notably, Joseph Esposito, Bruce Matthews, Jason Wirth and Tyler Tritten have compared the knowledge claims of both thinkers and arrived at various results.

Matthews emphasises Peirce's respect for Schelling's early attitude towards systematicity (reflected in our introduction under the title 'ablative systematicity') as well as an appreciation for Schelling's *Naturphilosophie*.[14] This appreciation is echoed by Esposito following the epigraphs above. Tritten, on the other hand, is more sceptical of Peirce's and Schelling's methodological closeness. In his *Beyond Presence* Tritten argues that Peirce's notion of abduction is too empirical for Schelling's taste, in that Peirce's model of hypothesis attempts to ground to the object of inquiry too quickly.[15] Furthermore, Tritten argues that Peirce's arbitrary guessing is too capricious for Schelling's model of freedom, since there is a kind of internal self-certainty which gives Schelling's investigative process more noetic, if not external, confidence.[16] As Tritten writes:

> Schelling does not arbitrarily posit a hypothesis among other possible ones but attempts to scientifically and objectively corroborate that for which subjective conviction already exists. Doubt and certainty are not theoretical but practical, and one does not test the practical by means of experimentation, just as one cannot afford to experiment and play with one's life but must always act with resolve. Abduction searches and hunts while for Schelling the hunting is over as he strives only after that having already seized him; one must only ask if a scientific path leading to the predetermined destination exists.[17]

Tritten's reading, in my view, overemphasises the epistemological function of revelation and grace at the cost of epistemological navigations, whether those navigations are of apparently external nature or are apparently internal mental episodes. In addition, being seized by powers or by objects as conglomerations of powers in the continuum of nature requires that one split oneself methodologically from the certainty of inner episodes of knowing in order to test that knowing. The certainty that Tritten highlights is thus by no means incompatible with abductive investigation. Schelling's notion of intuition treats the mind itself like an environment that abduction can navigate, but since our own epistemological and, in particular, reflective limitations require us to objectify our own thoughts, it is only by externalising ourselves that we abductively approach anything that we wish to investigate, even if that thing is our own certainty of investigation, that is, the activity of thought.[18]

Lastly, what many accounts of abduction and its relation to Schelling overlook, but what is clearly evident in the above epigraphs from Peirce, is the future-orientedness of abduction against what Peirce sees as crude nominalism. Peirce emphasises laws or universals not because he believes that these things can be definitively articulated for all time, but rather because he believes that pragmatic activity requires justification for its future or, in a spatial sense, possible non-local ramifications. Thus there must be something that guarantees future creation with and without us, and is necessary not in a metaphysical sense but in an explanatory sense. To use a simple example, the fact that stones fall when we drop them cannot be reduced to the pragmatic logic of 'because it works'. If this were the case, how would we augment or amplify our existing activities without being able to speculate as to their broader meaning outside that one particular activity? That is, how could we properly systematise our experience with nature if it were merely an accumulation of happenstance or an accretion of habits?

Given the emphasis on the local status of experience for thought in the *Erlangen* lectures and in *The Grounding of Positive Philosophy*, the immediacy of intuition is not that of a thinker being mentally 'attuned' with all of nature, but that of the continuity of nature allowing for the possibility of a local gesture or action to be more than a local account of synthesis. Examining the above epigraphs, it is no stretch on Peirce's thinking to argue that he is invested in the continuity of mind and nature, nor to affirm the importance of local wanderings or investigations to synthesise systems, however provisional they may be. It is in this sense that speculation and threats of idealistic vagueness orbiting intuition can be addressed, namely if they are tools in pragmatic engagement. This aspect of intuition, unlike abduction, is often ignored following a crude caricature of idealism, or of philosophy more generally. The idealist is portrayed as the armchair philosopher *par excellence* who philosophises so that she need not set out into the world. As Schelling puts it, to quote the *Erlangen* text yet again:

Those who dare set out to sea can certainly, due to storms or by their lack of skill, lose their way and be led astray, but those who never even leave port and whose entire endeavor, rather, consists in not leaving port and in preventing philosophy from ever beginning, by endless philosophizing about philosophy, those, of course, have no dangers to fear.[19]

But this is not merely to equate intuition and abduction. The reason for caution, I believe, is that of the core of pragmatism itself, that is, that navigations in the world inevitably alter our concepts, if those concepts were ever rooted in the world to begin with. Schelling is also taking aim at Kant's overly cautious schematism and his inability to accept challenges to the critical philosophy. Thus, it would be erroneous to claim that Peirce's abduction is only a repetition, or differently clothed form, of intuition. Abduction is the experimentally fuelled sceptical pragmatism that follows the locative function of intuition. Abduction functions as a formalised or ramified form of intuition. If intuition is the spatially immediate mental movement between methods, then abduction is this reading of intuition coextensive with experience. Experience, in the context of abduction, functions as 'experimental feedback', adding to the evolutionary paths of knowledge, which folds and unfolds the continuum through our concepts.

Less extravagantly, Peirce's abduction moves between deduction (or Schelling's naturalist derivation) and induction (Schelling's horizontal determination) as a progressive or evolutionary attempt at constructing a piecemeal net of conceptual reference that does not overdetermine its own internal composition, nor too stringently derive its derivations either into the past (as origin) or into the future (as a pre-thinkable human future). Thus the insuperability of thought and world does not entail that 'anything goes', but emphasises the necessity of experience in locating and contextualising reason. That is, because it *seems as if anything goes, we must be incredibly careful with our local activities.*

The speculative aspect of Peirce's pragmatism lies in his aforementioned anti-nominalism, against those who would claim that the facticity of things is more important than either their sensual or nomological (universal) ramifications. It is perhaps unsurprising that Peirce would be attracted to various forms of Objective Idealism as a third way of avoiding both speculative and anti-speculative excesses. We can ask then, to advance the experiment of Schelling and Peirce's proximity, if the sensual and universal stages (or Peirce's notions of firstness and thirdness) are to be found analogously or otherwise in Schelling's thought, and if this has consequences for the emphasis here on motion, space and nature.[20]

Beyond the connections between Schelling's intellectual intuition and Peircean abduction, there is a relation of spatio-temporality to cognitive continuity that links Schelling and Peirce. Schelling closes his *Essay on Human Freedom* as follows:

> We have the greatest respect for the profundity of historical investigations, and believe to have shown that the almost universal opinion of man only gradually arose from the dullness of animal instinct to rationality if not our own. Yet we believe the truth lies closer to us, and that we should first look for solutions to the problems stirred up in our day at home, on our own soil, before we wander to such distant sources. The time of mere historical faith is past when the possibility of immediate knowledge is given. We have an older revelation than all written ones – nature. It contains prototypes that no man has yet interpreted, whereas those of written revelations have long since received their fulfillment and interpretation.[21]

Take also the following quote from Peirce:

> How was it that man was ever led to entertain that true theory? You cannot say that it happened by chance, because the possible theories, if not strictly innumerable, at any rate exceed a trillion – or the third power of a million; and therefore the chances are too overwhelmingly against the single true theory in the twenty or thirty thousand years during which man has been a thinking animal, ever having come into any man's head. Besides, you cannot seriously think that every little chicken, that is hatched, has to rummage through all possible theories until it lights upon the good idea of picking up something and eating it. On the contrary, you think the chicken has an innate idea of doing this; that is to say, that it can think of this, but has no faculty of thinking anything else. The chicken you say pecks by instinct. But if you are going to think every poor chicken endowed with an innate tendency toward a positive truth, why should you think that to man alone this gift is denied?[22]

Thus, what is immediacy of action in relation to the immediacy of knowledge if the immediacy of knowledge is spatially determined? What becomes of the relation of activity and location, of the pragmatic maxim of 'what works' being what must be followed? These questions bring the general issue of intuition, abduction and navigation into the purported isolated interiority of thought. If intuition and abduction feed into navigation (both mental and pragmatic) because they allow us to fix points, objects or hypotheses in order to carry out any act whatsoever, then inverting this problem becomes one of determining the geometry or topography of a given mental space.

Given, for example, Schelling's minimalist definition of subjectivity in the *Erlangen* lectures, when he states that the subject is only the movement that is what it is and moves without remaining – how can the navigational model be made introspective?[23] Tracing Schelling's commitment to the book of nature in the quote above, we can say that his answer to this conundrum is his particular form of naturalism, of what in Chapter 5 was discussed in terms of the temporality of the vertical measure of the *Stufenfolge*. The question becomes: what form does Schelling's naturalism take in a contemporary context? As I will argue below, Schelling attempts to push the consequences of naturalising consciousness to the extreme, but in a way that amounts to neither panpsychism (consciousness is merely inserted everywhere) nor a pure scientific-naturalist treatment of consciousness where it is merely an effect of matter.

Clearly, Schelling is sceptical of any naturalist explanation concerning a smooth explanation of the emergence of reason. But rather than arguing that mind or thought is different in kind from nature, or from the natural processes of evolution, Schelling recognises the material effect of methodology on nature, because methodology is a part of it. However, this part cannot be defined in terms of its absolute location, because the cosmos is unbounded, and so mind can only be thought in relation to its effects on its neighbours, on those things and processes in its vicinity. How the seemingly unbound mental space of conceptualisation can be related to its localised material instantiation, the brain, may appear as an unnecessary detour here. However, as I will argue, the way in which one perceives the mind perceiving the mind, and the brain producing the concept of mind, becomes increasingly dilapidated without a robust theory of nature to support it. Furthermore, this apparent digression into naturalism will serve as an inroad into the thought of Wilfrid Sellars, who attempted to develop not only a transcendental naturalism, but also a theory of pure processes. While these facts may not themselves justify an investigation into Sellars's work, the fact that Sellars serves as the direct inspiration for a multitude of contemporary theorists utilising German Idealism warrants this path.

What does naturalism do to the brain? What does nature do to the mind?

In its ordinary functioning, science seems to limit itself to the gestures that guarantee the preservation of knowledge and leave undisturbed the patrimony of those that set it alight and multiply it. Those are also the ones that save it from indefinite accumulation and stratification, from the childishness of established positivities, from the comfort of the transits of the 'operational' and, finally, from the temptation of allowing itself to be buckled up in a grammar. They illustrate the urgency of an authentic way of conceiving information which would not be committed solely to communication, but would aim at a rational grasp of allusion and of the learning of learning. The latter, of course, would be far removed from the neuronal barbarism which exhausts itself in hunting down the recipient of the thought and in confusing learning with a pillaging of informational booty. Schelling perhaps saw more clearly: he knew that thought was not always encapsulated within the brain, that it could be everywhere, 'outside . . . in the morning dew.'[24]

Naturalism is generally divided into methodological and ontological strains. First, methodological naturalism can be discarded insofar as it merely claims that the methods of the natural sciences are the best methods *tout court*, especially when the historical and developmental nature of the methods of natural science is adequately situated. Ontological naturalism is most directly defined as the claim that nature is all there is, but a question arises from this definition: what is nature if it is not merely what natural science tells us? If the conceptual engagement with nature supersedes the methods of the natural sciences, then how can nature be conceptually separated from both physical nature and the concept? Or, to put this in a way that would fit Schelling's and Peirce's inquiries: what must nature be in order for it to continually test and allow for our amplified knowledge of it? Or, to put it in yet another way, in what philosophical cases does ontological naturalism (or some other strong form of naturalism) have a pragmatic function? Rather than outlining every form of naturalism, in the following I will attempt to address various thinkers who relate various forms of naturalism to Schelling and to the Sellarsian lineage (Sellars, McDowell, Brandom, Sebit) in order to determine what Schelling's form of naturalism, particularly as it relates to the role of consciousness, is.

Bana Bashour and Hans Muller's collection *Contemporary Philosophical Naturalism and its Implications* provides a succinct overview of various naturalist positions. A minimalist or tenuous naturalist position would simply be that of an anti-supernaturalism, that is, that only entities or processes we can at least vaguely describe should be said to be natural. From this minimalist naturalism the positions become more and more methodologically and ontologically strict regarding the place of reasons. Generally, this resolves around whether one can claim that reason evolved from primarily biological or other natural sources, or whether some normative emergence is required.[25] While Schelling's naturalised transcendental method rules out his adherence to methodological naturalism, a strict alliance to ontological naturalism is complicated, but not ruled out, by his utilisation of processes over things.

Immediately the challenge to relate *Naturphilosophie* to contemporary naturalism arises, under threat of anachronism. Since *Naturphilosophie* was a philosophical investigation of nature in its totality, it relied upon transcendental methods to critique scientific claims, if not necessarily scientific methods. Schelling's work in particular demanded that science think carefully about the claims it could make from particular fields of study, but he clearly saw more merit in some methods (such as field theory) than others (such as atomism). Clearly, Schelling fits neither into ontological or methodological naturalism. This leaves liberal naturalism and transcendental naturalism.

Liberal naturalism is generally described as a form of naturalism that recognises the explanatory power of scientific naturalism (as a combination of ontological and methodological strains), but argues that other forms of knowledge can explain the world as well and, perhaps, in better ways than a strictly reductive scientific approach. Schelling would seem to fit into this category straight away.[26]

Markus Gabriel, however, argues that Schelling's transcendentalism does not permit liberal naturalism. In *Transcendental Ontology* Gabriel associates liberal naturalism with John McDowell's position in *Mind and World*.[27] For Gabriel, liberal naturalism must assert a physical totality; the world must be one giant physically closed object, in order for its claims to hold. Yet, as far as I can discern, Gabriel offers no specific proof of why liberal naturalism, or any scientific theory, requires a closed world made of matter only in order to make scientifically valid claims. Gabriel notes that Schelling's notion of totality (or of what Schelling refers to as either the All or the Absolute) should be taken as meta-theoretical and not as a physically massive thing, yet this does not make Schelling's general thinking regarding nature anti-naturalistic.[28] Gabriel's argument for Schelling's concept of non-totality stems from the concept of the unprethinkable functioning as the tireless engine of logical predication, whereas I argue that the same argument can be made following a lean ontological structure of nature. Again, to assume Schelling's advocacy of non-totality, of a collection of systems as opposed to one system, does not override his insistence on the view that the cosmos pre-exists all logical construction. But, since the cosmos contains logical construction, since we exist and can logically construct, logical construction is not merely ideal, but always a mixture of particular acts of creation and their more than local consequences. The absence of this natural structure, I would argue, causes problems for both sense and logic, as well as for many fields beyond strictly human concerns, which justifies the speculation that non-totality and construction are not merely ideal.

If nature affects conceptualisation, then it becomes imperative to understand naturalism as a concept in the space of nature that gives rise to a space of reasons without cutting the ontological or generally constitutive tether between them. The division, following McDowell and other left Sellarsians, is anchored in a plea for coherence, in that the space of reasons cannot function (so normativists claim) with the impingement of nature. Yet without the acknowledgement of nature, the normative space has no material with which to work unless it amplifies the immateriality of thought and human action. The appeal to reason as a social exercise, put forth by Robert Brandom, attempts to circumvent this problem. Here we can investigate whether Schelling fits better in the category of transcendental naturalism as opposed to liberal naturalism since, for Schelling, the Hegelian-Brandomian socialisation of reason does not adequately address how reason occurs in nature in a structural sense.

But if naturalism is the thought that nature, as the nested set of physical systems, is what there is, then how does one explain the strange positionality of thought, able to abstract the cosmos – that a view knowing about nature as a non-totalisable whole or, following Paul Franks, a heterogeneous monism can be constructed? The claim that everything is nature is less problematic (in an ontological sense) than a two-worlds solution.

While I will address the normativists McDowell and Brandom as well as their forefather Sellars below, for now the question remains: what is the stuff of thought in relation to the very notion of totality? Is it methodologically efficacious to divide mind and world, or thought and nature, into kinds of spaces at all? Is it necessary that mind be ontologically or operationally separate from world in order for mind to abstract in terms of totalities? Or, perhaps more pertinently, to what degree do we need to think that thought operates independently from nature in order for thought to reach its 'proper' potential which is *a priori* unknowable?

Frederick Mortensen argues that Schelling's position is quite close to that of Thomas Nagel and, in particular, his *View from Nowhere*. If mind is in the world, and mind cannot be adequately explained through evolutionary means, then Mortensen argues that this opens the door for the religious naturalism of Nagel, which is closely aligned to liberal naturalism.[29] Both religious and liberal naturalism emphasise the importance of nature, of a world out there, but argue that other methodological approaches are integral to the investigation of nature as such. However, these approaches do not seem to adequately account for why it is then that the natural sciences are so apt at producing new entities and manipulating the external world.

In *Mind and Cosmos* Nagel attempts to get around this problem by claiming that the hard sciences, particularly biology, are fundamentally limited because they had to abstract mind from the world in order to set out to investigate it. Nagel claims that the physical sciences are therefore incapable of describing subjective experiences and argues that this disqualifies physical reduction as a means of explaining nature and thought's role and location in it. While Nagel's non-materialist naturalism appears, at first glance, very much like Schelling's form of naturalism, I believe that Schelling's investment in the physical sciences, particularly physics, means he cannot (*pace* Mortensen) be associated with religious or liberal naturalism.[30] While Schelling is a non-materialist in the sense that he argues for knowledge and science that is substratum-independent, he thinks that processes such as gravity, chemical decomposition and the like have a epistemic impact that is not on a par with other kinds of knowledge, at least when it comes to discussing nature. That is, when Schelling discusses light, gravity or the unfolding and enfolding of organic entities, the formal structure of these motions is extended into the all of nature. Furthermore, they are formal to the extent that we detect them operating in thought, but this operation within thought needs to be properly tested so that it is not merely in thought, or merely ideal. To assume that a form discovered by thought *belongs to thought only* does not properly account for the constructive subordination of thought to nature. Furthermore, Schelling's great heresy against Kant, beside his general attack on the critical system as merely negative, that is, non-creative, is his argument that existence is a real predicate. What is interesting is that Schelling's reason for this is not to reclaim an ontological proof of God, but instead to demonstrate that thought and actions have processual or physical (if we read physical in terms of fields and not hard stuff) effects, since they are in the world and there is only one world.

If nature is even partially similar to what we think it is, then we are natural beings with naturally endowed capacities. Assuming that mind is either unnatural, or functions primarily in an unnatural domain separate from nature, that is, that mind acts according only to its own rules, ignores the pre-existence of nature; nature as the processes and structures without which we cannot explain why anything holds together at all. As Michael Halley puts it: 'The concept of nature, does not entail that there should also be an intelligence that is aware of it. Nature it seems, would exist even if there were nothing that was aware of it.'[31] Yet how does the mind determine, or decide, from a degree, or space, of unnaturalness? A certain coherency is acquired following any kind of normative isolation, and yet why should this be taken as more than a methodological distinction? How could the advent of the normative, the space of reasons, be a cut in the real? How could the space of reasons be separated from the space of nature?

If the creation of a space of normativity is entailed by a need for coherency, then the space of nature must be fully abandoned to the natural sciences. The problem is not to question the authority of science as such, but to acknowledge the fact that if philosophy is to be as generic or universal as it claims, then it must apply to the sciences as well. Even if one separates the space of reason from the space of nature, it is granted that a degree of self-reflexivity allows for a process to identify itself. In the case of the normative system, this self-reflexivity allows a process also to isolate itself operationally, maybe even ontologically, from the natural world.

Intelligence, for Schelling, is a hyper-active (or, for us, proximal) form of self-relation. It is a form of self-relation that convinces itself that it is without limit, but its limit becomes the very fact that it thinks it has no limit. Thought appears to itself as a boundless trajectory, yet the path it has taken only matters if the material consequences are worked out, followed through. This pragmatism works against a normative space that would confuse, or at least conflate, cause, ground and reason. Grounds and reasons are held apart from one another in Schelling's work (*Vernuft* is a different term than *Grund*), since reason is a human capacity, whereas grounds are both human and non-human.[32]

Thus, the space of reasons cannot contain the space of nature, but the space of nature can be said to produce the space of reasons as a consequence, and thus reason can be viewed as an augmentation of nature, at least insofar as nature comes to know itself as nature for us and in itself. In both the space of reason and the space of nature, what is is that which structurally engenders the very base capacity for self-reflexivity. What does the very process of self-modification consist in? If reason is a later version of nature, in that it is another form of self-reflection, does this properly account for reason's capacities? For Schelling, only an appeal to the senses, but an appeal that remains aware of the transformation that reason and experience inflict on to what is sensed, can demonstrate the insufficiency of reason in the space of nature. As he writes:

> Of itself, reason cannot realize or prove any actual, real being even in the sensible world; it cannot realize or prove any present existence, for example, the existence of this plant or this stone. If reason wants a real being, if it wants as something real any type of object discovered within itself in a concept and, thus, as something merely possible, then it must submit to the authority of the senses. For the testimony of the senses is nothing other than an authority, since through it we know the present existence, the plant that exists here, which cannot be realized from the mere nature of things, and thus from reason.[33]

It is manifestly demonstrable that claims that the mind is a product and operator of nature do not deny the possibility of self-modification. Therefore, the question becomes: what does a theory of expansive or transcendental naturalism do to the mind, to the very concept of mind or mindedness? This raises a different, but not unrelated question: what does the normative mind think of the scientifically determined concept of brain or cognition? The question of what naturalism does to the mind becomes 'What directives are not engendered by naturalism for the mind?' What does it mean to be operating both according to nature and according to our own freedom or direction (to put it again in a navigational sense)?

There are thus two interrelated questions: 'What does naturalism do to the brain?' and 'What does nature do to the mind?' If nature is capable of self-modification (of augmentative recursion), then how is the self-modification that we seem to do to the mind and the brain related to how nature modifies the mind and the brain? Are the relations of mental and natural self-modifications themselves natural or normatively determined without concern for nature, or only concerned with nature after the fact?

The danger that arises here, in addressing liberal and/or religious naturalism, is that following a nature of processes, one falls into panpsychism to explain mind in general. That is, if thought is a process, and all that there is are processes, then does thought become a ubiquitous feature of the cosmos? Or, in other words, what are the adequate means of differentiating, but not sundering, thought from nature, given that we inhabit thought and, in a quite different sense, inhabit nature?

One temptation here is to follow numerous interpreters who see Schelling as endorsing either a traditional monism, or a panpsychism. Since the former has been addressed in Chapters 3 and 4, I will focus on the charge of panpsychism. Paul Hayner, in his *Reason and Existence* for instance, claims that Schelling's monism is a panpsychism following a complete identity of mind and nature.[34] However, Hayner seems to suggest that this is a traditional notion of identity and not one of copulation and genesis as outlined in Schelling's *Freedom Essay.* That is, as Daniel Whistler, Iain Hamilton Grant and others have pointed out, and as has already been discussed above, Schelling's notion of identity is a thesis of *univocal extension* such that the statement A = A does not mean that entity 1 is equal to or the same as entity 2, but that entity 1 is the ground of entity 2 and is expressed by its consequence. It is only in ignoring the difference between a literal understanding of identity, as opposed to Schelling's particular notion of identity, that Hayner can claim that the absolute is a category that ruins all of Schelling's early work both in the philosophy of nature and the identity philosophy.[35]

Michael Blamauer argues that Schelling's *Naturphilosophie*, which denies body or any other physical substratum at bottom, necessitates that Schelling is therefore a panpsychist.[36] He argues, for instance, that not every thought rewrites the brain, but that thoughts contribute to consciousness as self-modification of the state of things. Becoming convinced by an argument or watching an incredible film may adequately be described as natural occurrences, that is, as visual and/or auditory stimuli changing the way we think about some state of affairs or about ourselves. Thus, while there is clearly weak emergence of some kind, as things combine in a way that is predetermined by the qualities of their components, the question remains whether strong emergence, or radical novelty, occurs or not.

Strong emergence – the claim that reduction erases or fails to explain novelty – could be seen to be guilty of what Robert Batterman has referred to as property dragging; in other words, strong emergence does not appear to maintain any distinction between structure and change, between potency and actuality. Following the discussion of the potencies in Chapter 4, all creation is constrained, but all constraint is subsequently expressed (thus adding to creation). The world is as creative as it can be while still holding itself together. In this regard, and following Schelling's notion of identity as a thesis of extended univocity, he would most likely be critical of strong emergence, as it would negate the properly expressive relationship of the consequent from its antecedent.

The navigational character of Schelling's notion of creation can be expressed in creation being the production of constraints, of creation being the extending of boundaries and not the rupture of boundaries. Production, or creation, is the motion of inhibitions. Nature can be described in its most basic sense as merely self-deforming space, or as the universe's most plastic aspect. As Gabriel puts it in logical terms: 'the absolute necessity of the origin must therefore be compatible with the contingency of everything that originates'.[37]

Because self-modification and recursion occur within one world, or one space – namely a space of nature – it cannot be methodologically efficacious merely to naturalise epistemology fully, as thoughts act according to other thoughts, in a very particular way, and, at least for us, seem to be contained by the concept of the mental. Yet, as Grant emphasises in his *Philosophies of Nature after Schelling*, epistemology must undergo significant change if 'what thinks in me is outside of me'.

To address this, that is, the apparent externality of the world, as well as the apparent irreducibility of interior thoughts and/or experiences, we will now move on to the thought of Wilfrid Sellars, whose critical combination of nominalism, naturalism and process ontology allows for a nuanced approach to maintaining a space for reason's seemingly unnatural capacities, given the efficacy of naturalism, without falling into either crude empiricism, materialism or panpsychism.

Impure immediacies: Sellars and Schelling

The American philosopher Wilfrid Sellars has developed a novel attempt to deal with the problems of naturalism and epistemology, functioning moreover as a remarkable bridge between post-Kantian analytic thought and contemporary utilisations of German Idealism in the English-speaking world. Sellars's most important concepts for our purposes here are his synoptic image of the human, the myth of the given, and his later concept of pure processes. As I will attempt to show, Sellars's dual methodology and his reliance on a metaphysics of pure processes to link the two domains of knowledge appear broadly compatible with Schelling's general philosophical trajectory. Sellars's synopticism is simply the methodological dualism in viewing human beings either in terms of the manifest image or the scientific image. The manifest image treats humans as cultural, meaning centred, and concept-mongering creatures, while, in the scientific image, the human is treated as a mere biological entity, an animal subject to the laws of nature. As Sellars puts it in 'Philosophy and the Scientific Image of Man':

> The 'manifest' image of man-in-the-world can be characterized in two ways, which are supplementary rather than alternative. It is, first, the framework in terms of which man came to be aware of himself as man-in-the-world. It is the framework in terms of which, to use an existentialist turn of phrase, man first encountered himself – which is, of course, when he came to be man. For it is no merely incidental feature of man that he has a conception of himself as man-in-the-world, just as it is obvious, on reflection, that 'if man had a radically different conception of himself he would be a radically different kind of man'.[38]

He then later in the same text discusses the scientific image thus:

> The scientific image of man-in-the-world is, of course, as much an idealization as the manifest image – even more so, as it is still in the process of coming to be. It will be remembered that the contrast I have in mind is not that between an unscientific conception of man-in-the-world and a scientific one, but between that conception which limits itself to what correlational techniques can tell us about perceptible and introspectible events and that which postulates imperceptible objects and events for the purpose of explaining correlations among perceptibles. It was granted, of course, that in point of historical fact many of the latter correlations were suggested by theories introduced to explain previously established correlations, so that there has been a dialectical interplay between correlational and postulational procedures. (Thus we might not have noticed that litmus paper turns red in acid, until this hypothesis had been suggested by a complex theory relating the absorption and emission of electromagnetic radiation by objects to their chemical composition; yet in principle this familiar correlation could have been, and, indeed, was, discovered before any such theory was developed.) Our contrast then, is between two ideal constructs: (a) the correlational and categorial refinement of the 'original image', which refinement I am calling the manifest image; (b) the image derived from the fruits of postulational theory construction which I am calling the scientific image.[39]

Despite Sellars's daunting verbiage, the thrust of the argument is straight-forward. Simply put, Sellars wants to argue that we cannot avoid having a quasi-historical and pragmatic view of ourselves as a species, as being a type of thing located in a world. Yet at the same time, in order to navigate that world, we have to make speculations or theory constructions that redefine our position in the world as it allows us to move through it. The caveat is that our relation to ourselves is no less problematic or nuanced than our epistemological relation to facets of apparently external reality. This general attitude of Sellars, divided between naturalism and pragma-tism, is what leads him to the myth of the given as well as the theory of pure processes.

Sellars's myth of the given is outlined in his famous essay 'Empiricism and Philosophy of Mind'. Sellars wants to preserve inner episodes of con-sciousness (the fact that we have immediate experiences, or at least can reliably talk about these experiences in a scientific world-view) while not granting some special status to the given, or givenness, in philosophical theories of sense. In other words, Sellars wants to preserve internal states but argue that our purported immediate knowing of something is a loose attachment of language to a process, and that between language and process a game-like give and take occurs. This is often diagrammed via the inconsis-tent triad. Sellars, and his followers, argue that only two of three statements regarding the relation of sense and knowing can be true.

1. 'S senses red sense-content x' entails 'S non inferentially believes (knows) that x is red'.
2. The ability to sense sense-contents is unacquired.
3. The capacity to have classificatory beliefs of the form 'x is F' is acquired.[40]

In other words: 1) sense means one can know a fact, 2) we know what we sense is automatic and 3) our ability to claim a fact is learned. If we think that we have immediate access to sense, and that this also gives us unmediated knowledge, then we have fallen into the myth of the given. As Ray Brassier argues, Sellars selects the first and third capacities, leaving out the second. What this means is that for Sellars, the passage from recognising sense to making a fact about the world is conceptually coupled with the fact that facthood is something that must be learned. The process of saying that 'this apple looks red' therefore is possible because 'it is red' is automatically true for the interior thoughts of the observer, but for them to communicate with other observers, they must be trained to make classificatory beliefs (for them to know about redness generally).[41] Or, not all experience is conceptual, but all communicable experience is conceptual.

Sellars's view is, I believe, compatible with that of Schelling, since Schelling emphasises that the co-dependency of thought and world requires an appeal to intuition, but an intuition that is about immediate locality (objects in the field of sense), which may have deeper conceptual import for philosophical navigation of space. Furthermore, as I have begun to demonstrate above via Schelling's transition to positive philosophy, such a philosophy treats experience itself as a material to demonstrate the insufficiency of reason by itself. So while negative philosophy has its function (to say what something is, to make classificatory statements, in Sellars's language), it requires the immediacy of experience, but is locally limited (that x is this or that) in order to furnish the beginnings of a form of proto-pragmatism, to adequately grasp *how or why something exists.*

Practical activity tests the cut of the normative named above as occurring only within the normative, of being only according to the stability of reason, and thereby quarantining nature. Sellars's pragmatism is transcendental in Schelling's sense (in being about conceptual and not *merely conceptual* motion) because it makes reasons into causes. Sellars's pragmatism, in treating reasons like causes, is close to Schelling's positive philosophy, which treats experiences as if they are causes. For Sellars, nature, as a series of extended physical processes, is evident to us in our own doings and sayings (Robert Brandom will go on to emphasise the latter to great effect).

It is here that the importance of Sellars's late notion of pure processes emerges. Like Peirce's open notion of universal laws that are never known but only abductively approached, Sellars's notion of pure process does not only keep a space open for future knowledge, for what we might not know that we do not know, but also allows for the play-space between language, or pragmatic activity, and its grip on what seems to be a relatively stable physical world. This emerges in Sellars's Carus lectures.

Sellars's lectures, which were published in the *Monist* in three parts, re-examine his critique of the myth of the given in relation to an ontology of pure processes. In the first lecture, 'The Lever of Archimedes' (1981), Sellars re-presents his general account of sense. While Sellars maintains that a sensed quality such as red is already conceptually coded by the time we can refer to it, our experience of it is more or less immediate, but this immediacy is not conceptually accessible in the same way that the sense-as-quality is. However, Sellars argues, this access problem is not due to the fact that we have a concept of experience before we have experiences, but because of the complexity of quality-as-process.

In essence, Sellars argues that knowing the difference between 'the apple looks red' and 'the apple is red' does not hinge upon knowing, *a priori,* the iffiness of experience as such, that is, that it is intrinsically indefinable, but is rather based on the fact that our immediate conceptual grasp is not of objects *per se*, but of processes, of expanses of red.[42] Or, in other words, it is not because we know that experience is relative that we assume that we may experience a disjunction between 'is red' and 'seems red', but rather that the character of experience *is processual*, because we are always working to update our knowledge of redness. While the distinction may seem trivial, Sellars is advocating for reduction, but a reduction to processes. Therefore, he argues in an indirect but convincing fashion that adverbial forms are the most useful reductions we can perform. Thus, Sellars attempts to hang on to some notion of nominalism in the wake of his naturalism.

This is, I would argue, akin to Schelling's wholesale rejection of substratum reliance. It is quite telling that Sellars closes his third Carus lecture by quoting from his earlier 'Philosophy and the Scientific Image of Man', in which he states:

> But the scientific image is not yet complete; we have not yet penetrated all the secrets of nature. And if it should turn out that particles instead of being the primitive entities of the scientific image could be treated as singularities in a space-time continuum which could be conceptually 'cut up' without significant loss – in inorganic contexts, at least – into interacting particles, then we would not be confronted at the level of neurophysiology with the problem of understanding the relation of sensory consciousness (with its ultimate homogeneity) to systems of particles. Rather, we would have the alternative of saying that although for many purposes the central nervous system can be construed without loss as a complex system of physical particles, when it comes to an adequate understanding of the relation of sensory consciousness to neurophysiological process, we must penetrate to the non-particulate foundation of the particulate image, and recognize that in this non-particulate image the qualities of sense are a dimension of natural process which occurs only in connection with those complex physical processes which, when 'cut up' into particles in terms of those features which are the least common denominators of physical process – present in inorganic as well as organic processes alike – become the complex system of particles which, in the current scientific image, is the central nervous system.[43]

To point back to Chapter 5, we can see how Sellars argues that particles, or other entities, function as descriptive footholds for processes, particularly processes that are not, due to our naturalistic, albeit technologically appended, capacities, perceptible to us in the same way in which events such as thundering or running are. That is, a particle is an indexer of a process that we are attempting to come to grips with, while events we can perceive occurring between objects, as more sensibly accessible, can either be defined in the relation of the objects or can be reduced to the event. That is, the phrase 'Socrates ran on Sunday' can be productively reduced to 'a running took place'. Similarly, Sellars's discussion of particles, like Schelling's use of actants, demonstrates the difficulty in objectifying processes or qualities that requires the opposite move, that of added objects to explain the underlying event. Things are objects, which are logical cuts in the continuum. This, if they have operative or pragmatic efficacy, does not make them less real since, following Schelling, realness is a measure of consequence and not material composition (not what this particle is made of, but what it does in this particular instance).

Furthermore, Sellars is sceptical of the kind of fact ontology that Markus Gabriel utilises, since the immediacy of sense and the purported simplicity of fact cannot be aligned prior to the collective mediation of facticity either by inferential training (such as that of a child by its parents to know what facts are) or by social filtering and amplifying (as Brandom highlights in a Hegelian vein). Thus for Sellars and, I would argue, for Schelling, the problem is not immediate knowledge as long as one recognises the conceptual and local features of that immediacy which have already been processed prior to reflective acknowledgement.

Beyond these surface-level similarities, I believe that there are methodological congruities between Schelling and Sellars. The methodological bifurcations of Schelling's work (whether discussed as negative versus positive, or *Naturphilosophie* versus transcendental philosophy) can be compared (though as not strictly analogous to) Sellars's scientific image versus the manifest image, or viewing things as bundles of micro-physical processes on one hand, and as sensa or irreducible causes in and of experience on another. What is central here, as James O'Shea points out in relation to Sellars, is that physical grounds and logical grounds need not be collapsed. This ties in to Schelling's relation to Peirce discussed above. These divides, in both Schelling and Sellars, are due to underlying processes, but these processes are apparent because of the informative ambiguity of sensory experience.

For Schelling, the informative status of experience in *The Grounding of Positive Philosophy* is imperative for the very practice of philosophy itself, as well as for its non-sensorial or intuitive consistency. The necessity of experience as a material is not in order to bring philosophy 'down-to-Earth', so to speak, in an Aristotelian sense, but in order to account for the demands of dogmatic metaphysics without accepting their substantial metaphysical claims. Or in other words, taking experience as a material means taking its insufficiency as explanatory in itself, thereby absorbing the desire for a metaphysical structure but, at the same time, acknowledging that the extravagance of metaphysical systems can go and has gone far beyond being instructively compensatory in relation to sense.

Schelling's claim about the thirdness of the subject–object distinction is the claim that matter is synthetic, or constructed, in a way that makes it neither strictly subject or object (nor is it strictly potency), since it is and is existent, but not dead or brute as is often the case in materialism or mechanism (both of which Schelling railed against, particularly in the *First Outline* and in *The Ideas for a Philosophy of Nature*). The synthetic dimension is the creative dimension of metaphysics reduced (in a positive sense as discussed above) to the creative potentiality of subject and object.

Given his treatment of sense, it may not seem surprising that Sellars's work has, though with quite a temporal delay, fed into contemporary analytic utilisations of German Idealism by John McDowell, Robert Brandom, Robert Pippin and Brady Bowman, to name just a few. However, the form this reception has taken seems to be very much against Sellars's spirit, as the reception of his work has divided into what are commonly known as left and right Sellarsians, the former being Hegelians who emphasise the manifest image of Sellars's work, while the latter (who include Daniel Dennett, Ruth Milikan and Patricia and Paul Churchland) emphasise the scientific image. In addition, the Hegelianism of the left Sellarsians, which I will engage below, has been criticised as being a Fichteanism at heart, since it emphasises the *Logic* and the *Phenomenology* over and above all of Hegel's other texts, regardless of the subject matter being discussed. Furthermore, these left Sellarsians display little to no understanding of Schelling and, with regard to the legacy of Sellars, seem to overlook or purposefully ignore his emphasis on pure processes.

Johanna Seibt is the Sellarsian who has contributed the most to reinvigorating the process reading of Sellars's work. In her masterful 'Pure Processes and Projective Metaphysics', Seibt argues that despite Sellars's general emphasis on semantic games as the cornerstone for his thinking, processes function as a 'projective metaphysics', which is indispensable to his overall project.[44] Seibt states that Sellars's very notion of picturing, as well as the projecting and use of the scientific image and the manifest image, for example, are only possible with the concept of pure processes.[45] Ultimately, and in a way that I argue aligns itself with the discussion of Schelling's method, Seibt calls the utilisation of this process 'a transcendence from within'.[46]

This transcendence has to do with the fact that the processes are introduced by Sellars not only as a bridge for the manifest and scientific images, but because an altogether different technique of thinking is suggested by them. Seibt argues that processes go beyond the correlational techniques of the manifest image (such as the use of analogy to move slowly through the world), as well as beyond those techniques of the scientific image that propose entities (i.e. the techniques of either explaining events with objects, or constructing objects to explain events). Alternatively, she argues that the positing of the processes is about proposing new formulas for a potential new model.[47] The following statement sums up their function:

> In ontology as in science, then, the external significance of a theory is some-thing we assert 'from within', comparing the theory with its competitors rather than with 'reality'. Such external significance essentially remains comparative significance, since it derives from the comparative explanatory force of a theory relative to a data-set whose degree of picture correctness is unknown. Moreover, it remains projected external significance in the following sense. Sellars claims that ideal coherence and ideal picture-correctness go hand in hand, which allows for the possibility that in the sequence of frameworks leading up to the Peircean framework increases in picture-correctness and coherence or inferential integration may be occasionally out of step.[48]

In essence, Seibt is saying that framework independence, or admitting the limited ground from which one's knowledge claims begin, does not mean that those claims cannot have external significance. On the contrary, it is only through such an admission that one can see what is exterior. In other words, following the discussion of Schelling above, the speculative gesture can tell us about the actual ramifications of our local actions. The temptation, and one that Schelling rails against in a different form in his own time, is to overemphasise the degree to which reason is the sole capacity for stabilising and projecting a possible picture of the world. This over-reliance on the normative structure of reason will be addressed next.

Netting nature through norms?

> The whole world lies, so to speak, in the nets of the understanding, or of reason, but the question is *how* it entered these nets, since there is obviously something other and something *more* than mere reason in the world, indeed there is something which strives beyond these limits.[49]

We can now investigate, head on, the normative uptake of Sellars's work that engages with the broad themes of German Idealism (though never Schelling specifically). It is Schelling's difficult method, as well as his emphasis on nature, that removes him from the Sellarsian use of German Idealism.

What is nevertheless interesting here, with regard to the concepts of space and motion, is that a spatial division is made by left Sellarsians in order to defend the very process of reason: the division between the space of reason and the space of nature. Our guiding question here will be: how can these thinkers divide nature from reason in a spatial metaphor in order to justify a movement within, but not across, these spaces, given the naturalist roots of consciousness and the non-normative explanatory power required to discuss movement and space as such?

As Gabriel points out, all post-Sellarsian Hegelians interpret the division of mind and world, reasons and causes, or thought and nature in different ways, following Sellars's famous, and already discussed, 'Empiricism and Philosophy of Mind'.[50] However, while Brandom and Gabriel emphasise the semantic aspect of this division, the later Sellars complicates the strictly semantic character of the treatment of such spaces, as we have seen in the work of Seibt. If the tissue of the world is made of processes or occurrings, it appears that Brandom, Pippin and to a lesser extent McDowell take the division of spaces that justifies its act of cutting in merely normative terms, that is, there are two kinds of processes that are different in kind. Normativity becomes a netting of nature that then proceeds by splitting nature into two halves and throwing out the nature part.

Given this, it can hardly be surprising that in the ongoing adoption of German Idealism by contemporary analytic philosophers, Hegel has been the star, Fichte the understudy, and Schelling the *enfant terrible*. Schelling receives little or no mention, other than as kook, romanticist or half-stepping stone, half-obstacle to Hegel's meteoric rise to greatness. But given the contemporary emphasis on German Idealism as helping to navigate the gap between the logical space of reasons and the logical space of nature, it is odd that Schelling is ignored, as his work is tremendously focused on the relation of thought and nature, or mind and world.

The purported dubiousness of Schelling's *Naturphilosophie* is often held up as the glaring metaphysical hex damning him from contemporary appropriation; yet his critics fail even to consistently critique him, oscillating between accusing him of being a bad influence on the physical sciences of his time and claiming that he had no influence at all, citing little proof in either case. As a corollary, Schelling's work on Absolute Identity (or what he saw as the ur-logical form undergirding his numerous systems of philosophical inquiry discussed in geometrical language) is dismissed by reputation alone following Hegel's infamous statement that Schelling's conception of the Absolute was the 'night in which all the cows are black'. Thus Schelling is critiqued for simultaneously being too specific in his empirical claims and too vague in his philosophical claims, with little or no attention given to Schelling on his own terms, or to the positive citing of his work in the physical sciences by figures such as Humphry Davy, Michael Faraday and Hans Christian Oersted.

Against this reputation, and following the work of contemporary Schellingians such as Iain Hamilton Grant, I will argue that Schelling's work can be brought to bear on the nature and mind divide in a way that can inform the take-up of Hegel by figures such as John McDowell and Robert Brandom. Specifically, Schelling's work can account for a more positive description of the space of nature than that demonstrated by the aforementioned Pittsburgh Hegelians.

A brief overview of McDowell's work and the motivations behind it would serve well here. McDowell's *Mind and World* aims to clear the philosophical field of a large swathe of misunderstandings. Following Kant and Sellars in particular, McDowell argues that contemporary philosophical problems stem from an inability to accept the idealistic power of human thought above and against the sense of world. He argues that too much hand-wringing has been done in concern over a world 'out there' and in attempting to explain how our minds may or may not be able to map it.[51] For McDowell the problem stems from either giving into Sellars's aforementioned myth of the given (the claim that the outside is somehow immediately compatible with human thought) or worrying excessively about the dualism between sense and intuition in the wake of Kant.

McDowell's solution, following from his Sellarsian reading of Kant, is to argue that there is no fundamental limit to the conceptual.[52] That is, in order to avoid the myth of the given, spontaneity and receptivity must be co-constitutive. In essence, receptivity and spontaneity are always-already working in conceptual space, and therefore it is fundamentally contradictory to draw a line between conceptual space as interior and natural space as exterior. For McDowell the relation between mind and world must be a normative one and hence the world (or nature) will be understood in normative terms or as empirical laws.[53] Following a particular reading of Sellars, McDowell defines the logical space of nature negatively, as functioning according to different rules from the space of reasons. Beyond this, nature and naturalism are only to be operated upon in terms of epistemological description. While McDowell argues that receptivity and spontaneity co-construct reason, he must seriously downplay the latter as having any contribution other than as suggesting epistemological images of what nature may be.[54] For McDowell, freedom can only describe itself in its own terms, and thus nature must be navigated away from, based on following normative rules alone. Or, as he later states: 'independent reality exerts a rational control over our thinking but without falling into the confusion between justification and exculpation'.[55] Here I find it difficult to ascertain how McDowell can account for the infinite speed of reason, for reason being embedded in nature in such a way that is completely conscious to us. McDowell ends his short text with an appeal to a kind of 'naturalized Platonism'.[56]

As should be evident from the above discussion of the various forms of naturalism, McDowell works under a mode of soft or liberal naturalism that attempts to accept the ramifications of nature, but only to the extent that they are produced by the natural sciences. Furthermore, he claims that, because of the emergence of the space of reasons, nature is transformed into a second nature, over which our own human spontaneity allow us control.

Robert Brandom, who in many ways takes up the reins of McDowell's project, and is classified as a left Sellarsian alongside him, further distances nature from reason. Like Robert Pippin, Brandom argues that McDowell does not go far enough in downplaying the *active role* of the space of nature. Brandom attempts this by emphasising the social aspect of reason. In his impressive *Reason and Philosophy*, Brandom argues that reason is fundamentally normative due to the centrality of the concept of recognition – recognition of any and all ingredients to normativity and to the efficacy of normativity itself as the giving and taking of reasons in order to explain and justify behaviours in ourselves and other (presumably) rational agents.[57] Brandom justifies his engagement with Hegel in asserting that 'We are social, normative, rational, free, self-consciously historical animals. This powerful and finely conceptually articulated vision of ourselves is the crowning achievement of German Idealism.'[58] For Brandom this achievement is possible because, in following Kant, the German Idealists (which for Brandom means Hegel foremost) took the activity of searching for a unity of apperception as the ground of rationality itself. Rationality, for Brandom, becomes a triangulation of the conceptual via inferences and incompatibilities of the use of numerous predicates. Brandom effectively argues that, at base, the subject is simply that which attains definiteness in a social setting.[59] An essentially naturalistic account of the individual and its acquisition of language skills is facilitated by social (or normative) existence, as Brandom argues that Hegelian recollection (*Erinnerung*) utilises the Kantian integration of concepts into reason and casts it in a broader and historicised light.[60] Brandom argues that 'Kant replaces the *ontological* distinction between the physical and the mental with the *deontological* distinction between the realm of nature and the realm of freedom: the distinction between things that merely act regularly and things that are subject to distinctively normatively sorts of assessment',[61] and hence Hegel historicises this process and socialises it. In this regard, within the normative realm, Brandom's rational Hegelian agent is capable of determining both the behaviours of itself and others (via the linguistic giving and taking of reasons) as well as ordering historical or other grand narratives in order to construct a progressive or evolutionary account of reason's or, in a more embodied sense, humanity's ascension.

Brandom emphasises, in summoning the figure of Minerva's owl, that the Hegelian dialectic gives contingency the form of necessity.[62] Within this discussion he emphasises the 'newness' of Hegel's concept of determinateness, although it appears, albeit in an slightly more abstract form, throughout Maimon's work as the law of determinability, as was discussed in Chapter 2. Whereas Brandom's account acknowledges the heuristic and pedagogical roots of determining, the very form of the act is mystified beyond being the propellant of language. Brandom explains determination as occuring through the giving or taking of reasons. Whereas McDowell offered some space for nature, for Brandom determination as such occurs only with normative reasonable *discourse*. In addition, Brandom's erasure of Sellars's pure processes can only raise the question of how it is that the relation between saying and doing can be *fully* articulated with human-controlled normative functions. Here Brandom goes even beyond Fichte in asserting that activity, *as such*, is the sole purview of human beings.

In *Tales of the Mighty Dead* Brandom again connects Hegel to determination as a form of subjective-objectivity that centres upon processes of individuation.[63] Here I believe that Brandom, once again, overdetermines the linguistic skeleton of determination itself in order to better stitch together mind and world with tools crafted from and within the logical space of reasons, without recourse to the space of nature (to say nothing of whether this latter space is logical as such). My point here is not that there is an easy alternative by which we could describe the space of nature as it asymmetrically forms the space of reason (or normative space), but to argue that the patchwork means by which we construct theories about anything is naturalism at work, in that our senses (although they may already be present to us consciously as always-already conceptual content via Sellars) are nature at work in us. But this does not speak to the spatio-temporal kinematics of ourselves in relation to those concepts locally isolated. To return to the discussion of Seibt above, and to Schelling's discussion of experience and sense in the *Grounding*: just because our sensed world is already conceptually riven, categorised and formed does not mean that everything subsequently affected by that content must be fully conceptually graspable. Nor, however, does it mean one should throw out the conceptual codedness of the world and claim that we can sneak thoughts into the world before epistemologically treating it. The difficulty here is the following: once experiences or senses have been recognised to have been conceptually coded, how are we to extend our concepts of those experiences while at the same time acknowledging that the 'matter' of those concepts is not only conceptual?

To reconnect to the discussion of naturalism above, one can also engage with some of the right Sellarsians' critiques of Brandom and McDowell. The cognitive scientist and philosopher Daniel Dennett has critiqued the division of normative space from the space of nature, albeit for reasons different than those of this book. In his essay 'The Evolution of Reasons' Dennett points out the difficulty in distinguishing questions of 'what for?' from those of 'how come?' from within the so-called normative space of reasons.[64] While Dennett admits that reasons of 'what for?' can be discussed effectively in terms of socially mediated practices, those of 'how come?' generally require a more practical or engineering model to explain their function.[65] A consequence of this is to say that termites and architects both have reasons for why they construct the way they do, but humans can represent those reasons to one another whereas termites cannot.[66] But this difference does not adequately justify the normative form of 'what for?' replacing or overriding the questions of 'how come?'. Dennett argues that Brandom and other Pittsburgh Hegelians use the space of reasons in a way that effectively terminates inquiry if it keeps reason so isolated from nature.[67]

As I hope to show, while Schelling and German Idealism writ large similarly endorse closing the ontological gap between mind and world (or between thought and nature), the way in which McDowell proposes such a suture does not provide an adequate grounding for the ambit of the practical for which he argues. Furthermore, it remains to be seen how exactly the very split between mind and world (between thought and nature) is merely *ideal for us*, and how this split for our own sake maps on to the split (or perhaps more tentatively the emergence) of thought from nature ontologically. Or in other words, a de-ontologised account of nature and myself as a thinking being cannot account for natural impediments to my capacity to think in the same way my giving of reasons affects nature.

Tethered *ekstasis* and the speculative mousetrap

But a glimpse into its recent history provides adequate material for melancholy reflections on philosophy; this is because until now there has been no way to philosophize, or, as one otherwise says, none of the different philosophical systems has been able to survive over the course of time. I contend that it is also the duty of the teacher to reveal this side of philosophy, which repulses more than it attracts. For whoever considers how many people have shipwrecked on this rocky sea, how some with no vocation for philosophy have consumed the best years of their life, emptying their very soul in the fruitless and foolish pursuit of philosophy, who, without mentioning the desolate halls of prehistoric schools of wisdom, wander among the weather-beaten tombstones of former doctrinal systems.[68]

To start our project upon grittier wheels, we must appreciate how easily humble and natural musings about concepts and attributes can insinuate themselves into our practical affairs and lead us onward to unhappy conclusion. Sometimes the process resembles a familiar species of nightmare. We have been cheerfully ambling along a pleasant country lane when we notice that our surroundings have turned grim. Now we seem trapped within some vast cemetery that sprawls endlessly over gray hills. We find nothing but huge mausoleums that honor dynasties of abstracta of which we've never heard. 'Where did all these edifices come from?' we ask and wonder what faulty turn in the road could have led us into this disconcerting City of the Dead. It's better that we do not linger long amongst the marble but instead retrace our way back to that sunny lane.[69]

How to unite transcendental, *Naturphilosophical* and pragmatic (or positive) sciences as well as bring Schelling's thought into the twenty-first century? The enduring legacy of Schelling's thought is that nature, as inexistent powers, topologically viewed as a self-deforming space, is a necessity, reverse-engineered from the momentum of there being thinking creatures in a world – a world that depends upon a physical history but one that generates not only technological objects but also fictional entities, contradictions and a self-altering neuronal architecture. Put otherwise, the great problematic that Schelling outlines is that we humans are products of nature who have a capacity (thought) so powerful that it constantly *appears to contain* all of nature, or exclude nature, when, in fact, it is nature that is always thinking through us. Thus, nature is always inexistent because it is always trying to become an object to itself, and yet it fails to do so and instead contructs through extaining, generating time and space. Nature produces more constraints, and this failure of its easy access to itself produces distance, a self-altering topology that in turn engenders more extainment (*Ausschließung*). Thinking, just as much as it can point to the inexistence of the past, of what has gone and left only traces or no traces at all, points to the creativity of the future, of a more-than, but a more-than in which we have a current creative stake. What does the conjunction of speculation and pragmatism mean in Schelling's view of a freedom that is bound to its antecedents but uncontainable in the form of its potentially countless consequents?

One threat is a tendency to wander, to have to explore the consequences of ideas that may have no tooth or claw to them. But is not the advantage of thought the generally 'low-cost' simulations of the potential consequences of ideas? As hopefully was shown in the previous section, the strictly normative approach of the Pittsburgh Hegelians sacrifices too much in the name of discursive and rational stability. Broadly speaking, the normative approach overloads the restrictions on concepts before deploying them, while emphasising clarity over extension. In emphasising clarity, however, the normativists cut short the model of conceptual use for philosophy, in that concepts, overwhelmingly, re-emphasise their own groundlessness at the cost of exploration. Schelling, on the contrary, attempts to synthesise an ecstatic account of embodiment (taken from his extrapolations on

Aristotelian naturalism) with the Platonic realist approach to the life of the idea. While this would seem far afield from any pragmaticist concerns, this tension regarding conceptual use is central to the contemporary pragmatic thinker Mark Wilson.

Wilson's mammoth text *Wandering Significance* aims to redraw the map of conceptual use broadly, arguing that both the linguistic turn in philosophy and the classical picture of how language and concepts grasp meaning are presented in either too loose or too stringent a light. While addressing the function of language in Schelling would be its own project, it is the linguistic ramifications of the conceptual that I am interested in connecting to the relation of pragmatic and speculative navigation. Why pragmatism and speculation?

Schelling's fascination with the classic Leibnizian question 'Why is there something rather than nothing?' has been interpreted in a multitude of ways but, I would argue, it is precisely this question that captures Schelling's thought as pulled between pragmatic and speculative concerns.[70] By 'pragmatic' I here mean thought that is driven to do justice to action, that is, to both the productive processes we can observe and the very activity or process of thought, which is arguably the most basic fact of our existence. By 'speculative' I do not intend to invoke the pejorative sense of the arm-chair philosopher who creates out of her mind alone, pulling monads and explanatory spectres from the ether, but the sense shared by the German Idealists broadly – namely, the possibility of unbinding thought from the obvious and apparent in order not only to service thought itself, but also to dismantle potential barriers to action if one were to focus on only the immediate horizon.

The question 'Why is there something rather than nothing?' is essentially Schelling's way of asking why individuation occurs, given the fact that, at bottom, there seem to be only processes. It is this question that haunts Schelling for his entire life in letters; it manifests itself in a process- or powers-based meontology that has no determinable origin and no determinable end. It is a meontology that must cut this continuum of powers, which are speculative and can be said to inexist in that they allow for the retro-revisal of epistemological practices as well as the ongoing production of new forms of knowledge.

Schelling's interesting move is to use these desires to philosophise in order to check and balance one another: to reduce the world to navigate it (pragmatic maxim) and to expand the world to truly understand it (speculative maxim). The difficulty here is that the figure of the philosopher becomes a lonely wanderer, not only of the world, but a figure who must attempt to engage in *ekstasis* – to float above the world without leaving it, a leaving the world that pushes against its edges. *Ekstasis* should be taken to be the embodiment of conceptual abstraction in the most literal sense. The question that now naturally follows is this: how can this procedure be fleshed out in a pragmatic and speculative sense?

Just as Schelling attempts to navigate between Kantian restrictions and metaphysical inebriation, Wilson attempts to show the importance of finding a place between inflexible classical definitions of concepts and the conceptual play of post-modern thinkers. Wilson's difficult task is to demonstrate how it is that concepts can be plastic yet robust, without appealing to a definitively realist sense of the world 'out there' that the concepts necessarily grip on to, and on the other hand, without reducing conceptual use to a merely socially mediated language game unfolding over time.

Wilson argues that it is by investigating dull things, such as concepts, that pragmatism is at its most powerful as a philosophical field. Furthermore, this application of pragmatism, of the maxim 'do what works', to abstract capacities such as conceptualisation further indicates the important difference between practical and pragmatic, one that, as hopefully was seen above, the normativist camp elides. Practical thought takes the immediate horizon for granted as it sets about its tasks. A pragmatic view, on the other hand, is constantly distilling a greater horizon in order to act in a way that is local, yet future-oriented. Wilson argues that a pragmatic approach allows one to avoid both associating conceptual authority with hidden desires of domination while also critiquing concepts for being overly rigid, for not allowing transformation or movement between domains.[71] Furthermore, Wilson's pragmatism is constantly in contact with a conceptualisation of nature, albeit an abstract one. As he writes:

> It is then commonly presumed that Nature's uncooperative tendencies with respect to descriptive acquiescence emerge mainly with the rise of relativity and quantum mechanics but this is not true; allied difficulties glower sullenly even at the core of what we may mistakenly regard as the most stolid and respectable corners of engineering.[72]

He then goes on to say:

> The main consideration that drives the entire argument of the book is the thesis that the often quirky behaviors of ordinary descriptive predicates derive, not merely from controllable human inattention or carelessness, but from a basic unwillingness of the physical universe to sit still while we frame its descriptive picture. Like a photographer dealing with a rambunctious child, we must resort to odd and roundabout strategies if we hope to capture even a glimpse of our flighty universe upon our linguistic film.[73]

Wilson's proximity to Sellars, *contra* Brandom and McDowell, should begin to become clear. Wilson's doubt about the self-consistency of the so-called space of reasons begins to emerge and, in addition, he draws the ontological strings tighter between pragmatic activity and concept-use. This is possible, which is again evident from the quote above, because of Wilson's focus on engineering, on what in a conceptual sense could be called applied physics. He is thus particularly focused on construction both in an ideal and in a real sense (to transpose his concerns to Schellingian language). It is from this middle ground of concept-into-action that Wilson makes his philosophical stake in favour of pragmatism and against the normativists explicit. But this requires a brief detour through his notion of ur-philosophical concepts.

Wilson warns against ur-philosophical concepts or those concepts that under-gird, with almost utopian naïvety, the general thrust of a philosophical endeavour. Just as one can, looking at the above epigraph, get lost in the graveyard of forgotten abstract concepts, one can also advance too quickly along the sunny lane of non-contingency.[74] This ur-philosophical favouritism that asserts that the world is fully graspable is exactly the kind of bias that Schelling attempts to torpedo with both the unprethinkable and the inexistence of the *Potenzen*.[75] That is, Schelling opens up the beginning and the end of the world and runs it through with a plurality of processes – not in order to explain it dogmatically, but to make it possible for us to think its complexity and our role in that complexity, but never in a complete manner.

While a strict sense of the pragmatic maxim might seem, on the face of it, to rule out speculative entities, the inexistence of the potencies and the singularity of the world of powers allows pragmatism to apply to both thought and action, to treat thought as a kind of activity that our limited access, and not our ontological or theologically decreed finitude, makes pertinent. Inexistence and the potencies are speculations which in fact function as meta-pragmatic, in that they keep pragmatic thinking functioning into the future epistemologically and meontologically. If the world is closed via a philosophy of immanence (Spinoza and his heirs), or if we resort to a fact-based ontology (Gabriel), then pragmatism would become nothing other than a local adumbration of philosophical riches, whereas, in fact, the world as discovered and as created is only rich because of local activities; furthermore, these activities are local because of the limitations of our particular individuations and locations within bigger processes and not because things are, in and of themselves, unknowable or ungraspable. As Wilson illustrates through and against Hume, one cannot simply ban oneself from speculation, keeping one's nose to the immediate conceptual ground, as to do so would be to fail to locate the local space of action in any meaningful sense.[76]

One can take the various forms of naturalism above as a case in point. How could one in good faith claim that biologists, or even technicians working in biological fields, should not, or could not, benefit from grand theories of biological development such as Darwinian evolution? Only with such theories does local pragmatic work in biological realms have more than local meaning. This does not mean that such acts are only in service of a particular theory, but it is only when couched in a theoretical or speculative context *of some kind* that such activities could ever even contribute to a new theory.

It is here that we can investigate Wilson's direct critique of the normativist approach to nature and reason. While Wilson supports Brandom's general objective in terms of trying to identify what human mental capacities are in the wake of the failure, or insufficiency, of our past attempts at self-reflexivity, he becomes increasingly sceptical of the socially normative tissue that Brandom and his enclave aim to articulate.[77] Wilson begins by critiquing John McDowell's claim that conceptual authority can be easily replaced by social agreement and that, as a result of this, the purposes of science are conceptually limited, because a concept's proper home is in the space of reasons as opposed to the space of causes.[78] Wilson furthers his critique by stating that he does not think that the normative move of segregating human use of concepts from their sub-personal or neurophysiological activity will hold over time. One can return to the Schellingian approach to naturalism above, as well as the concerns of the previous chapter, as Schelling articulates this problem, though in a very different historical context, in terms of the epistemological conundrum of 'what thinks in me is outside of me'. Schelling's conclusion is that concepts must not only be flexible in terms of their observable content (as was emphasised via Sellars above) but also in terms of the point of their generation, that is, in terms of it being 'my' concept as well as a concept of a locality within the mind and an intuitive locality of immediate surroundings. That is, universal inexistence and local conceptual use may function differently, but this does not mean that two different concepts are at play.

As Wilson puts it:

> With respect to the terms of macroscopic classification we have investigated, public norms, however formulated, are implausible as a final magistrate of conceptual correctness, simply because our chief objective is to make practical headway within an often uncooperative external world. Getting matters right with respect to those externals usually matters more to us than the opinions of our chums.[79]

He then concludes the sentiment with the following:

> Once we are concerned with building a skyscraper or laying down long extensions of telegraphic cable, the standard 'get the right answer' represents our avatar, not any norms promulgated by civic rigorists. Indeed, these are the exact

concerns that led us to conclude, long ago, that environmentally determined standards of correct use apply even to the lonely mumblings of a Robinson Crusoe, at least when he is busy counting his goats or planning a mousetrap.[80]

If pragmatism operates on thought in relation to questioning what a thing does, then Schelling's thought focuses on the where and when of creation or generation. A concern with nature is all too quickly written off as appealing to pre-critical metaphysics, as wanting merely to go on speculative fancies without constraint or measurable consequence. Yet once again, this caricature ignores the generative and regulative powers of nature on the pragmatic.

As Wilson makes clear, conceptual use is always interfaced with the environment in which one is engaged and, at times, the same environment in which one became conceptually trained. Again, following Sellars above, it is only this kind of training that allows us to amplify our naturalistically granted capacities, in order to get a better sense of the world in which we are forced to navigate.

Schelling applies this problematic to the very nature of philosophy itself via the notion of *ekstasis* in 'On the Nature of Philosophy as a Science', in which the philosopher makes the world into an object of thought, while recognising that the philosopher herself is only ever operating on the world second-hand, and that this conceptual delay applies to the thinker viewing herself *as a philosopher*. As Schelling writes outlining the dire task of philosophy as navigation:

> Those, then, who want to find themselves at the starting point of a truly free philosophy, have to depart even from God. Here the motto is: whoever wants to preserve it will lose it, and whoever abandons it will find it. Only those have reached the ground in themselves and have become aware of the depths of life, who have at one time abandoned everything and have themselves been abandoned by everything, for whom everything has been lost, and who have found themselves alone, face-to-face with the infinite: a decisive step which Plato compared with death. That which Dante saw written on the door of the inferno must be written in a different sense also at the entrance to philosophy: 'Abandon all hope, ye who enter here.' Those who look for true philosophy must be bereft of all hope, all desire, all longing. They must not wish anything, not know anything, must feel completely bare and impoverished, must give everything away in order to gain everything. It is a grim step to take, it is grim to have to depart from the final shore. This we can infer from the fact that so few have ever been capable of it.[81]

Thus Schelling's speculative sailor, the one who engages in apparently reckless *ekstasis*, if she cheats death, can only hope to become Wilson's Crusoe and pragmatically attune such explorations on stable land even if such stability is only temporary. But does this mean that Schelling's philosophy implies or even requires the lonely thinker, one who must abjure the collective labour of thought and practice so celebrated by McDowell and Brandom? I do not believe that this is the case.[82]

The upshot of Schelling's entire philosophy, I believe, is the importance of the worldliness of ideas or their collective formation, where unworldliness, or mere ideality, is replaced by inexistence – by that which has not yet come to be. This, in fact, burdens the thinker with responsibility for the future. At the same time, it disallows any privileging of thought or action – for instance, giving action the typical advantage over thought since thought is somehow of another world (even when Platonism is attacked). An example of the purported advantage of thought over action would be that thought, or rationality, has a modicum of purity, and this is also disallowed. Following the general thrust of Schelling's thought, if realness is measured in terms of consequences, then action for its own sake, or armchair thinking for its own sake, may not appeal to being either only or never of this world. That is, actions are not immediately more valuable because they are right before us, nor are ideas only things to be aspired to. In fact, actions are not merely before us at all, nor are ideas merely above the world, as there is only one world in Schelling's philosophy, his Aristotelian naturalism combined with his Platonic realism. The world is a natural Aristotelian world, stripped of its essences and its perfection, haunted by the open-ended temporality of a Platonic universe, a world that restlessly churns with chaotic change.

This is why the subject for Schelling, whether engineer, philosopher, naturalist or geometer, is nothing but an instance of eternal freedom. But it is a freedom that does not mean freedom from something, as, once again, there is only this world and no free realm beyond – rather, it is the freedom to adopt a form, to carve out a space and navigate nature.[83]

Notes

1. C. S. Peirce, *The Collected Papers of Charles Sanders Peirce*, ed. Charles Hartshorn and Paul Weiss (Cambridge, MA: Harvard University Press, 1931–35), 21–2.
2. Peirce, *Collected Papers*, 2182.
3. Letter of C. S. Peirce to William James, 1894, quoted in Esposito, *Schelling's Idealism*, 203.
4. Quoted in Iain Hamilton Grant, interview by Leon Niemoczynski, http://afterxnature.blogspot.fr/2013/04/iain-hamilton-grant-interview-with.html, 10 April 2013 (accessed 4 August 2018).
5. Schelling, *First Outline*, 41.
6. Schelling, 'On the Nature of Philosophy as a Science', 216–17.
7. Ibid., 221.

8. Ibid., 234.

9. Extainment is Iain Hamilton Grant's translation of *Ausschließung*, which is more commonly translated as separation. Grant borrows the term from Châtelet as one that is not merely opposed to containment, but is a spilling outwards that retains its connection to that which it appears separated from. See Grant, 'How Nature Came to be Thought', 40–1.

10. Schelling, 'On the Nature of Philosophy as a Science', 209, 213.

11. Ibid., 210–11.

12. K. T. Fann, *Peirce's Theory of Abduction* (The Hague: Martinus Nijhoff, 1970), 7.

13. Ibid., 8.

14. Matthews, *Schelling's Organic Form*, xi.

15. Tritten, *Beyond Presence*, 61–3.

16. Ibid., 62.

17. Ibid., 63.

18. This difference hinges on the degree to which one sees the importance of God or of the theological in Schelling's work. While I do not have the space to engage with such an enormous issue, my intuition is that Schelling's ungrounding of God in the *Weltalter* drafts, as well as his general scepticism regarding treating God as equivalent with a justificatory absolute in general, seriously questions this theological emphasis.

19. Schelling, 'On the Nature of Philosophy as a Science', 212.

20. As we will see below, Sellars advocates the use of analogy in relating the known to the unknown, as Brassier will later emphasise.

21. Schelling, *Philosophical Investigations*, 76–7.

22. C. S. Peirce, 'Methods for Attaining Truth', in *Collected Papers*, 415.

23. Schelling, 'On the Nature of Philosophy as a Science', 215.

24. Châtelet, *Figuring Space*, 14. While he does not cite the source, Châtelet is no doubt referring to a passage from Schelling's *Clara*, 22.

25. Bana Bashour and Hans Muller (eds), *Contemporary Philosophical Naturalism and Its Implications* (New York: Routledge, 2014).

26. A central flaw of liberal naturalism, which is important to note here, is that it generally collapses reduction interior to particular scientific fields with reduction that is eliminative, i.e., it believes that scientific explanation necessarily eliminates entities in other fields. As we saw in Chapter 5, this confuses ontological and methodological meanings of reduction, as Robert Batterman argues.

27. Gabriel, *Transcendental Ontology*, 3.

28. Ibid., 11.

29. Mortensen, 'The Fate of Finitude', 17.

30. Nagel, *Mind and Cosmos*.

31. Michael Halley, 'Schelling's Empiricism: A Transcendentalist's Conversion', *Idealistic Studies*, 37.2 (2007): 114.

32. This is evident in the example of legal jargon which separates grounds and reasons. Whereas one's reasons might be understood, they may not count as legal grounds for performing an action, i.e., grounds require justification outside an individual's desires or individual reasons for doing something.

33. Schelling, *The Grounding of Positive Philosophy*, 210.

34. Paul Collins Hayner, *Reason and Existence: Schelling's Philosophy of History* (Boston: Brill, 1967), 41, 47.

35. Ibid., 51–2.

36. Michael Blamauer, 'Schelling's Real Materialism', *Minerva*, 16 (2012): 3, http://www.minerva.mic.ul.ie/vol16/Schelling.pdf (accessed 1 July 2015).

37. Gabriel, *Transcendental Ontology*, 66.
38. Wilfrid Sellars, 'Philosophy and the Scientific Image of Man', in *Empiricism and the Philosophy of Mind* (London: Routledge & Kegan Paul, 1963), 6.
39. Ibid., 19.
40. Ray Brassier, 'Bergson, Lived Experience, and the Myth of the Given', talk given at 'To Have Done With Life – Vitalism and Antivitalism in Contemporary Philosophy' conference at MaMa, Zagreb, 17–19 June 2011.
41. Here I follow Ray Brassier's reading of how Sellars treats the inconsistent triad, as opposed to Robert Brandom's. Brandom argues that Sellars merely drops option 1. See Robert Brandom, 'Guide to Empiricism and Philosophy of Mind', available online, http://www.pitt.edu/~brandom/me-core/downloads/EPMGuide11496a.docx (accessed 20 August 2018). For further discussion of the inconsistent triad, see James O'Shea, *Wilfrid Sellars: Naturalism with a Normative Turn* (Cambridge: Polity Press, 2007), as well as John McDowell, *Having the World in View: Essays on Kant, Hegel, and Sellars* (Cambridge, MA: Harvard University Press, 2013), 235–7.
42. Wilfrid Sellars, 'The Lever of Archimedes', *The Monist*, 64.1, (1981): 7–10; Wilfrid Sellars, 'Foundations for a Metaphysics of Pure Process', *The Monist*, 64.1 (1981): 37–65.
43. Wilfrid Sellars, 'Is Consciousness Physical?', *The Monist*, 64.1 (1981): 87–8.
44. Johanna Seibt, 'Pure Processes and Projective Metaphysics', *Philosophical Studies*, 101 (2000), 254.
45. Ibid., 266.
46. Ibid., 267.
47. Ibid., 275.
48. Ibid., 284.
49. F. W. J. von Schelling, quoted in Christopher Lauer, *The Suspension of Reason in Hegel and Schelling* (London: Bloomsbury, 2010), 194.
50. Gabriel, *Transcendental Ontology*, 35–6.
51. As Ray Brassier has pointed out, however, this elides the emphasis on Sellars's use of processes in his later work, namely the Carus lectures.
52. McDowell's reading of Kant is also heavily influenced by P. F. Strawson's book *The Bounds of Sense: An Essay on Kant's Critique of Pure Reason* (London: Methuen, 1966).
53. John McDowell, *Mind and World* (Cambridge, MA: Harvard University Press, 1996), xii.
54. Ibid., 9.
55. Ibid., 27.
56. Ibid., 92–5.
57. Robert Brandom, *Reason and Philosophy* (Cambridge, MA: Harvard University Press, 2013), 2–4.
58. Ibid., 17.
59. This speaks to a tension between continental and analytic readings of Hegel, where the former emphasise his metaphysical aspects whereas the latter emphasise his historical uses modified for the present. These lines have become significantly blurred in works such as those of Adrian Johnston, Brady Bowman and Markus Gabriel, to name but a few.
60. Brandom, *Reason and Philosophy*, 90–1.
61. Ibid., 115.
62. Ibid., 102.
63. Robert Brandom, *Tales of the Mighty Dead: Historical Essays in the Metaphysics of Intentionality* (Cambridge, MA: Harvard University Press, 2002), 179.

64. Daniel Dennett, 'The Evolution of Reasons', in *Contemporary Philosophical Naturalism and Its Implications*, ed. Bana Bashour and Hans Muller (New York: Routledge, 2014), 54.
65. Ibid., 51.
66. Ibid., 54–6.
67. Ibid., 59.
68. Schelling, *The Grounding of Positive Philosophy*, 97.
69. Wilson, *Wandering Significance*, 17.
70. See, for instance, Tritten's *Beyond Presence*.
71. Wilson, *Wandering Significance*, 2–3.
72. Ibid., 9.
73. Ibid., 11.
74. Ibid., 16–17.
75. Ibid., 600.
76. Ibid., 602.
77. Ibid., 30–1.
78. Ibid., 613–14.
79. Ibid., 615.
80. Ibid., 616.
81. Schelling, 'On the Nature of Philosophy as Science', 217–18.
82. Interestingly, Wilson discusses the importance of nautical metaphors in Peirce with regard to conceptual behaviour (*Wandering Significance*, 42).
83. Schelling, 'On the Nature of Philosophy as Science', 220–1.

Bibliography

Works by Schelling

Schelling, F. W. J. *The Abyss of Freedom/Ages of the World* (1813). Trans. Judith Norman. Ann Arbor, MI: University of Michigan Press, 1997.

Schelling, F. W. J. *The Ages of the World* (1815). Trans. Jason Wirth. Albany, NY: State University of New York Press, 2000.

Schelling, F. W. J. *Bruno, or On the Natural and Divine Principle of Things*. Trans. Michael Vater. Albany, NY: State University of New York Press, 1984.

Schelling, F. W. J. *Clara, or On Nature's Connection to the Spirit World*. Trans. Fiona Steinkamp. Albany, NY: State University of New York Press, 2002.

Schelling, F. W. J. 'Exhibition of the Process of Nature'. Trans. Iain Hamilton Grant. Unpublished manuscript, 2013.

Schelling, F. W. J. *First Outline of a System of the Philosophy of Nature*. Trans. Keith Petersen. Albany, NY: State University of New York Press, 2004.

Schelling, F. W. J. *The Grounding of Positive Philosophy: The Berlin Lectures*. Trans. Bruce Matthews. Albany, NY: State University of New York Press, 2007.

Schelling, F. W. J. *Historical-Critical Introduction to the Philosophy of Mythology*. Trans. Mason Richey and Markus Zisselsberger. Albany, NY: State University of New York Press, 2007.

Schelling, F. W. J. *Idealism and the Endgame of Theory*. Trans. and ed. Thomas Pfau. Albany, NY: State University of New York Press, 1994.

Schelling, F. W. J. *Ideas for a Philosophy of Nature*. Trans. Errol Harris and Peter Heath. Cambridge: Cambridge University Press, 1988.

Schelling, F. W. J. 'Of the I as a Principle of Philosophy'. In *The Unconditional in Human Knowledge: Four Early Essays (1794–1796)*. Trans. F. Marti. Lewisburg, PA: Bucknell University Press, 1980.

Schelling, F. W. J. 'On Faraday's Most Recent Discovery: Lecture to an Open Sitting of the [Bayerische] Akademie [des Wissenschaften] on May 28, 1832'. Trans. Iain Hamilton Grant. Unpublished manuscript, 2014.

Schelling, F. W. J. *On the History of Modern Philosophy*. Trans. Andrew Bowie. Cambridge: Cambridge University Press, 1994.

Schelling, F. W. J. 'On the Nature of Philosophy as Science'. In *German Idealist Philosophy*. Ed. Rudiger Bubner. New York: Penguin, 1978.

Schelling, F. W. J. 'On the True Concept of Philosophy of Nature and the Correct Way of Solving its Problems'. Trans. Judith Kahl and Daniel Whistler. *PLI: The Warwick Journal of Philosophy*, 26 (2014): 58–81.

Schelling, F. W. J. *On University Studies*. Trans. E. S. Morgan. Athens, OH: Ohio University Press, 1965.

Schelling, F. W. J. *Philosophical Investigations into the Essence of Human Freedom*. Trans. Jeff Love and Johannes Schmidt. Albany, NY: State University of New York Press, 2006.

Schelling, F. W. J. *Philosophy and Religion*. Trans. Klaus Ottman. Putnam, CT: Spring Publications, 2010.

Schelling, F. W. J. *The Philosophy of Art*. Trans. Douglass Stott and David Simpson. Minneapolis, MN: University of Minnesota Press, 2008.

Schelling, F. W. J. *Presentation of My System of Philosophy*. In J. G. Fichte and F. W. J. von Schelling, *The Philosophical Rupture between Fichte and Schelling: Selected Texts and Correspondence (1800–1802)*. Trans. M. Vater and D. Wood. Albany, NY: State University of New York Press, 2012.

Schelling, F. W. J. *Sämmtliche Werke*. Ed. K. F. A. Schelling. 14 volumes. Stuttgart and Augsberg: J. G. Cotta, 1856–61.

Schelling, F. W. J. 'Stuttgart Seminars'. In *Idealism and the Endgame of Theory*. Trans. and ed. Thomas Pfau. Albany, NY: State University of New York Press, 1994.

Schelling, F. W. J. *System of Transcendental Idealism*. Trans. Peter Heath. Charlottesville, VA: University Press of Virginia, 1978.

Schelling, F. W. J. *Timaeus*. Trans. Adam Arola, Jenna Jolissaint and Peter Warnek. *Epoche*, 12.2 (2008). Online.

Schelling, F. W. J. 'Universal Deduction of the Dynamic Process of the Categories of Physics'. Trans. Iain Hamilton Grant. Unpublished manuscript, 2013.

Secondary works

Aristotle. *Metaphysics*. In *The Basic Works of Aristotle*. Ed. Richard McKeon. New York: Modern Library, 2001.

Authier, Andre. *Early Days of X-Ray Crystallography*. Oxford: Oxford University Press, 2013.

Bashour, Bana, and Muller, Hans (eds). *Contemporary Philosophical Naturalism and Its Implications*. New York: Routledge, 2014.

Batterman, Robert. *The Devil in the Details: Asymptotic Reasoning in Explanation, Reduction, and Emergence*. Oxford: Oxford University Press, 2002.

Beach, Edward Allen. *Potencies of the God(s): Schelling's Philosophy of Mythology*. Albany, NY: State University of New York Press, 1994.

Beiser, Frederick. 'Dark Days: Anglophone Scholarship since the 1960s'. In *German Idealism: Contemporary Perspectives*. Ed. Espen Hammer. 70–90. New York: Routledge, 2007.

Beiser, Frederick. *The Fate of Reason: German Philosophy from Kant to Fichte*. Cambridge, MA: Harvard University Press, 1993.

Beiser, Frederick. *German Idealism: The Struggle Against Subjectivism, 1781–1801*. Cambridge, MA: Harvard University Press, 2008.

Beiser, Frederick. 'Maimon and Fichte'. In *Solomon Maimon: Rational Dogmatist, Empirical Skeptic: Critical Assessments*. Ed. Gideon Freudenthal. 233–48. New York: Springer, 2003.

Bell, David. 'Transcendental Arguments and Non-Naturalistic Anti-Realism'. In *Transcendental Arguments: Problems and Prospects*. Ed. Robert Stern. 189–220. Oxford: Oxford University Press, 2000.

Blamauer, Michael. 'Schelling's Real Materialism'. *Minerva*, 16 (2012): 1–24. http://www.minerva.mic.ul.ie/vol16/Schelling.pdf. Accessed 1 July 2015.

Bowie, Andrew. *Schelling and Modern European Philosophy*. New York: Routledge, 1994.

Bowman, Brady. *Hegel and the Metaphysics of Absolute Negativity*. Cambridge: Cambridge University Press, 2013.

Brandom, Robert. *Making it Explicit: Reasoning, Representing, and Discursive Commitment*. Cambridge, MA: Harvard University Press, 1998.

Brandom, Robert. *Perspectives on Pragmatism: Classical, Recent, and Contemporary*. Cambridge, MA: Harvard University Press, 2011.

Brandom, Robert. *Reason and Philosophy*. Cambridge, MA: Harvard University Press, 2013.

Brandom, Robert. *Tales of the Mighty Dead: Historical Essays in the Metaphysics of Intentionality*. Cambridge, MA: Harvard University Press, 2002.

Brassier, Ray. 'Bergson, Lived Experience, and the Myth of the Given'. Talk given at 'To Have Done With Life – Vitalism and Antivitalism in Contemporary Philosophy' conference at MaMa, Zagreb, 17–19 June 2011.

Breazeale, Daniel. 'Kantian Questions/Fichtean Answers'. In *The Transcendental Turn*. Ed. Sebastian Gardner. 74–95. Oxford: Oxford University Press, 2015.

Burke, John G. *Origins of the Science of Crystals*. Berkeley, CA: University of California Press, 1966.

Buzaglo, Meir. *Salomon Maimon: Monism, Skepticism, and Mathematics*. Pittsburgh, PA: University of Pittsburgh Press, 2002.

Caneva, Kenneth L. 'Physics and *Naturphilosophie*: A Reconnaissance'. *History of Science*, 35 (1997): 35–106.

Chamayou, Gregorie. 'Fichte's Passport: A Philosophy of the Police'. Trans. Kieron Aarons. *Theory and Event*, 16.2 (2013).

Châtelet, Gilles. *Figuring Space: Philosophy, Mathematics, and Physics*. Trans. Robert Shore and Muriel Zagha. London: Springer, 1999.

Châtelet, Gilles. 'Interlacing the Singularity, the Diagram, and the Metaphor'. Ed. Charles Alunni. In *Virtual Mathematics: The Logic of Difference*. Ed. Simon Duffy. 31–45. Bolton: Clinamen, 2006.

Crowe, Michael J. *A History of Vector Analysis: The Evolution of the Idea of a Vectorial System*. Mineola, NY: Dover Books, 2011.

Deleuze, Gilles. *Pure Immanence: Essays on a Life*. Trans. Anne Boyman. Minneapolis, MN: Zone Books, 2001.

Dennett, Daniel. 'The Evolution of Reasons'. In *Contemporary Philosophical Naturalism and Its Implications*. Ed. Bana Bashour and Hans Muller. 47–62. New York: Routledge, 2014.

Dretske, Fred. *Naturalizing the Mind*. Cambridge, MA: MIT Press, 1995.

Edwards, Jeffrey. 'Spinozism, Freedom, and Transcendental Dynamics in Kant's Final System of Transcendental Idealism'. In *The Reception of Kant's Critical Philosophy: Fichte, Schelling, Hegel*. Ed. Sally Sedgwick. 54–77. Cambridge: Cambridge University Press, 2007.

Ellis, Brian. *The Philosophy of Nature: A Guide to the New Essentialism*. New York: Acumen, 2002.

Esposito, Joseph. *Schelling's Idealism and Philosophy of Nature*. Lewisburg, PA: Bucknell University Press, 1977.

Fann, K. T. *Peirce's Theory of Abduction*. The Hague: Martinus Nijhoff, 1970.

ffytche, Matt. *The Foundation of the Unconscious: Schelling, Freud, and the Birth of the Modern Psyche*. Cambridge: Cambridge University Press, 2011.

Fichte, J. G. *The Science of Knowing: J.G. Fichte's 1804 Lectures on the Wissenschaftslehre*. Trans. Walter Wright. Albany, NY: State University New York Press, 2005.

Förster, Eckart. *Kant's Final Synthesis*. Cambridge, MA: Harvard University Press, 2000.

Förster, Eckart. *The Twenty-Five Years of Philosophy: A Systematic Reconstruction*. Trans. Brady Bowman. Cambridge, MA: Harvard University Press, 2012.

Frank, Manfred. 'Schelling and Sartre on Being and Nothingness'. In *The New Schelling*. Ed. Judith Norman and Alistair Welchman. 151–66. London: Continuum, 2004.

Franks, Paul. *All or Nothing: Systematicity, Transcendental Arguments, and Skepticism in German Idealism*. Cambridge, MA: Harvard University Press, 2005.

Franks, Paul. 'From Quine to Hegel'. In *German Idealism: Contemporary Perspectives*. Ed. Espen Hammer. 50–69. London: Routledge, 2007.

Franks, Paul. 'Transcendental Arguments, Reason, and Skepticism'. In *Transcendental Arguments: Problems and Prospects*. Ed. Robert Stern. 111–43. Oxford: Oxford University Press, 1999.

Franks, Paul. 'What Should Kantians Learn from Maimon's Skepticism?' In *Solomon Maimon: Rational Dogmatist, Empirical Skeptic: Critical Assessments*. Ed. Gideon Freudenthal. 200–32. New York: Springer, 2003.

Freidman, Michael. *Kant's Construction of Nature: A Reading of The Metaphysical Foundations of Natural Science*. Cambridge: Cambridge University Press, 2013.

Freudenthal, Gideon. 'A Philosopher between Two Cultures'. In *Solomon Maimon: Rational Dogmatist, Empirical Skeptic: Critical Assessments*. Ed. Gideon Freudenthal. 1–17. New York: Springer, 2003.

Freydberg, Bernard. *Schelling's Dialogical Freedom Essay: Provocative Philosophy Then and Now*. Albany, NY: State University of New York Press, 2008.

Gabriel, Markus. *Transcendental Ontology: Essays in German Idealism*. London: Continuum, 2011.

Garre, Arran. 'From Kant to Schelling to Process Metaphysics: On the Way to Ecological Civilization'. *Cosmos and History: The Journal of Natural and Social Philosophy*, 7.2 (2011). http://cosmosandhistory.org/index.php/journal/article/view/263. Accessed 30 June 2015.

Goudeli, Kyriaki. *Challenges to German Idealism: Schelling, Fichte, Kant*. Basingstoke: Palgrave Macmillan, 2003.

Grant, Iain Hamilton. 'Being and Slime'. *Collapse: Philosophical Research and Development*, 4 (2008): 286–322.

Grant, Iain Hamilton. 'Does Nature Stay What It Is?'. In *The Speculative Turn: Continental Materialism and Realism*. Ed. L. Bryant, G. Harman and N. Srnicek. 66–83. Melbourne: Re:Press, 2010.

Grant, Iain Hamilton. 'The Eternal and Necessary Bond between Philosophy and Physics: A Repetition of the Difference between the Fichtean and Schellingian Forms of Philosophy'. *Angelaki: Journal of the Theoretical Humanities*, 10.1 (2005): 43–59.

Grant, Iain Hamilton. 'How Nature Comes to be Thought: Schelling's Paradox and the Problem of Location'. *Journal of the British Society for Phenomenology*, 44.1 (2013): 25–44.

Grant, Iain Hamilton. Interview with Leon Niemoczynski. http://afterxnature.blogspot. fr/2013/04/iain-hamilton-grant-interview-with.html. 10 April 2013. Accessed 4 August 2018.

Grant, Iain Hamilton. 'The Law of Insuperable Environment: What is Exhibited in the Exhibition of the Process of Nature?'. *Analecta Hermeneutica*, 5 (2013): 1–12.

Grant, Iain Hamilton. 'The Movements of the World: The Sources of Transcendental Philosophy'. *Analecta Hermeneutica*, 3 (2011): 1–17.

Grant, Iain Hamilton. *Philosophies of Nature after Schelling*. London: Continuum, 2006.

Grant, Iain Hamilton. 'Prospects for Post-Copernican Dogmatism: The Antinomies of Transcendental Naturalism'. *Collapse: Philosophical Research and Development*, 5 (2009): 415–54.

Grant, Iain Hamilton. 'The Remains of the World: Grounds and Powers in Schelling's Later Naturphilosophie'. *Schelling Studien*, 1 (2014): 3–24.

Guyer, Paul. 'The Unity of Nature and Freedom'. In *The Reception of Kant's Critical Philosophy: Fichte, Schelling, Hegel*. Ed. Sally Sedgwick. 19–53. Cambridge: Cambridge University Press, 2007.

Halley, Michael. 'Schelling's Empiricism: A Transcendentalist's Conversion'. *Idealistic Studies*, 37.2 (2007): 105–20.

Hayner, Paul Collins. *Reason and Existence: Schelling's Philosophy of History*. Boston: Brill, 1967.

Heidegger, Martin. *Schelling's Treatise on the Essence of Human Freedom*. Athens, OH: Ohio University Press, 1985.

Heinrich, Dieter. *Between Kant and Hegel: Lectures on German Idealism*. Cambridge, MA: Harvard University Press, 2008.

Heuser-Kessler, Marie-Luise. 'The Significance of *Naturphilosophie* for Justus and Hermann Grassmann'. In *From Past to Future: Graßmann's Work in Context*. Ed. H.-J. Petsche et al. 49–59. Basel: Springer, 2011.

Jaspers, Karl. *Schelling. Größe und Verhängnis*. Munich, 1955.

Johnston, Adrian. *Adventures in Transcendental Materialism: Dialogues with Contemporary Thinkers*. Edinburgh: Edinburgh University Press, 2014.

Kant, Immanuel. 'Concerning the Ultimate Ground of the Differentiation of Directions in Space'. In *Theoretical Philosophy 1775–1780*. Ed. and trans. David Walford. 361–72. Cambridge: Cambridge University Press, 2003.

Kant, Immanuel. *Critique of the Power of Judgment*. Trans. Paul Guyer and Eric Matthews. Cambridge: Cambridge University Press, 2000.

Kant, Immanuel. *The Critique of Pure Reason*. Trans. Norman Kemp Smith. Basingstoke: Palgrave Macmillan, 2007 [1929].

Kant, Immanuel. *Kants gesammelte Schriften*. 29 volumes. Berlin: de Gruyter, 1902.

Kant, Immanuel. 'On Creation in the Total Extent of Its Infinity in Both Space and Time'. Trans. Martin Schonfeld. *Collapse: Philosophical Research and Development*, 5 (2012): 379–414.

Kant, Immanuel. *Opus Postumum*. Trans. Eckhart Förster and Michael Rosen. Cambridge: Cambridge University Press, 1993.

Kant, Immanuel. 'What Does It Mean to Orient Oneself in Thinking?' In *Religion and Rational Theology*. Trans. and ed. Allen Wood. 1–18. Cambridge: Cambridge University Press, 1996.

Kerslake, Christian. *Immanence and the Vertigo of Philosophy*. Edinburgh: Edinburgh University Press, 2009.

Krell, David Farrell. *Contagion: Sexuality, Disease, and Death in German Idealism and Romanticism*. Bloomington, IN: Indiana University Press, 1998.

Lauer, Christopher. *The Suspension of Reason in Hegel and Schelling*. London: Continuum, 2010.

Lenoir, Timothy. *The Strategy of Life: Teleology and Mechanics in Nineteenth Century German Biology*. Chicago: University of Chicago Press, 1989.

Lord, Beth. *Kant and Spinozism: Transcendental Idealism and Immanence from Jacobi to Deleuze*. New York: Palgrave Macmillan, 2011.

Lovejoy, Arthur. *The Great Chain of Being*. Cambridge, MA: Harvard University Press, 1936.

Maimon, Salomon. *Essay on Transcendental Philosophy*. Trans. Nick Midgley, Henry Somers-Hall, Alistair Welchman and Merten Reglitz. London: Continuum, 2010.

McDowell, John. *Having the World in View: Essays on Kant, Hegel, and Sellars*. Cambridge, MA: Harvard University Press, 2013.

McDowell, John. *Mind and World*. Cambridge, MA: Harvard University Press, 1996.

McGrath, Sean. *The Dark Ground of Spirit: Schelling and the Unconscious*. New York: Routledge, 2012.

Matthews, Bruce. *Schelling's Organic Form of Philosophy: Life as the Schema of Freedom*. Albany, NY: State University of New York Press, 2011.

Meillassoux, Quentin. *After Finitude: An Essay on the Necessity of Contingency*. Trans. Ray Brassier. London: Continuum, 2008.

Meinong, Alexius. 'The Theory of Objects'. In *Realism and the Background of Phenomenology*. Ed. Roderick M. Chisholm. 76–117. Glencoe, IL: Free Press, 1960; repr. Atascadero, CA: Ridgeview, 1981.

Mendelsohn, Joshua. 'Teleology and the Scientific Image in Schelling's Philosophy of Nature'. Unpublished manuscript.

Molnar, George. *Powers: A Study in Metaphysics*. Oxford: Oxford University Press, 2007.

Mortensen, Frederick. 'The Fate of Finitude: Schelling and the Question of the World'. PhD thesis, University of Copenhagen, 2012.

Mumford, Stephen, and Rani, Lill Anjum. *Getting Causes from Powers*. Oxford: Oxford University Press, 2011.

Nagel, Thomas. *Mind and Cosmos: Why the Materialist Neo-Darwinian Concept of Nature is Almost Certainly False*. Oxford: Oxford University Press, 2012.

Nassar, Dalia. 'The Absolute in German Idealism and Romanticism'. In *Edinburgh Critical History of 19th Century Philosophy*. Ed. Alison Stone. 29–46. Edinburgh: Edinburgh University Press, 2011.

Nassar, Dalia. *The Romantic Absolute: Being and Knowing in Early Romantic Philosophy, 1795–1804*. Chicago: University of Chicago Press, 2013.

Negarestani, Reza. 'Rainbows and Rationalism'. Unpublished manuscript, 2013.

Negarestani, Reza. 'Synechistic Critique of Aesthetic Judgment'. In *Realism, Materialism, Art*. Ed. Christopher Cox, Jenny Jaskey and Suhail Malik. 231–44. Annandale-on-Hudson, NY/Berlin: Bard College/Sternberg Press, 2015.

Nuzzo, Angelica. *Ideal Embodiment: Kant's Theory of Sensibility*. Bloomington, IN: Indiana University Press, 2008.

Oken, Lorenz. *Elements of Physiophilosophy*. Trans. Alfred Tulk. London: The Ray Society, 1847.

O'Shea, James. *Wilfrid Sellars: Naturalism with a Normative Turn*. Cambridge: Polity Press, 2007.

Palmquist, Stephen. *Kant's System of Perspectives: An Architectonic Interpretation of the Critical Philosophy*. Lanham, MD: University Press of America, 1993.

Peirce, C. S. *The Collected Papers of Charles Sanders Peirce*. Electronic Publication, 1994.

Peirce, C. S. 'Methods for Attaining Truth'. In *The Collected Papers of Charles Sanders Peirce*. Vol. 1. Ed. Charles Hartshorn and Paul Weiss. Cambridge, MA: Harvard University Press, 1931–35.

Pinkard, Terry. *German Philosophy 1760–1860: The Legacy of Idealism*. Cambridge: Cambridge University Press, 2002.

Plato. 'The Statesman'. In *Plato: Complete Works*. Ed. John Cooper. 294–358. Indianapolis, IN: Hackett Publishing, 1997.

Plato. 'Timaeus'. In *Plato: Complete Works*. Ed. John Cooper. 1224–91. Indianapolis, IN: Hackett Publishing, 1997.

Rajan, Tilottama. 'First Outline of a System of Theory: Schelling and the Margins of Philosophy, 1799–1815'. *Studies in Romanticism*, 46 (2007): 311–35.

Rawes, Peg. *Space, Geometry, and Aesthetics*. New York: Palgrave Macmillan, 2008.

Richards, Robert. *The Romantic Conception of Life: Science and Philosophy in the Age of Goethe*. Chicago: University of Chicago Press, 2002.

Ritter, Constantin. *The Essence of Plato's Philosophy*. Memphis, TN: Jackson Press, 2007.

Schechter, Oded. 'The Logic of Speculative Philosophy and Skepticism in Maimon's Philosophy: *Satz der Bestimmbarkeit* and the Role of Synthesis'. In *Solomon Maimon: Rational Dogmatist, Empirical Skeptic: Critical Assessments*. Ed. Gideon Freudenthal. 18–53. New York: Springer, 2003.

Sedgwick, Sally. 'Introduction'. In *The Reception of Kant's Critical Philosophy: Fichte, Schelling, Hegel*. Ed. Sally Sedgwick. 1–18. Cambridge: Cambridge University Press, 2007.

Seibt, Johanna. 'Pure Processes and Projective Metaphysics'. *Philosophical Studies*, 101 (2000): 253–89.

Sellars, Wilfrid. 'Foundations for a Metaphysics of Pure Process'. *The Monist*, 64.1 (1981): 37–65.

Sellars, Wilfrid. 'Is Consciousness Physical?'. *The Monist*, 64.1 (1981): 66–90.

Sellars, Wilfrid. 'The Lever of Archimedes'. *The Monist*, 64.1 (1981): 3–36.

Sellars, Wilfrid. 'Philosophy and the Scientific Image of Man'. In *Empiricism and the Philosophy of Mind*. 1–40. London: Routledge & Kegan Paul, 1963.

Shaw, Devin Zane. *Freedom and Nature in Schelling's Philosophy of Art*. London: Continuum, 2011.

Smith, John H. 'Friedrich Schlegel's Romantic Calculus: Reflections on the Mathematical Infinite around 1800'. In *The Relevance of Romanticism: Essays on German Romantic Philosophy*. Ed. Dalia Nassar. 239–57. Oxford: Oxford University Press, 2014.

Snow, Dale. *Schelling and the End of Idealism*. Albany, NY: State University of New York Press, 1996.

Steffens, Henrik. *The Story of My Career*. Trans. William Gage. Boston: Gould and Lincoln, 1863.

Steigerwald, Joan. 'Epistemologies of Rupture: The Problem of Nature in Schelling's Philosophy'. *Studies in Romanticism*, 41 (2002): 545–84.

Steigerwald, Joan. 'Natural Purposes and the Purposiveness of Nature: The Antinomy of the Teleological Power of Judgment'. In *Romanticism and Modernity*. Ed. Robert Mitchell and Thomas Pfau. 29–46. New York: Routledge, 2011.

Strawson, P. F. *The Bounds of Sense: An Essay on Kant's Critique of Pure Reason*. London: Methuen, 1966.

Sturma, Dieter. 'The Nature of Subjectivity: The Critical and Systematic Function of Schelling's Philosophy of Nature'. In *The Reception of Kant's Critical Philosophy: Fichte, Schelling, and Hegel*. Ed. Sally Sedgwick. 216–31. Edinburgh: Edinburgh University Press, 2007.

Thielke, Peter. 'Intuition and Diversity: Kant and Maimon on Space and Time'. In *Solomon Maimon: Rational Dogmatist, Empirical Skeptic: Critical Assessments*. Ed. Gideon Freudenthal. 89–124. New York: Springer, 2003.

Torretti, Roberto. *Philosophy of Geometry from Riemann to Poincaré*. London: Reidel, 1978.

Tritten, Tyler. *Beyond Presence: The Late F.W.J. Schelling's Criticism of Metaphysics*. Boston: De Gruyter, 2012.

Vater, Michael. 'Fichte's Reaction to Schelling's Identity Philosophy in 1806'. In *After Jena: New Essays on Fichte's Later Philosophy*. Ed. D. Breazeale and T. Rockmore. 81–90. Evanston, IL: Northwestern University Press, 2008.

Weyl, Hermann. *The Open World: Three Lectures on the Metaphysical Implications of Science*. Woodbridge: Ox Bow Press, 1989.

White, Alan. *Schelling: An Introduction to the System of Freedom*. New Haven, CT: Yale University Press, 1983.

Williams, L. Pearce. *The Origins of Field Theory*. New York: Random House, 1966.

Wilson, Mark. *Wandering Significance: An Essay on Conceptual Behavior*. Oxford: Clarendon Press, 2006.

Wirth, Jason. *The Conspiracy of Life: Meditations on Schelling and His Time*. Albany, NY: State University of New York Press, 2003.

Wolfendale, Pete. *The Noumena's New Clothes*. Falmouth: Urbanomic, 2014.

Wood, Allen. 'The "I" as Principle of Practical Philosophy'. In *The Reception of Kant's Critical Philosophy: Fichte, Schelling, Hegel*. Ed. Sally Sedgwick. 93–108. Edinburgh: Edinburgh University Press, 2007.

Wood, David. *Mathesis of the Mind: A Study of Fichte's Wissenschaftslehre and Geometry*. Amsterdam: Rodopi, 2012.

Yakira, Elhanan. 'From Kant to Leibniz? Salomon Maimon and the Question of Predication'. In *Solomon Maimon: Rational Dogmatist, Empirical Skeptic: Critical Assessments*. Ed. Gideon Freudenthal. 54–79. New York: Springer, 2003.

Zalamea, Fernando. *Synthetic Philosophy of Contemporary Mathematics*. Trans. L. Fraser. Falmouth: Urbanomic, 2012.

Žižek, Slavoj. *The Indivisible Remainder: On Schelling and Related Matters*. London: Verso, 2007.

Žižek, Slavoj. *Less than Nothing: Hegel and the Shadow of Dialectical Materialism*. New York: Verso, 2012.

Žižek, Slavoj. *The Sublime Object of Ideology*. London: Verso, 1989.

Žižek, Slavoj. *Tarrying with the Negative: Kant, Hegel, and the Critique of Ideology*. Durham, NC: Duke University Press, 1993.

Index